Active / Passive

Edrita Fried, Ph.D.

Associate Clinical Professor of Psychiatry
New York Medical College

Training Analyst and Senior Supervisor
Postgraduate Center for Mental Health, New York

Passive

The Crucial
Psychological Dimension

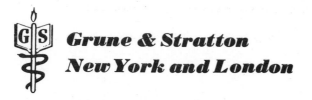

Grune & Stratton
New York and London

LIBRARY OF CONGRESS CATALOG CARD NUMBER 78-115013
INTERNATIONAL STANDARD BOOK NUMBER 0-8089-0647-X

Printed in the United States of America (CB)

Contents

Preface

To restore or build the emotional and mental roads that lead from dependency, narcissism, and passivity to vitality and activeness is an essential goal of psychotherapy. It is also one of the most difficult tasks with which the therapist is entrusted. It was for these reasons that I decided to plunge into the issue of the activity-passivity dimension.

In my practice and teaching, it had become ever clearer to me to what degree depression and anxiety, which are among the foremost plagues from which body and mind suffer, are connected with the hostile and immobile passive condition. It seemed to me imperative that, in order to liberate individuals from their passive fetters, we develop new methods and therapeutic steps, *not in opposition but in addition* to those commonly subsumed under the heading of psychoanalytic psychotherapy.

Inquiry into the *how* of building roads that lead to activeness — a term that includes action but is defined much more broadly in this book — seemed important for another reason. The passive individual is troubled relatively little by the quagmire of his passivity. His main disturbance comes from the symptoms flourishing in this quagmire: depression, loneliness, failures of every kind, including a slackening of sexuality. But other people in his environment — and this does not exclude the therapeutic community — become alternately uninterested in and irritated with the passive patient, as the deep hostility which his withdrawal implies is felt. Hence, the passive person not only removes himself from contact with others, but induces, through his effect on others, the very alienation from which he suffers. Therefore, let us make it possible for those troubled by dependence and passivity to speak out and be heard. This possibility of expression gives them a better chance eventually to become initiating, enterprising, and alive adults possessing enthusiasm and vision.

In my dealings with the activity-passivity dimension I have been encouraged by my patients. As I learned better how one might steer a mind toward a vital future, as I learned how to induce emotional activity, they started to glow and to reach out. I thank them for making it possible for me to work and progress along with them.

For one year, while my husband was on an assignment in Nepal, I became acquainted with a good many Buddhists. I did not study their philosophy on a systematic level, but I became convinced that these lovely people were predominantly active, though in ways that were gentle and calm. Their own perceptions were important to them. Exploration of anything that could be seen was a source of joy. The men and women, small of stature, did not shuffle their bodies along but moved freely through the rice fields and along the bumpy roads. Play, song, smiles, and joyful emotions were predominant. Nearly all foreigners who lived in this region felt that it was a good life. It appealed to me because it was active, not in vigorous deeds, toward which these people showed no conspicuous inclination, but in perception, emotion, play, and, among the educated, thought.

My warm gratitude for other experiences underlying the writing of this book goes to several institutions where I worked. First, I am grateful to the Albert Einstein College of Medicine and especially to Dr. Jack Wilder, now director of the Soundview–Throggs Neck Mental Health Center. He has created a therapeutic community with many branches which helps patients move toward genuine activeness. I appreciate the atmosphere at New York Medical College, with which I am now associated, and wish to express my sincere gratitude to the Department of Psychiatry. Its spirit is inquiring and enterprising and does not shy away from new ideas. The Postgraduate Center for Mental Health and its director, Dr. Lewis R. Wolberg, have been a continuous stimulus toward investigation and always a source of support, for which I am most grateful.

With much warmth I wish to acknowledge the encouragement and aid of my long-time friend Dr. Helen Durkin. She read some chapters of the manuscript carefully, and her valuable suggestions were of great help. Mr. William Evans of the British Psychoanalytic

Society also expressed his support for my investigation of this topic. My thanks go also to my husband for commenting succinctly on some chapters and putting up with my difficult time schedule.

Miss Marcia Picker read two chapters in rough draft with exceptional care, and I wish to thank her for insightful comments and suggestions. Finally, my gratitude and love go to Ruth Marcus. She has helped me with secretarial work for many years and undertook the chore of typing several revisions of these chapters. Not only is she a most patient secretarial assistant, but through her efficiency and optimism she keeps up the spirits of those with whom she works. I am fortunate that this includes me.

EDRITA FRIED, PH.D.

Active / Passive

1. The Basic Need for Activeness

People want to be users of life. They wish to expose themselves to experiences, even when this exposure involves challenge and danger. They have the desire to explore other people and the world. And this urge to act on the environment and to effect movement and change is universal.[1] Although the human species is highly susceptible to dangers (and particularly to internal dangers), although many people respond to these dangers with anxiety, while many others seem to cling to languorous, masochistic suffering — even as these surface phenomena of passivity and withdrawal are apparent everywhere — *one of the most basic needs of the human race is activeness.* To tackle life, to make human contacts, to experience vivid emotions, and to exercise will and skills are prime desires.

It has been a regrettable mistake to adopt on a broad scale Freud's assumption that pleasure derives from the reduction of tension. And we have misled ourselves in accepting the idea that the chief human motivation is to maintain a steady equilibrium with an unchanging level of energy and with desires at a low ebb. Equally questionable is Freud's and Ferenczi's claim that the deepest, most nearly universal, and always existing (though often unconscious) longing is to return to the prenatal protection of the womb.[2,3] This idea, which has stimulated much psychoanalytic thinking, holds true only during strong ego regressions in illness, in extreme fatigue, or in the moments before falling asleep.

Observations of recent years show that there are permanent wishes — indeed, urges — for activeness and efficacy which far outweigh the wish to live untroubled.[4] Not everyone, not even the majority, prefers the still pond or the safe mainland to the churning of the sea.

Only those who have deep problems wish to avoid activity, exploration, and tension. For such people, the already existing high level of tension threatens to exceed ego endurance. Many assumptions about human nature at large have been based on studies of the abnormal. To complete our comprehension of man we must add a thorough acquaintance with health, with all the processes of vitality, and with the nature of activeness as well as of withdrawal.

The affirmative personality that modifies the world rather than adjusts and conforms becomes the new object of study — and the new ideal. Self-expression, a clamor to secure satisfactions (and I am not talking of simply hedonistic pursuits), the exercise of the senses, the enjoyment and expansion of perceptual and thinking discoveries, the strengthening of inventive language, these and much more constitute self-affirmation and emotional-psychological activeness. In ego psychology today, compassion for the masochistic sufferer is dwindling. The self-depreciating and self-hurting life style is no longer the mode. This change is partly an expression of new ego ideals that permeate society. It is also a result of growing psychoanalytic understanding of the masochistic phenomenon and the development of techniques suitable for dealing with it.

Criteria of mental health, aims of therapy, and processes of activeness must be specified, at least in part, to make clear what we are talking about. Some of the signposts are these: Emotions are brought to light, and the individual is enabled to be in touch with them, using them as road signs that tell what troubles or desires are stirring. Men and women whose development was tampered with in childhood are enabled to move ahead along a step-by-step continuum of human relations that leads from narcissism, through symbiosis, beyond individuation-autonomy to reciprocal love (object constancy). Though a measure of adjustment is necessary — imaginatively conceived and executed, it is hoped — people learn to act on their environment. Passivity is the engulfing pitfall on their road.

Mental and emotional activeness offers the most reliable protection against that slyest and most formidable psychological enemy, anxiety. But we have to add a very important modification. Activeness must be, for the most part, *straight* — that is, largely conscious, goal-directed, and based on authentic emotions. It must be distinguished from defensive activeness. Authentic contacts with others, a deliberate (though often necessarily subtle) assertion of one's rights or desires, the use of self-made resources rather than of borrowed strength, a clear perception of what exists and is dangerous, all these are *straight activities*, which will be discussed more fully later. Wishing dangerous facts away, relying on fancied omnipotence, repressing awareness of dangers, or taking refuge in withdrawal, these are *defensive activities*. They belong largely in the category of defensive living which in the long run offers no protection against anxiety. Of course, everyone needs to rely on certain defenses during crises, but defenses can be chosen discriminatingly and given up when trouble recedes. This wise use of defenses was shown by a man who was about to go to an essential meeting when he got a message that a relative had died. His immediate response was, "What a sad day that will be tomorrow." He knew that one can defend against pain by delaying one's reaction, should urgent circumstances call for it.

At times, if the individual wishes to fight for self-determination and the exercise of straight activity but cannot summon sufficient energy to take the risks and consequences, the need for activeness goes underground, but it does not disappear. Pressures build up and then surface in the form of discontent and depression. Simultaneously, a fuzziness begins to affect thought and feeling, which, in turn, breeds anxiety. In some such instances the individual lives on two levels at the same time. One is marked by caution, silence, and defense; the other by an inner gnawing and urgency. The individual is anxious that his behavior might shift uncontrollably from the defensive, passive level to that of activeness.

Norris never emancipated himself from the pressures of his mother which had led to his most marked character trait: timidity. When he married, he felt the same kinds of pressures — imagined, suspected, and often real — from his wife, Marcia. One day in therapy he said, "I'm fed up with the domestic scene. It's too confining because I let my wife push me around. I want out. I feel like uttering screams, but I stifle them. I'm just about to start conducting myself as I choose. At last I feel I have the inner strength to go my own way. But there is something screwy about my thinking. A double layer of thought is going on all the time. On the top I hide my murderous anger against her and tell myself that while it is here today it will be gone tomorrow. But underneath there is a funny image: I have a clear vision of myself as a criminal. It's not that I will kill her, but that I have already committed the crime. I have murdered her because I permit her to confine me to passivity. But I can't get the double layers of thought and emotion together into one clear focus for a straight and free life."

The final impetus that prompts disturbed people to seek treatment is usually an obvious symptom such as sleeplessness, sexual impotence, a work problem, or depression. But it is interesting how soon many patients, and particularly the younger ones, speak of their wish to "get with it" and how quickly they are able to relate their lethargy, apathy, and depression to the underlying narcissism and passivity. Though passivity is often hidden behind such facades as synthetic casualness, love of leisure, languor, suffering, and, astoundingly enough, hyperactivity, the discontent it creates gnaws at the mind and makes for uneasiness. *A greater emphasis on the fact that genuine activeness is a necessity of life, just like unpolluted air ana water, will do much to clarify the nature of what is too often a vague but perpetual discomfort.*

> Jane, the depressed, middle-aged wife of a professor, came for a consultation with a therapist. Her husband, long genteelly poor, was at last earning an adequate income, relieving his wife of the pressure to work. She reported anxiously that she looked with suspicion on her ever-longer dawdling in bed. "I don't keep my dining table pretty, I hardly bother to cook, I feel and think black emptiness. I am slipping into something sinister. The external circumstances that used to get me going — for instance, getting the children to school — don't exist any more. I can just glimpse that I must stop myself from slipping into a do-nothing, feel-nothing state of mind. I want help to come back to life."

The wish for activeness underlies in pathological ways (which need further study) the paranoid life strategies. Patients with paranoid character traits fight, scheme, litigate in the courts, and invent distortions. They are, to be sure, in constant danger of being fired or confined or abandoned. Yet, I believe that the people who incline toward the paranoid and schizophrenic strategies take a good deal of pride in their conduct, self-destructive as it is. Compared with the masochists who give in to passivity and complaining, the paranoid patients are more active. Their arrogance does not stem solely from grandiosity but also from a conviction that they are maintaining some measure of action and initiative. Rarely do people with paranoid inclinations part with their pathological activity unless they have been helped to form a core of true self-esteem and have started to apply their initiative in constructive areas.

The Processes of Activeness

Brain studies show that the human organism is active and not reactive.[5,6] It seeks stimulation even if it has to go out of its way to get it. If the input is low or nil, as in isolation experiments, the mind goes ahead and creates mental products, albeit in the form of hallucinations and delusions. Vital activity — for example, certain fair and decent fights [7] — tones up mind and body. It enhances the capacity to solve problems and even to resolve inner conflicts by strengthening a kind of mental "ready-set-go" orientation.

Even at the beginning of life, infants and children struggle fiercely against those parental injunctions that stem the forward movement from narcissism, through symbiotic union with the mother, to self-differentiation and individuation. The eight-month-old who needs his mother screams wildly for attention. The three-year-old, whose motility is reasonably developed, throws a temper tantrum or runs away if the parent wants to restrain him.[8] Repeating the phases of child development on new and different levels, adolescents and young adults who are held back swing to extremes to summon the strength to assert their rights to activity.

To illuminate the essence of activeness, some processes that go into its making will be singled out. If such processes are not present in an individual, they can often be developed through suitable psychotherapy. Here are examples: (1) Problem-focused, inventive thinking predominates over evasive, routine thinking.* (2) Freshly coined, selectively chosen language outweighs slogans and general-

* For more on this, see chapter 7, "Active Thinking."

ities.* (3) New perceptions are found in familiar surroundings, and new impressions are captured through excursions into new territory, be it only a walk around a new corner. (4) Interventions that consider the other's needs outweigh ritualistic exchanges and marginal gestures. (5) Inquiry into another person's idiosyncratic ways prevails over assumptions that he is just like oneself. (6) A certain measure of self-exposure is considerably more frequent than is carefully guarded or rationalized isolation. (7) An ongoing (and not necessarily grim) search for the essence and solution of inner conflicts replaces narcissistic, masochistic, passive behavior, and stewing over old problems. (8) The development and refinement of new mental skills (ego functions) go on constantly and are a source of joy. (9) The range of emotions is maintained and expanded.

Timothy, treated in combined individual and group therapy, actually came to treatment in imitation of his humorous, gifted, and enterprising boss, who had been a patient. Timothy had very little to say and usually mentioned a technicality in his work when he did get around to talking. When he tried to think or reported that he was thinking, he often turned around in his mind six or seven pronouncements his wife had made. Avoiding self-exposure in all circumstances, and especially in treatment, he talked primarily about other people — his wife, his boss, his boss's wife — and had to be reminded many times that he, not these others, was the star of the therapy session. When Timothy divorced his wife, a cold but very bright and enterprising girl, he spent weekends in bed masturbating. In group situations he often said, "I'm sorry" or "I don't mean that," pretending through the facile use of the apologetic phrase that he was concerned with the feelings of other group members. But in actuality he had no interest in anyone else — he always forgot names, for instance — and he showed little or no comprehension of the mind of others.

Everything was done in therapy to point out to Timothy his unrecognized but simmering rages and also to help him, by alternately teasing or challenging him, to articulate anger. He was encouraged to admit his grandiose — and inaccurate — view of himself. Since his dreams showed a lot of negativism

* See chapter 10, Escape From Semantic Jungles."

(he would, for example, dream of climbing snow-covered mountains backward, with his skis pointing down as he ascended, and of driving his car in reverse gear), the therapist told Timothy that often when he was outwardly polite he didn't mean it. When the patient was talked to, challenged, teased, or questioned by the group, he was requested firmly to respond with *anything* except silence or withdrawal.

Gradually this passive, self-isolating man turned into a fun-loving person. He bought a motorbike and explored all of Manhattan, previously seen only through half-shut eyes. From being a verbal reactor who responded to questions simply by reiterating them, like an automaton, he took the leap into humor and initiative. Timothy's boss noticed that his steady but unimaginative employee was changing. When he asked questions, he found that Timothy often shifted queries to more fruitful angles or brought hidden implications or overlooked facts into the open. Timothy soon found and accepted a much more interesting and lucrative position and finally, after four years of treatment, went abroad for a year to explore the world and try himself out.

Timothy's escape routes from inertia to activeness were several: self-understanding (insight); expression of rage; response to challenge (in this case, to moderate and good-humored attack by the therapist and some group members); active thought; and, once it was made clear that withdrawal was taboo, expressions of affects other than rage — for example, occasional enthusiasm and warmth.

If emotional and mental alertness, direct and authentic self-expression, maintenance of contact with the external world, and the development and exercise of human (ego) skills are such desirable and necessary experiences, and indeed have been proclaimed as the very goal and essence of life,[9,10,11] then why are there so many people who fail in these essentials?

Among many answers to this key question three stand out.* (1) Behind all inertia, passivity, and abstinence from vitality are the scars of extremely harsh and repeated parental injuries in early infancy and childhood. When parents cannot make contact with the

---

* For more on this, see chapter 8, "The Passive Stalemate," and chapter 9, "The Subjective Advantages of Passivity."

periodically changing needs of their child, the young mind invents
or instinctively finds countermeasures and self-protections. Withdrawal and apathy, which later often become permanent character
traits, are prime defenses. People forfeit activeness out of habit
(defensiveness). They also seek to punish everybody by sulking and
by refusing to participate in others' enterprises. (2) If mental in-
surance policies in the form of retreat predominate because of childhood scars, the personality has only an underground life. In the
subterranean world, fantasies, rages and related affects, and a jungle
of defenses flourish. Quite likely those defenses are produced by
neurological restraint processes with which we are as yet not familiar.
We do believe, though, they probably are qualitatively different
from the processes that underlie straight participation in the flux of
life. It may be that if such special forms of restraint prevail, they do
not leave sufficient room for the growth and strengthening of the
energies or processes that are the root of straight, deliberate, largely
conscious activities. (3) A psyche that has not developed ego skills
because of withdrawal reactions and abstention from contact, competition, and open participation is lame. Activeness is often avoided
because a person feels or knows that his mind, perceptions, and
body are not sufficiently supple to let him immerse himself successfully in life.

The following case illustrates the first-mentioned reason for inactiveness — namely, the wish to get even with others through sulking
and nonparticipation.

> Lee, the daughter of parents who hardly touched her when
> she was a baby, was so pained by her longing for stimulation
> that even as a small child she would withdraw into darkened
> rooms. Emotionally she turned to an underground life of rage
> and defenses. In adult life she went to great trouble to per-
> petuate withdrawal: She held in her rage and used a maze of
> defenses. Despite occasional breakthroughs of engaging charm
> and wit, repressions, long periods of withdrawal, and masoch-
> istic suffering designed to get even with uncaring parents
> spread like weeds. In a rare fit of open rage that heralded her
> beginning improvement, Lee exclaimed, "How I hate this waste.
> The dark rooms, the timid ways that I don't need because I
> am mischievous and shrewd enough to stand my ground. It's

all pretense. I ruin my life to get even with parents who don't even realize I am making myself unhappy in order to punish them. I am tired, tired of self-extinction."

Some people are active in some sectors of their mental-emotional territory and passive in others. Quite frequently these persons have psychopathic inclinations. They see some problems with merciless clarity and have extraordinary skills and talents, often in the area of visual perception where they are enterprising, innovative, and daring. In this field of functioning they have managed to preserve autonomy, independence, and activeness. Another area that often has been protected against invasion and curtailment by parents is the spending and investing of money. Other aspects of the personality are stunted. There may be little or no ability to carry on relationships of any duration or consistency with family members (although the capacity for loyalty toward employees is, interestingly enough, often much more pronounced, probably because employees do not as readily become the object of carryover [transference] feelings). In other cases, the range of affect is as narrow as that of a four-year-old, and hence vital reactivity is limited to standardized, empty responses: "Oh!" "Ah!" "Terrific!" In therapy sessions childlike and empty expressions occur over and over again.

The half-active, half-passive patients we have been discussing often feel such urgent needs to get into the swing of activeness, whether halted in life or in therapy, that in a treatment session they start to tap with a foot or hand, to twist in a chair, anything to come to life again.   •

Ivan was sometimes daring and impetuous. At other times he was passive to such a point that he had no thought, association, or question and sat on a chair twisted like a pretzel. He had, however, an unceasing need to become active at all costs. In the pursuit of psychological activeness, he became hectically active in a physical way. He traveled all over the world. He built himself houses and plowed land. Ivan was original, inventive, and completely his own master when it came to one faculty, visual perception. He was a successful and distinguished photographer. Whenever he was called upon to tap this uncontested and uncontaminated skill — the source of his luxurious livelihood — anxiety and passivity disappeared as well as his physical restlessness. "When I am behind my camera," Ivan would say, "I feel vibrant, alive, six feet tall. I don't even remember what anxiety feels like."

Self-Esteem, Mastery Over Anxiety, Reality Confrontation

Self-Esteem. Privileges and reassurances, more effective than bank accounts, come to the vital, active, and affirmative person. Because he possesses mental and emotional strength and flexibility,[12] a high degree of self-reliance is available to him. Though encouragement by others and mutual exchange are always welcome, the source of energy, the only reliable steering and pulling power of the vehicle of life, rests in the self.

Where activeness prevails, the self can come to the aid of the self because it is well equipped with what it takes to move ahead — if not always, then often. The active person commands the courage to look at problems and conflicts straightforwardly — if not always right away, then after some self-search. He can do this because he knows that he has access to many alternatives. He need not rely on the assistance of others. If his car gets stuck, he can drive to a service station or fix it himself.*

When the personality feels fortified by contact with the emotions, when it can make reasonably accurate diagnoses as to what is wrong, when it can anticipate what correctives are needed to set things straight, when contacts with others are straightforward and clear rather than manipulative and fuzzy (as they are when defense operations becloud what goes on), when ego skills, well-assorted and perpetually practiced, are on call, then self-esteem runs high.

The person who is affirmative, vital, and active resembles the free farmer who owns his land, while the passive person, like a peon, depends for sustenance and the fruits of harvest largely on the whims of the landlord. Needing little protection and patronage, which always command a price, individuals who have acquired the daring to be active on their own behalf need not strike emotional bargains in return for assistance. The distance between what they need and

---

* Dreams show how often the pursuit of life is symbolized by the motion of a car.

what they can procure by themselves is relatively narrow. This, according to most definitions,[13,14] allows for a high and stable level of self-esteem. Vitality and activeness invite the benevolent presence of hope.[15]

As we have said, the original activeness that exists in every living organism at birth can be extinguished because childhood injuries make necessary an energy-consuming maze of fake emotions and defenses that are perhaps shaped by neurological curtailing processes. If these processes weaken the bases of vitality, self-esteem is lowered because the pillars on which it rests are corroded. As one example of a defensive operation that clearly reduces self-esteem we can take a look at masochism. Characteristically, masochism demands that personal initiative and efficacy be largely extinguished.[16,17]

The mother or father of many a child who becomes masochistic demands directly or in veiled ways that the child remain helpless. Childlike ineffectiveness is more acceptable to such parents than strength and independence. If masochism becomes permanent, as is often the case, a seeming incapacitation continues, and the masochist learns to enlist the aid of others through various manipulations. Of course, the chosen protectors who are expected to stand by in case of danger or defeat also get blamed a great deal. Among the contributions to the complex phenomenon of masochism, a tie to a patron — a mate, a parent, a boss, or a homosexual partner — is a psychological necessity. At times it is the masochist's own stern, scolding superego from which instructions and blame are expected and which is hated in return. In any event, to maintain the favor of the patron, the passive person must make himself pleasing. He represses his own opinions, acts like a court jester, and humbles himself, all with a lot of underlying resentment.

In sum, the attack on self-esteem in cases of masochistic defenses is perpetual. Who can remain self-reliant and look proudly upon his powers if he curtails his efficacy while he cringes and woos a patron? When passive people, highly defended through masochism, survey in psychotherapy the terrain of their lives, they begin to see that they have alternatives. They note that they can continue to suffer the gnawing pangs of a dwindled self-esteem or can choose instead the growing pains of becoming independent and strong. Usually the vote is cast for the acquisition of self-esteem.[18]

Other defenses detract from self-esteem because they deplete energy to a point at which nearly no vitality is left for vibrant and direct life participation. Someone who maintains very many repressions, for instance, spends so much effort scanning impressions and potential responses that his mind is too busy to relate or to venture forth. If one constantly watches over the output of reactions and weeds out most impulses, the defensive operations take over so much of the mental territory that little space is left for such active engagements as are the wellspring of self-esteem.

Mastery Over Anxiety. Another advantage of a vital mind is the occasionally swift, sometimes slow, mastery of anxiety. The active person can afford to rely on his own skills and decisions to run his psychic household. He need not depend on outside help. He can therefore forget the anxiety-producing question of whether the others who are supposed to keep the psychological unit together will be available and successful.

Activeness and independence are intricately connected. Not only can active personalities shift for themselves, but they can also spare themselves the ambivalent emotions that every dependent person feels toward a patron. The individual who becomes dependent loses emotional clarity. As the patron becomes ever more important, he is also more and more hated since he is perceived as the source of confinement, largely self-imposed though this confinement is. The coexistence of need, gratitude, and resentment, like all ambivalences and confusions, makes for anxiety. A whirlpool of pulls, one of the chief causes of anxiety,* builds up: the person feels the wish to run away, revulsion toward the protector, guilt feelings over such disloyalty, and the wish to stay put. Like a swimmer caught in an undertow, the person who has thrown away his chance for activeness and has given in to passivity feels he is drowning. As he again expresses activeness and independence, immense relief and a loosening of anxiety set in.

Norris confused his confining mother with his wife, who was alternately thoughtful and shrewishly demanding of her husband. When, under the influence of psychotherapy, Norris began to take his first independent steps, he was gripped by anxiety. One day as he went to buy some cigarettes, despite

* For more on this, see chapter 4, "Mastering Danger and Anxiety."

his wife's petulant request that he stay home because she felt sick, he asked himself, "Where will I go if she throws me out of the house?" Immediately he chuckled over the spontaneous answer that came to him, "Why, I shall be free to sleep on a park bench or hike to Canada where I would much rather be than in this distasteful home."

Another time, Norris suddenly realized in a treatment session that despite his wife's likely opposition he could go ahead and dig a garden in the back of his house. Seeing that he could be as independent and active as he wanted, he said: "Now I feel weird. For the first time in years spring is underway. It is both eerie and wonderful. I sense that the muscles in my upper arm are getting taut and strong. Now I want to say nothing more. That is my determination. I am becoming my own man. These vague feelings of anxiety have gone."

Reality Confrontation. Because vitality is, by definition, an initiating state that transmits energy to the environment and generates ideas, it sparks contact with others. Contact, in turn, guarantees that *the world is perceived as it is.* Reality-testing is shored up. As Freud said, "We need to love and keep in touch in order to be healthy." He meant in part that genuine contact keeps narcissistic self-involvement at bay. Creating interest in and understanding of the needs and mental makeup of others, authentic contact reduces the danger of falling back upon an image of a world where wishes and magical thought rather than facts rule. Among the many reasons why human beings seek out the love of their fellow men, not the least is the need to have their image of the world checked. By comparing impressions with others, through what the social psychologists call consensual validation, and even through informative gossip, we make sure that the world actually resembles the picture we create of it. In touch with others, we are exposed to a guidance toward normality. Teasing and criticism keep a check on narcissism and help deflate nascent feelings of omnipotence. They help to straighten out feelings, thoughts, and observations.

Beverly, who tried to be the alluring woman her parents wanted her to be, lived on a diet of dreams rather than realistic evaluations. Out of contact with others (for eventually she also shunned her parents), she yearned for ecstatic love. She had a grandiose wish to find a very special man.

When Beverly learned gradually to face the real world of courtship, love, and the complexities of marriage, she severed what had once seemed a precious, ecstatic, and unreal love relationship. She learned to distinguish between the real interest and concern of male acquaintances and the romanticism of her lover who, although brilliant in his search for ecstatic moments, was basically ungiving and often pretentious. Like some other patients described, Beverly was in combined individual and group therapy. The questions of group members, often based on points of view and experience entirely new to Beverly, at first set off rages. She was reluctant to relinquish her fantasy world and enter the real world that required activeness, persistence, and genuine contacts.

Although passivity and withdrawal promise protection, individuals gradually become aware of the high price they have to pay for these defenses. With this awareness, slowly they will turn to the active life that exists potentially in everyone. Even in those who are passive as a form of revenge, in those whose defenses have overgrown and throttled the wellsprings of vitality, in those who withdraw to hide their incompetence at living there slumbers someone who wants to get out, be with it, experience real emotions, and live.

Active living, which is always creative, is a sentinel against dependency, anxiety, narcissism, feelings of omnipotence, hyperactivity, and alienation from reality. Obversely, passivity, by braking active living, ends in the sullen determination to stay put. It forfeits self-confidence. It leaves the individual behind the movement of life, with a minimal sense of mastery over danger, and unwittingly allows maximum intrusion of anxiety. As a form of strike, a refusal to cooperate with fellow beings, it escapes their corrective arguments and leads to a loss of reality-testing. Every therapeutic investigation shows that the sulker, the hostile passive person, and the timid soul who stay in their corners endanger their emotional and mental health. Yet, as experience shows, when helping hands are extended, passivity can be shed, not instantly but with gradual and growing relief. The exchange of permanently applied brakes for controlled starting and stopping is always welcomed in the end.

Straight Activity

As we have seen, what matters is not just that the mind be active. The most passive person's mind is not entirely inactive. Even in sleep it does not rest totally; indeed, it then produces some of its most surprising and original creations. Rather the point is that the active mind produces a *preponderance of* emotional openness and of probing, venturesome, undisguised mental activeness which is here called *straight activity.** Primitive functioning, as it emerges in dreams or pops up in horseplay and humor, represents one of the many cores of artistic productiveness. It is in the *straight* category. So are, of course, the plain undisguised emotions, their deliberate control, and the skills of the ego. Included also is a reasonable measure of once chosen, now automatic reactions, which cut down the expenditure of psychic effort when we have to carry out fairly meaningless tasks. Only when automatisms spread like weeds — as in the obsessive-compulsive personality, for instance — do they stifle enterprise and alienate the patient from his basic, original emotions.

Of course, not every legitimate goal can be reached by aiming at it directly. As we often cross unknown and difficult territory by traveling roundabout pathways, so mental detours are a *sine qua non* of reaching many desirable and difficult destinations. But to remain in touch with emotions, to sustain authentic contact, and to stay affirmative, detours must be chosen deliberately and conscientiously. We cannot allow them to become the rule rather than the necessary exception.

Similarly with defenses. A measure of defensive activity is necessary to all people. The psyche is bombarded early by internal pressures, the release of which would cause retribution, and by overwhelming external stimuli or injurious acts on the part of caretakers. It needs the protection of defenses. Repressions, withdrawals, masochistic surrenders, and so on provide the first emergency shelters in which refuge is found. Only when defenses overgrow the psyche, becloud the emotions, and shift the psychic balance away from activeness for extended periods of time does human existence become more and more a waste.

* Henceforth in this book, the terms *activity* or *activeness* will always denote what is here defined as straight activity.

Internal (intrapsychic) conflicts, which pit one wish against another or a desire against a fear, and external (interpsychic) clashes between people, in which the interests and emotions of one person go against the interests and emotions of another, can be solved more often than is generally assumed by using concentration, a vital, straight approach, and will. When all these are expected and encouraged at appropriate times and in the right cases by therapist or by therapy-group members, progress is accelerated. It is, of course, true that a patient's defensive aim of remaining unaware and staying put (resistance) is maintained for very good reasons. There are periods and occasions when a person has to hold on to the status quo and abstain from a vital push forward, so as to preserve the shaky relationships he has been able to develop.[19] But this is not always the story. Many patients from whom, after careful deliberation, we require a courageous self-inspection and forward movement are able to cut through the defensive jungle. They surprise themselves by possessing a greater potential for well-aimed mental motion than they gave themselves credit for. In various mental hospitals and clinics, patients are told early in their treatment what their dilemmas, their basic problems, and their deep fears are. The results of these well-planned confrontations prove that a kindly directness and an open appeal to the patient's own resources serve at times better than an indiscriminate respect for self-hiding and self-arrestation.

Gregory, who was an immature though perceptive man when he came to treatment, suffered in his work and marriage from a severe character disorder. His mind was cluttered by obsessive-compulsive habits (defenses). When Gregory first came, he contradicted all the therapist's explanations of his problems. When it was suggested to him that he needed to be suspicious because he was all too readily sucked in by others, he refuted the idea. The explanation that he was stingy because he felt himself to be too vicious to be entitled to financial and professional success was rejected offhand as preposterous. He ridiculed the therapist's observation that one reason he constantly announced his intent to divorce his wife was his desire to be a step ahead in case *she* wanted out.

Eventually, during a group session in which Gregory was

sure to have allies, the therapist challenged him and asked outright that he stop repeating old phrases and arguments. He left in an obvious rage, muttering that he would never return. But he did come back, and amazingly and gratifyingly he opened up for the first time. He spoke of the ruthless uncle who brought him up and who repeatedly deceived him; he acknowledged a gnawing sense of worthlessness; he vividly described his dread of losing his wife. Allowed occasional moves backward into defensiveness and chant-like repetition of worn-out explanations, Gregory, from that point on, cut through many deep problems. He became a more affirmative man, turned increasingly to humor and laughter, and was impatient to shed his old psychological skin.

In a climate in which straight and open communications prevail, these repetitive responses are absent, problems are tackled straight-forwardly, and ego skills grow strong, effective but supple. Like trees that move with the wind, these skills remain flexible. But many mental capacities developed in a climate of derision and confusion resemble dwarfed arbors. Their shapes are arresting, yet the twists and turns into which they have been forced do not allow for sustained thrusts of growth nor for natural flexibility. It is true that twisted ego functions often give others and the individual himself the impression that he is prodigious and extraordinary. They create a fanciful self-esteem and an eccentric identity. In the long run, though, the mental skills that have grown in a healthy climate and have developed as one biological and psychological phase naturally followed upon the next [20,21] afford a robust and unshakable self-esteem and clear identity.

Identity comes about through the continuity and clear recall of what a person feels, thinks, and does. The greater the predominance of what is here called straight mental activity and of mental capacities that are upright yet supple and not warped, the more delineated and stable the sense of identity and authenticity.[22,23]

Knowledge of the neurological foundations of straight activeness, like that of defensive activity, is still nearly nonexistent. Yet we can name some criteria of mental processes that are straight and charged with vitality: they register readily and clearly in consciousness; they are accessible to fairly swift learning and change; we can recollect them without much effort; they create a feeling of joy. The feeling of tiredness experienced by the mind that has moved about and undertaken clear-cut projects is pleasant. It resembles the satisfying fatigue a skier feels after a day on the slopes.

By contrast, defensive mental and emotional processes, rearguard actions that go on underground in a battle of perpetual self-insurance, effect quite different mental states. They are not accompanied by clear awareness. Though more susceptible to remodeling than many therapists believe, defenses and defense strategies are nevertheless only tardily changed and abandoned. They exhaust rather than refresh, and when their use outweighs the direct and open activities, they lead into a cul-de-sac of perpetual fatigue. A decline of initiative and, eventually, depression follow.

Among the almost unlimited variety of defenses, identification — especially with a threatening person — occupies a danger spot comparable to that of masochism, of which it is, in fact, often an integral part. To placate a supposed traitor or enemy the individual may shed his own skin and slip into that of the antagonist. The result is confusion of identity, depression, and pessimistic fatigue. To reinstate straight activity, the defenses that squelch self-expression and identity must be removed.

Faye, a young wife and the mother of three children, enjoyed the company of unconventional friends during the day when she could act as she pleased and do what "came naturally." When her husband came home at night, she was usually dejected and eventually became very depressed. Faye was also puzzled and disturbed by regular depressive moods that overwhelmed her when she visited her parents, who were also, at least in part, very controlled personalities. Faye was relieved when it was pointed out that she was sacrificing her own identity as soon as she encountered tightly controlled people who were close to her. She had to learn and indeed did learn to detect how burdened she was by *their* defenses, so alien to her own personality. As she spotted these burdens and cast them off, like a puppy reasserting his natural friskiness, she became cheerful and enterprising. In fact, she became an artist of daring and stature.

When passivity, induced largely through defensive overactivity, finally wanes through therapeutic intervention, when a wider range of options is exercised and the range of responses expands, spirits lift and body postures change. A feeling of vitality, outward-directed gestures, and more spontaneous and frequent smiles emerge.[24] One of the reasons why a moderate dose of alcohol give many people a lift is that their defensively busy preoccupation dwindles along with the pressures of conscience (superego). The freedom and fun that emerge more naturally, gradually, and lastingly through the liberating effect of psychotherapy may well be due to the increase of neuropsychological effects, equaling those that alcohol and some drugs have on the mental system.

The emotional companions of vitality and activeness are zest and optimism. Patients get even stronger by using and refining their potential skills. Like athletes who develop muscle during physical performances, they develop a constantly growing and expanding ego. As this takes place, they turn to optimism and humor. With free access to existing emotions, these newly alert human beings enjoy the pleasure of a rich, uncluttered affect life, and they can rely on their feelings to steer the way through human contacts. In direct contrast, inertness is always found to consort with depression and pessimism. Every therapeutic improvement in the direction of freeing of energy, increased reliance on life participation, and emergence of real rather than pretended feelings is accompanied by an emergence of good humor, zest, and, indeed, optimism. Enterprise shoots up from the previously stony soil of caution, and more vivid perceptions emerge.

Martin, a forty-year-old musician, had become so passive that he spent nearly the whole day near the kitchen where his wife (whom he resented but to whom he clung) busied herself with domestic chores. Despite his clinging, however, he couldn't even describe just what his wife's activities were. As he got better, his perceptions multiplied and were tinged with pleasure sensations born of improved memory. Beaming with a joviality hitherto unknown, he told his therapy group: "Ah, that delicatessen around the corner, it's a better joint than I knew, and they carry my favorite beer. In fact, the bottles are displayed in the window, but I'd never noticed them before. I am looking around me these days. Those pretty legs in the bus, they ought to put a patent on them". On another occasion he told the girl next to him, "You are nice, and I'd like you to come lie on my bear rug. It's the rug in front of the fireplace where I make love. It tickles me to talk to you like that. I am getting quite tippy-tongued [used to saying what's on the tip of the tongue]. Makes me feel a little tipsy. Wonderful!" With the lid of repression removed, he hit on new expressions and felt the lift associated with creation. No wonder he felt good.

The vitality that produces keen and alert observers, doers, and coiners of language is particularly apparent in certain schizophrenics, whose pathology, though exacting its own severe price, often stems partially from determined and long-term efforts not to be squelched by a hostile and confusing environment.

Priscilla, a brilliant forty-year-old schizophrenic, was alert to minute changes in the therapist's office. Unfettered by convention, she looked at everything as though seeing it for the first time. Because she was frightened of injury, her antennae were always up. She always reported her discoveries with glee. She was delighted that her mind was alert, and her accurate perceptions filled her with a sense of triumph over the therapist who was often not equally agile.

Vitality in Our Society

Observations about idea-constriction, the shadows of atomic or ecological doom, and increasing government-imposed conformity are often linked with assumptions that psychological health is impossible in the age we live in. Such complaints are as untrue as they are vociferous. As new modes of extinction occur, new ways to express productivity, creativity, and individual vitality can be discerned all around by those who want to look. Painting and music are ubiquitous, poetry flourishes as never before in the arts — and even in fashion and advertising. Our world sparkles. And the younger generation has shown that it will not be put down. The youthful counter-culture has as one of its aims the freedom of self-expression and self-determination. The desire to be turned on, to be with it, visible behind many false and unwise methods, expresses the preference for activeness and adventure. We are, with the help of new psychological knowledge and experience, learning how to be users of life, not merely consumers of goods.

2. Female Passivity:
A Half-Truth

The confusing idea — still widely upheld, perhaps because it is appealing — that the female needs to be enormously passive to make a good lover, mate, and mother, grows from the soil of prejudice. It is borne out by neither fact nor observation.

The female position on the passivity-activity continuum is still too often misjudged because we remain hampered by Freud's early thesis. For a time he championed the idea that true femininity and passivity are inevitably linked. Despite Freud's later revisions of this view and the newer, more complex notion that the sexually functioning woman needs to draw on a mixture of passivity and activity,[1] the old notion lingers on. Perhaps the old formulation owes its tenacious survival to male fears of all-powerful mother-women. After all, if the good and desirable woman is one who is exclusively, or even primarily, passive, this dread can more easily be laid to rest.

The Victorian mores, confining women to quiet passivity and secondary roles, have been challenged forthrightly and forcefully for many decades. Nevertheless, here too there is a holdover. While the present-day mores that predominate in the Western world, and even begin to affect other cultural areas, allow the woman initiative and strength,[2] disbelief and confusion still hold sway. Many a woman who seeks therapeutic help is mixed up as to whether to steer toward the timidly passive or the alertly active pole. What further perpetuates the muddle are unwarranted links between, on the one hand, healthy, adult, female outspokenness and calm assertiveness and, on the other, destructive, neurotic, female "bitchiness."

But the truth, as always, has several facets. The neurotic woman feels compelled to rely on aggressiveness, a perpetuation within her personality of early hostility invoked against an abandoning step-mother-like mother who is a prime cause of neurotic development. Also, some women who are disturbed continue to employ aggressive tactics which they acquired in childhood, emulating a father or brother in the attempt to find an ally against the injurious mother. But undisturbed women approach the world with helpful and con-structive self-affirmation. Their assertiveness, coupled with flexibility, is the benign heritage of a good relationship with a relatively accept-ing mother who could be trusted rather than suspected and fought off.

Woman's Complex Sexuality

To move toward sexual climax the woman, especially in her pelvis, must produce and tolerate both passive and active movements. Placid, unvarying, and tepid readiness does not give her sexual ful-fillment. Indeed, these descriptive terms do not capture the essence of female sexuality. The chain of emotions and body experiences that climaxes in female orgasm is quite different from what the man feels. The female emotions and experiences do not simply con-sist of lowered activity and empty, flaccid passivity. Quite the contrary, full sexuality on the part of the woman calls for the active involvement of both the emotions and the body. To achieve a full climax the woman shifts back and forth between a softening and a tightening of the membranes and muscles of the vaginal walls. She can come to orgasm only if she possesses the ability to tolerate and, in fact, to produce changes of muscle tonus.

> Cora, a patient who had been married for six years, became preoccupied with the shortcomings of her quite timid and awkward husband. Blinding herself to her mate's loyalty, wit, and actually colorful physical appearance, Cora told herself stubbornly that she wanted out of matrimony. As her anger ran its course she unwittingly turned off the currents that had previously flowed through her mind and body — and especially her pelvis. With her husband, Cora was either limp and apa-thetic or stiff, as her muscles tensed up to express her angry

rebellion and rejection. Her body and sexual organ had lost the previous range of tonus. As she frequently put it, the sexual experience and life as a whole were just "blah," implying that a tepid, low responsiveness had become all-prevailing. In short, Cora, previously not frigid, had turned herself into an unresponsive woman through resentment and anger which affected the condition of her sexual organ. As this patient gradually became aware of her husband's many good qualities, and as she began to take reluctant looks at the connections between her rebellious body stiffening and her frigidity, she was considerably startled. Then, through self-understanding and deliberate, though not forced, body changes, Cora recaptured her previous responsive pelvic condition. Affectionate feelings toward her husband made her body and her sexual organ again receptive and soft. As the tense condition of the pelvis waned, it was replaced alternately by receptivity and firm and yet resilient responses.

The expanding and blooming female sexuality, far from being passive, taps the woman's capacity for flexibility and variation. To move toward complete orgasm the woman entertains and endows with pleasure an image of the inserted penis and the male who makes love to her. The expressions of pleasure through sound and word spark off in the male articulations of his own. All these variegated experiences are not the harvest of mental and physiological placidity. In fact, they suggest complex processes, many of which are active. As the case of Cora shows, only when physiological and mental currents are sparse and monotonous does frigidity ensue.

Partial female frigidity is more common than the comparable sexual disturbance of the male because in coitus the female sexual organ is expected to perform a more complex sequence than is that of the man. As a prelude to intercourse, the vagina is soft, relaxed, and extended. Lubrication is provided by an involuntary process of the membranes, and a state of quiescent readiness prevails. Such a prelude has been falsely equated with passivity. This is a misleading description. Indeed, the whole female being is permeated by lively, pulsating feelings of longing, anticipation, and yearning. In true passivity the mind is inert, the body is unresponsive, and the level of consciousness is low.

When the male organ has moved into the female pelvis, the emotional response is one of welcome, and physiologically the vaginal membranes close tightly over the penis, making experiences of friction possible and pleasurable. The tonus of the vaginal walls is high. But frigid women cannot accept the male with pleasure nor admit his organ receptively. Neither softly ready for the male nor later tautly reactive, the walls of the female organ contract rigidly.[3] Or else, if the female is uninterested rather than anxious, the vaginal walls remain insensitive and lack tonus, with little or no friction registered.

When the sexually responsive woman holds the male organ in what amounts to a pelvic embrace, the image of lover and penis is vivid and enhances responsiveness. Some semifrigid patients have been helped to activate their vagina and achieve climax when, after fears and resentments of the male were reduced, they were encouraged to develop concrete and love-tinged images of the inserted male organ.

Just before orgasm is reached and while it occurs, the pelvic muscle tone and firmness give way once more to internal softening. Involuntary pelvic contractions set in, and the entire body yields to softness and relaxation, the essence and finality of the female orgasm.

No similarly complex physiological pattern accompanies the male sexual act. His body and sexual organ remain taut and firm up to climax, and it is unlikely that there are parallels to the described alternations between tautness and softness. Only after the peak of orgasm does the male organ go from firmness to softening. No wonder that the complexity of female biology accounts, at least partially, for female sexual frustration such as, for instance, the achievement of a mere clitoral excitation.

Obviously the idea that clitoral and vaginal orgasm are equivalent,[4,5] and that one can be substituted for the other, is not shared here. While most women do indeed need clitoral stimulation as a prelude to vaginal excitement, the suggested equivalence of the two should be further examined. Many women have no basis for comparing either the antecedents or the final body reactions to the two kinds of orgasm. The proportion of women who enjoy vaginal climax is fairly small. Hence it is quite likely that some subjects who were questioned in recent studies had never experienced vaginal orgasm and therefore could not validly weigh the essence and aftereffect of the two connected yet essentially different forms of female climax.

Joanne, a twenty-year-old divorcée used to achieve clitoral orgasm by masturbating in a special way. She merely pressed her legs together and imagined angry male voices nearby. During her brief and unhappy marriage she had often found herself irritated after having been stimulated clitorally by her unloved husband and reaching a climax.

Following divorce and during the course of psychoanalytic psychotherapy, this patient began a love and sexual relationship with a man whom she at first adored but gradually learned to love deeply without ecstatic overevaluation. While she did not reach vaginal orgasm for a long while, new vaginal sensations were awakened that lasted for days after intercourse. The young woman felt that her pelvis was deeply immersed in sensuous longing, and her inside felt enlarged and expanded. The patient clearly distinguished the different experiences of intercourse. Previously she was detached during intercourse and had clitoral orgasms that left her nervously agitated and irritated. But her new lovemaking was accompanied by love-charged images of her lover and unprecedented vaginal reactivity. Invariably the newer sexuality, though not ending in climax, left her partially relaxed. And as the patient put it, "After a little pause I often come out with something showing a sense of humor that takes moody and irritable me by surprise."

Impatience, irritability, and perpetual pursuit of sexual conquests, all these suggests that vaginal orgasm was neither approached nor realized. Women who have remained bereft of the passionate feelings and the final relaxation of complete lovemaking crave more stimulation in the ill-begotten hope that other lovers or more clitoral excitement will bring peace and satisfaction to body and mind.

In some respects woman has to learn what her sexuality is all about. Misled by the idea that flaccid passivity is the road to the goal of satisfaction, many a woman restricts herself to false quiescence rather than reaching for the challenges of emotional and physical participation in lovemaking. Passive, and probably silently hostile to begin with, a large proportion of women complicate their sexual failures through sheer ignorance. True enough, it is on account of their opposition to and fear of the male that they cannot allow their vaginal walls to be responsive, at first softly allowing male entry and later firmly embracing the penis and eventually giving in to the feelings that have been called feminine surrender.[6] But the rigidity, aversion, or apathy that exist to begin with can be perpetuated by sheer sexual confusion. Sexual hurdles are overcome in two ways: if the hostility to the male gradually diminishes and if new avenues of emotion and body experience are knowingly explored.

> Francine, a young schizophrenic woman, recently divorced, with two children, asked what an orgasm was like. A week later she reported with some suspicion and surprise, "I made love and it worked. What you told me about how a deep orgasm comes on slowly and how it helps to get wrapped around the penis made a difference. I had always thought it would happen like a firecracker popping. I was not to participate, just lend myself to lovemaking. This time I just kept from going numb, and today I feel that my insides are all stirred up. I never did dislike Mel [her lover], but now I like him better."

Rigidity and passivity are but one side of the coin of female sexual malfunctioning. The other side is hyperactivity and hectic sexuality. The frenetic woman, fiercely striving after power and using promiscuity as a means of achieving it, is driven by forces she cannot control. She often suffers from confusion. She has learned falsely to equate a hyperactive life with the pure gold of genuine aliveness, passion, and pelvic sensitivity.

Little girls and many female adolescents are unaware of their inner sexual organ. They are gripped by jealousy of the noticeable and manipulable genitals of the boy. While penis envy does not determine female psychology and pathology as deeply as has been claimed, the absence of a noticeable female organ at a time when body feeling focuses on the genital area can do harm. A sense of deprivation, inferiority, and angry envy often emerges. One way of rendering such feelings less painful, prolonged, and perturbing is to explain to little girls their anatomical structure once they begin to raise questions. Mothers can tell their little daughters that inside their body lies a pocket that is nice. Addressing themselves visually to the imagery-demanding mind of the child, mothers can show their daughters a jewelry box or pocket to concretize the comparison with a receptively empty organ.[7] Assisted by such demonstrations and explanations little girls form more appropriate body images and gradually even entertain the idea that at some time ahead their pockets will be filled.

Not all women can acquire the yielding-active alternations that lovemaking requires because present-day treatment techniques do not always produce altered physiological responses. Yet many learn to permit some measure of "letting go." Even females who cannot move all the way to climax can relinquish brittleness of ego and body boundaries where it exists. The mental image of a hard self and a cautiously tightened body can be exchanged for a vision of more flexible emotions and a sometimes soft, sometimes taut pelvis. Though the temporary dissolution of self (regression) which is a prelude to and part of orgasm is not always within reach, the image of a flexible female body steers the woman in that direction. Body roundness, the discharge of the womb lining during menstruation, the swelling and changes that pregnancy produces, and the female organ itself, all these can create, if properly perceived, the mosaic of a body image in which softness and pliancy are part of the design. An appropriate body image, perhaps one corrected by psychotherapy, together with social expectations that a woman's appearance and conduct should display both resilience and softness, can help a woman achieve a yielding-active stance. Where the sexual problem is body rigidity, new ideas of the self can assist the relinquishment of firmness and unyielding ego boundaries in favor of sexual surrender.

Female Masochism:
Being a Mother's Daughter

How the personality shapes up in adult life is influenced by a multitude of bodily events.[8] The anatomy sets basic tunes which the listening mind uses to form the variations and compositions of character. The vicissitudes of the female anatomy provide the melodies that reverberate throughout female life. Yet, just what variations, what individualized responses a female evolves in orchestrating and playing the melodies of her physiology, these are determined by other than the anatomical facts.

The expectations, restrictions, and encouragements that society offers have a hand in what happens.[9] Mores are road signs. They mark the highways as well as the by-ways of self-protective behavior (defenses). A woman has a choice of paths to travel in her life.

Yet still more decisive than social mores is another factor — the early relationship between the mother and her baby girl which forms the core of the female personality. More than social possibilities or life's happenstances, this relationship guides or misguides the female's reactions to anatomy. Psychoanalysis, mental health education, and the change in woman's social status have helped mothers to accept their daughters more readily. The conscious and declared intention of most mothers is to grant their daughters first-class citizenship in the family, instead of the old stepchild position to which many a daughter used to be condemned. Yet the baby girl's relationship to the mother still remains precarious, especially in the not infrequent instances in which a mother, herself antagonistic to the female fate, is a poor parent to the daughter. Whether a mother overprotects, critically rejects, or neglects her daughter, either directly or in still more damaging but veiled ways, the daughter's life as a female is fraught with danger.[10] Frustration, rage, hypochondriasis, masochism, and sadism, all these abound in female personalities that were shaped under the influence of unmotherly mothers. Poorly aided or even harmed by out-of-tune mothers, daughters do not meet anatomical reality and emotional demands as adventures that call forth strength and ingenuity. Rather these daughters are forced to regard them as catastrophes, and this produces massive anxiety. It is challenging to delve into new physiological experiences under the guidance of a mother who possesses the chief attributes of good parenting: intelligent patience, attentiveness, and attunement. However, if the daughter is left alone to struggle clumsily and unaided with life, it taxes the young mind to the point where neurotic countermoves are tried out and eventually adopted permanently.

Since all women share the same physiology and, within the same culture, similar social demands, female irascibility, still a rather frequent phenomenon, can no longer be explained in old ways.

Neither anatomy nor social pressures are alone responsible because equality between the sexes has become close to a fait accompli. If it is still true that *la donna è mobile,* if it still holds that many women are irritable creatures, the explanation must lie elsewhere. The thesis here is that in good measure it is poor mothering that makes for a daughter fraught with problems. Women who either had the good fortune of having accepting mothers or else have climbed over psychological hurdles with the help of psychotherapy are strong as well as soft, with flexibility one of their chief distinctions. But women who are brittle, complaining, and sadistic often owe their personal disturbances to the effects of bad mothering which have remained unrelieved.

To be a mother's daughter is a dangerous fate when the mother has herself had inadequate maternal care. The harsh vicissitudes of a bad relationship with the mother during the formative years of infancy and childhood determine the unfortunate choices of protections and facades that mar the adult personality. Indeed, even healthy females owe their specific character traits not only to their anatomy, not only to social expectations, but also to the daughter role. How different their situation is from that of the male who is a mother's son. As such, he has different character tendencies. In cases in which the mother is disturbed, he faces entirely different emotional problems.

It is not sufficiently highlighted by the psychoanalytic literature that the girl, especially if she is the first or the only child, gravitates towards certain problems among which the following stand out: she tends to be masochistic; she is sporadically or continuously sadistic; she meets the mother's frequent demand that the daughter be a parent to the mother with reluctant submission, apathy, or outright anger.

If we throw into one pot the chief ways females use to cope with their lot as a daughter — and in turn with anatomy and society — we encounter a broad though not infinite spectrum of possibilities. Depending on the base lines of individual female adaptation, specific personality traits emerge. Together these make up something like a female psychology. It is one by no means characterized by passivity alone.

Much has been made quite recently, as well as in the past, of woman's inclination toward a masochistic style of life. Since her body has to cope with some happenings that can easily be regarded as suffering, it has been said that woman finds a modus vivendi by elevating pain to virtue. Either that which she has to tolerate becomes comfortable, like an old shoe, or, as some psychoanalysts have claimed, pain is imbued with pleasure. Masochism, always centering on a large core of passivity, has been attributed to woman by many an amateur and expert.[11,12,13] The startling readiness of many women, especially in other periods of history and in other than the Western part of the world, to accept second-rate status and heavy physical labor has added natural fuel to the claim that the female is unavoidably masochistic. If women have in so many settings and to this day accepted the deprivations and frustrations handed out, it is argued, is this not a sign that they incline toward masochism?

A refreshing, more complex, and hence probably truer survey is furnished by another set of up-to-date observations. All together these observations seem to separate the members of the female sex into something like a tripartite classification. First we have the subdivision of the healthy modern woman who is neither suffering nor notably weak. Rather, she sets examples that enrich everyone as she proves to be zestful, resilient, and highly imaginative. These women are the offspring of healthy and predominantly daughter-accepting mothers. As the imprint of bodily development appears within the total setting of the personality, such women are the bearers of but the faintest masochistic pain. Indeed, the mere touch of masochism that cannot be totally avoided despite fine maternal care lends the hue of graciousness to the healthy female personality.

In a second subdivision of the tripartite female classification we find women who cover up basic depression, apathy, and masochism with frenetic hyperactivity. In the childhood of such frenzied women we not infrequently discover maternal neglect rather than either overprotection or outright rejection. Maternal absences are frequent, and substitute care by baby sitters or neighbors is erratic. Psychopathic patterns, characterized among other criteria by a superego that is shot full of holes, begin to develop early, together with a hunger for contact that accounts for an early, continued, and indiscriminate search for friends, parent figures, mates. The frenetic woman thinks at a furious but fragmented pace. She speaks quickly and likes exaggerations that stem from the search for omnipotence. Manners and appearance are as frequently changed as boy friends, mates, and employers. If ever the brittle and frenetic overlay that covers apathy and depression is punctured, the bubbly zest collapses fast and gives way to depression.

Slim was the unwelcome, illegitimately conceived though legitimately raised daughter of an unfeminine mother. She was told every Sunday at breakfast that the mother would send Slim to an aunt and take into her home in Slim's place a nice obedient boy. Frustrated that she herself could not become a famous scientist, the mother pushed her daughter, from the age of three on, to obtain fame. At the same time the mother threatened that Slim would end as a failure who would never herself bear a healthy child. When evening came around Slim sat forlorn on her bed, her mother away in a bar. By her eleventh year this patient had already adopted a furious life pace. Her speech was agitated, her movements hectic. At the age of sixteen the patient was already quite a prominent entertainer who used her hyperactivity to amuse others. But when alone she kicked the furniture around and smashed window panes. Unless she could get hold of liquor or make a quick date with a friend, she fell victim to depression. After three suicide attempts she entered psychotherapy, but she only gradually admitted the yearning for contact and the longing for love that underlay her hectic and frenetic search for amusement.

Finally we have a third subdivision into which many disturbed women fit. These women share with one another a deep core of passivity, a quite apparent masochism, and a more concealed resentment.

The masochistic suffering, which goes back developmentally to the first and second years of life, the so-called preoedipal period, is so complex that only some basic features can be outlined. For one thing, the female masochist usually makes sure that her slip is showing. She slyly half-reveals her pain through skillful hide-and-seek games with those who are close. Unexposed, because of early withdrawal reactions, to the stark realities of the world, the masochistic female is filled with infantile omnipotent wishes. She is intolerant of frustrations because of her craving for omnipotence. Because her ego has remained weak, rage alternating with irritation is the usual response if things go wrong. At the time when her major task was to induce the rejecting mother to look on her child as harmless and thus to offer some protection, a kind of self-restriction was developed. Never recognized for its true intent, this self-paralysis has become embedded in the character. Unsure bodily gestures, a groping walk, and self-induced failures reflect the eventually automatic self-curtailment of the masochistic girl. Appearance is often neglected. But invariably the masochistic system includes all-permeating though often well-hidden rage, explosively ventilated only from time to time.

Women who have adopted masochism as their chief line of self-defense resemble flowers nipped in the bud. Formerly preoccupied with the hope of keeping rejecting mothers at bay by appearing needy and harmless, they eventually forfeit their spunk for good, unless therapy intervenes. Tiredness and a drugged feeling are the prime emotions. But of course in the background there hovers heavy and violent anger that becomes directed at the self.

> Bodha was a young woman who came for help when she realized that she was about to destroy her marriage. She was, in effect, brought up by two mothers, each rejecting and hurtful in her own way. One was the real mother, a diffident, depressed, and hypochondriac woman who spent long periods of time in bed. The other "mother" was the very young maternal grandmother, a real shrew. She screamed if Bodha ran about exuberantly and accused her of being a "bad seed" who would disgrace the family. Where the real mother harmed the child by her demands that the daughter mother the mother, the grandmother obstructed the pathways toward independence by angry shouts and accusations.

> In treatment, Bodha dwelt on her failures and woes although she barely acknowledged them in everyday life. She reported to the therapist at length how sick she herself, her mother, and the rest of the family were, and she ended her enumeration of calamities with the question, "Do you think I will end up in an asylum?" These queries, running parallel to constant exhibitions of pain and fear within her marriage, were designed to alert the therapist to the emergency state in which the patient wanted to see herself. When it was explained to Bodha that in her home life she behaved so as to "let the truth show through" and exhibited suffering designed to reveal as well as to hide distress, the condition began to improve.

Exceptionally talented and intelligent, Bodha played the role of an incompetent and silly girl. She was a master at enacting a stepdaughter-like, or orphan-like, role. When the therapist laughingly stated that such self-paralysis, though interestingly displayed, was not a convincing reflection of the patient's true and capable self, Bodha was enraged. But gradually her spunk and competence shot up through previously arid soil.

This young wife, who had pretty features and a winsome smile if she permitted it to break forth, neglected her body and appearance to highlight her misery, her harmlessness, and self-extinguishing conduct. Quite overweight, she made sure that her physical self remained as fettered as her psyche. Bodha's walk, described by her as "clumpy," and her angry nail-biting reflected the inner battle. Self-extinction (docility) and fury (self-assertion at a primitive level) struggled with one another. The patient felt "dopey" much of the time. These moods mirrored her far-reaching self-alienation and self-extinction, originally undertaken to achieve an undangerous modus vivendi with the two bad mothers.

All suffering and self-extinction have their own sweet rewards. Deprived of love from others, the sufferer who stays in a corner or who moves about slowly is left to herself. She can direct her attention and her unspent love toward herself in many indulgent and sweet-tasting ways. Like certain kinds of masturbation, masochism resembles dwelling in a never-never land where the self gives to the self. For this and other reasons it is a difficult, though nevertheless possible, task to pull the female masochistic victim who is about to be dragged down by a vortex of her own making back onto the safe and clean shores of health.

Poor mothers, standing emotionally with one foot outside and another inside the home, threaten to desert the female child. Themselves abandoned by their own rejecting mothers, they demand, knowingly or unwittingly, that their daughter mother the mother. Out of the fear of being deserted many a female child heeds the cry. She begins to wait on her mother and takes to clinging habits early in life. She attaches herself symbiotically to the mother so as to make sure that the female parent does not slip away.[14]

Lee, a married, lonesome young musician, was an only child.

Her mother had amply evidenced her dislike of being a wife and parent by neglecting the home, taking vacations for long periods, and watching absent-mindedly the often dangerous excursions and play activities of her little daughter. Seized with anxiety lest the absent mother never return home, Lee at the age of five had already assumed a mothering role. She tidied up the house, set the table in her clumsy little way, and cooked dinner. She heroically kept up daily trips to a neighborhood drug store where she looked for a house and a sister to buy. Although this patient during the first six years or so of life managed to hold on to some zest and initiative, she gradually became enveloped by sadness and depression. From the age of seven on she slid into grief. Her large, sad, and expressive eyes were part of her eventual appeal as a musician. Apparently the audiences for whom she performed were attracted to her because of strong desires to come to the aid of such a sad young woman.

Neither hyperactivity nor the described masochistic patterns nor direct hostile aggressiveness furnish reliable protection for the female exposed to past and present sufferings that go back to negligent, deserting, and rejecting mothers. Psychotherapy demonstrates that the only alternative forms of behavior that stand up and do not backfire lie in the development of healthy activism and the unfolding of given potentials. Once the endangered daughter of a formerly disappointing and deserting mother realizes that as a grown-up she can extend her dealings to persons who understand and love her, including males, she is ready to expand and use many strengths previously beclouded and underdeveloped. Her safety is guaranteed when she finds out how to spot personalities who are different from the childhood mother. She discovers that she can develop and exercise her potentials without risking the danger of desertion by the new cast of characters in her present life.

Female Sadism: A Show of False Strength

Many deeply masochistic women deny the feeble roots of their existence. Placing strength on top of weakness like a gardener grafting a strong plant on a weak stem, they draw attention to a display of power. But it is a fake power, superimposed on a confused and weak personality. For a time the display of bravado and the waving of the flag of independence take in both the woman herself and many who give her merely a superficial glance. When worldly circumstances take an adverse turn, when a seemingly strong but basically weak and masochistic woman loses a person who offered emotional support, and when sudden catastrophe befalls her, the seemingly strong front collapses, and she sinks into depression.

Another strategy to hide inner weakness and masochistic clinging is the turnabout. In this case the helplessness and the suffering are shifted to someone else, and the woman who felt herself to be the original victim now seeks out situations in which she gains triumph and satisfaction by taking on the role of victor. Records of acts by which a victimized woman fortifies herself by stepping on a person who is weaker than she abound in the practice of the psychotherapist. Humiliating her victims, both male and female, the boss-woman recovers from her own sealed-off pangs of weakness by dealing out to weaker victims the blows once aimed at herself.

Why are women so often feared as employers? Why have some been depicted as a mean and inconsiderate part of the human race? Surely one of the prime answers is that, feeling themselves to be victims and often fearing the strong powers of their own superiors (especially if these superiors are women whom the masochistic females cast in the mother role), they are on the lookout for means of defense. One of the most destructive is the attack on weak human prey who will lend themselves to expressions of contempt, to shabby treatment, and to condemnation to an inferior role. It is only the disturbed person who turns to this kind of defensive attack to secure reparation for injustice. Of course the guilt feelings created by this particular form of defense are excruciatingly deep. Many a victimizing woman conceives of herself as evil, ugly, and witch-like, but her guilt does not usually bring her exploitations and derisions to a halt. Indeed, it may intensify both self-flagellations and sadistic exploits unless therapy intervenes.

In treating women who are thus split down the middle — harsh, demeaning, and sadistic toward those who are perceived as weak and deferential and pacifying vis-à-vis the powerful — it is useful to remember always that it is helplessness and masochism that appear first in childhood development. The impetus behind the pathology is fear. It is not the display of sadism that matters most, but the desperate restraint of anger and rage toward the real target and the misplaced expression of these feelings toward the substitute figures later set up in its place.

Basically masochistic women who protect themselves through their sadistic acts become resistant in treatment when the therapist takes their cruelty and derision to be the prime expression of the true self. They feel totally misunderstood and turn angry and even suicidal. It is when the major currents of the personality are uncovered and the defensively sadistic female is convinced that her basic masochistic suffering is comprehended that she becomes willing to cooperate as a patient. She might be ashamed of her emerging weaknesses, now seen in clear light; she might insist that some of her strength is genuine, as indeed one portion always is; but she will be grateful when attention is focused on the core of her being rather than on the layers of powerful sham spread over it. This is not to say that the way to treat masochism is to ignore its surface manifestations and to get lost in sympathy with the patient's suffering. It does mean that several therapeutic acts need to be initiated simultaneously: the masochistic core has to be identified; the sadism and aggressiveness have to be perceived as cloaks that hide underlying weakness; and the masochistic sufferer, no longer a helpless child but an adult with partly formed potentials, needs to be encouraged to stand up for her rights. To shed both the masochistic nucleus and the sadism, the woman need not shout, reproach others, or seek retributions for past injustices. What matters is that she begin to fend for herself in the present and use fair weapons in the fight. Otherwise she will feel guilty and exclude herself once more from human camaraderie.

Lee, walking around with deep sadness and dejection in her eyes, regarded her inability to love and her readiness to torture others through ridicule as the ugly core of her personality. Alternating between the exploitation of others, and particularly of basically homosexual men, she was filled with self-accusations.

Lee was married to a man who obviously represented to her a mother figure. He provided well, frequently cooked their meals, and was exceptionally fat. The patient often described him as a woman-man. During her marriage the patient had love affairs with three men whom she encouraged to exploit her, thus playing victim to them. But inexorably she triumphed over them in the end through her own deception. All of the patient's lovers were chosen with an eye to finding in one and the same person both a protector and a victim, and Lee detected such possibilities with exceptional shrewdness. At first she lured her lovers into a false sense of safety. She brought them gifts, did chores, and demeaned herself sexually. When a lover had become off guard, she got ready to destroy him by her derisive attacks.

An almost unfailing instinct for spotting people who are just right for the sadistic maneuver is a talent that dwells with many masochistically sadistic, disturbed women who look at the world with a greedy eye, deciding who could deliver the right mixture of mothering and protectiveness that masochism demands and the appropriate weakness that sadism requires.

Lesbian relationships rest on many of the strategies mentioned, including the masochistic attempt to find protection against the dreaded trauma of desertion and the sadistic need to take continued revenge on the mother. The ménage of two lesbians inevitably represents traumatic enactments of protectiveness, self-humiliation, desertion, counterdesertion, and attack. Both women involved in a lesbian setup vie for one-upmanship. They constantly probe the question of who is to be the winner and who the victim.

Diane, the middle child between two successful sons, had always been treated with contempt by her mother who despised femininity. The patient came to treatment in a state of panic. She drank heavily, took large doses of tranquilizers, had slipped into mild paranoid delusions, and was numbed by depression. Diane's despondency and anxiety were soon found to be related to anguish over her desertion by her lesbian friend Rhona, with whom she had lived for two years. Rhona, whom Diane had supported through college, was seduced by Norma, the very woman who had initiated Diane into the lesbian way of life. Diane was devastated by Rhona's abandonment and Norma's deception. While Diane was in therapy (to which, it might be noted, her resistance was great), she ran into Elizabeth, an undernourished, poorly dressed, and timid teacher. It did not take long for Diane to latch on to this girl who was younger and less efficient than herself. She first induced Elizabeth not only to move in with her but also to get rid of all her own furniture, thus rendering her totally dependent on Diane for shelter. Diane, once she was sure of her partner's confinement to the lesbian home, stopped telling Elizabeth her plans and stopped coming home on time for meals. She spent her weekends with her own powerful and destructive mother whom she alternately hated and courted. However, a series of shocks started when, after four months of such sadistic and abandoning treatment, Elizabeth seized the initiative and stayed out for whole nights with male companions. Her sadistic desertions were aggravated by frequent derogations of Diane's looks, especially an emphasis on her heavy arms. Nearly slipping once more into the familiar role of despondency, self-incrimination, and fear of desertion, Diane, her ego strengthened, was able to pull herself up by her bootstraps. She showed her friend, Elizabeth, some genuine warmth, fortitude, and good judgment. As a result, this lesbian drama ended before it became another tragedy.

Many marital failures are due to the woman's inability to resolve her masochistic dilemma and get rid of the sadistic defenses against it. Casting around for a male at the time she reaches a marriageable age, the disturbed and weak woman selects a male who assumes the responsibilities of mothering. As the wife awakens to the very weaknesses on the part of the husband which underlie his readiness to take a mothering role — and which indeed induced her to choose him as a mate — she casts aspersions on him. Unable to see, or still fearful of seeing, that the disturbed mother was the first real cause of her problems, confused and therefore unaware that as an adult she can bury her rages altogether, the victimizing woman keeps hunting suitable prey. Habitual blunderers, handicapped men or males who develop slowly, perpetual losers, and other insecure people become the targets of her scorn. When therapeutic experience breaks the vicious circle, the blame directed at victims and the underlying self-blame gradually fade away.

The Aggressive Female Facade

Some disturbed women lose all traces of inner vulnerability and masochistic clinging. They have given up the search for mothering from either male or female. Rather than alternating between their courtship of a powerful mother figure and their exploitation of victims weaker than themselves, they are exclusively power-focused. Finding that no show of passivity, self-derogation, and masochism is rewarded, they make a defensive swing of 180 degrees. These women hold on to fierceness and attack even though this posture creates and perpetuates problems. Like many attackers, they guard their capacity for assault and aggression like a precious asset because it lends more personal power than does submission.[15]

The once rejected and subsequently masochistic woman can hide her wounds behind a powerful facade because she has learned to copy and internalize efficiency and power. Women who adopt defense systems that consist primarily of a power show conceal their suffering self. Even as little girls they become entrenched in foxholes of aggression. Often quick learners, they adopt the skills, talents, and power of attack observed in others near them, especially in the prime aggressor, the mother. We often find in the case histories of women who appear made of rock the existence of a particularly harsh and aggressive mother. Hiding all soft spots, women who adopt a Maginot Line defense appear totally insulated from further hurt. Their all-encompassing brittleness, aversion to demonstrations of love, and apparent insensitivity, though defenses and not outgrowths of innate aggressive instinct,[16] threaten whatever marriages these females have contracted.

> Lillian was the daughter of a mother who was forty years old when her first and only child was born. The little girl soon proved to be exceptionally gifted academically and equally proficient as an athlete. Moreover, she was unusually practical and efficient, having adopted both her efficient father's and her unrelenting mother's assertiveness. From her father she copied a seemingly inexhaustible endurance, fearlessness, and a negation of emotional or physical hurt. She practiced physical and acrobatic skills for so many hours that at the end of her self-imposed training periods she collapsed, fatigued by hunger of

which she had taken no notice. Lillian learned to type flaw-lessly and fast by the time she was nine and contracted for small clerical assignments which she farmed out to teenagers older than herself. She collected commissions from jobs she handed down to her crew of assistants. From her mother — a woman rejecting her own female characteristics and disliking her daughter — Lillian learned devastating sarcasm. Only brilliant writers, artists, actors, and scientists, some of whom she met in Europe, where she worked as a social secretary to wealthy Americans, could match her in a battle of wits.

Eventually, and rather late, Lillian got married to a success-ful, handsome, sarcastic, and detached man. As soon as it turned out that her mate had a rheumatic heart, a fact he did not know or claimed not to have known when the couple got married, the patient scoffed at him. When his real estate opera-tions ran into difficulties, Lillian treated his failure with deri-sive contempt. It did not take long until she made fun of the way her husband ate, walked, or brushed his teeth. The husband, the first person to offer Lillian emotional comfort (which she had been eager to accept), decided that he wanted to leave his talented but incessantly critical wife, and he asked for a quick divorce. At this point Lillian's compact aggressive facade collapsed. A deep depression set in. Lillian came to treatment distraught, suicidal, and convinced more than ever that she was incapable of love or any other warm human feelings.

To help the patient it was imperative to convince her of the purpose of the aggressive, derisive — indeed, seemingly in-human — barricade with which she had surrounded herself from early youth on. It was equally urgent to convince the patient that, though she shrank from the idea, she yearned for love, emotional shelter, and acceptance as unquestioningly as a two-year-old child who feels that she is omnipotent and can have everything. The patient was helped by her acknowledg-ment in word and action of the depth and the stormy urgency of these feelings of longing, never before allowed to show. As layer after layer of the aggressive behavior melted, Lillian, of course, felt extremely vulnerable. She often wondered which was better: to rebuild a marriage she basically desired or to crawl back into the formidable shell in which she had remained hidden and invulnerable. Gradually Lillian's wish to join the human race won out. Her cynicism turned into whimsical humor. Her display of physical invulnerability took on merely human proportions. Her ability to use every angle of a situation became useful when she employed it not destructively but as a cooperative director of a branch of her husband's far-flung business.

When the toughness that covers up the underlying passive, masochistic orientation is poorly integrated, the emerging female personality is confusing not only to others but to the woman as well.

Sonja was like a chameleon. Sometimes she was gruff yet playful like the old grandfather who was the closest companion of her childhood. At other times she became soft and showed her yearning for love. And on yet other occasions she was coldly polite and unapproachable like her detached, pretentious, and rigid father and her resentful, rejecting mother. When Sonja "got tough," she refused to listen to anyone, including, of course, the therapist. She engaged in monologues designed to prove that the only sensible opinion was her own. The rapid alternations between sensitivity and these various forms of invulnerability were never integrated, and they gave the patient the feeling that she behaved like a whirling dervish or else that she was really nobody at all.

The Attachment to Mothering Males

Some fathers step into the role vacated by wives who are either ambivalent or rejecting toward their female child. These fathers take on the physical care of their little girls, seeing that they get their bottle on time, fondling them (not seductively but like a loving mother), and accompanying and guiding each step of development. Sometimes they turn into ideal male playmates. They may even teach their daughters skills ordinarily instilled by a mother.

This situation is not infrequent, and it opens the way for yet another line of female defense. Fathers assume mother roles when thcy thcmsclvcs fccl shortchangcd by their wives and get too little love and attention. They solve their own problem in a constructive way by becoming good caretakers who restrain their erotic impulses toward their daughters. If a father manages to steer clear of erotic temptations, he will not aggravate the oedipal problems of his daughter to a point that would destine her for severe adolescent and adult disturbances. However, although we need not expect the confusion that ensues when a mother is a rejecting or absentee parent and the father supplies the mothering to be hopelessly damaging to the girl, some consequences do lead to problems.

When fathers do the mothering, the girl regards her male parent very early in life as her chief protector, and he will be the most beloved parent at a time when other girls still think of mother as the main island of safety. As a result of the care and attention the father gives very early to the female child, the personality of father-reared daughters bears a male imprint in addition to female features. The child develops into a kind of boy-girl. This type proves highly attractive to disturbed men, who see in the male identifications and projections a promise that they will be understood. Moreover, men whose own identity is confused and who combine strong mothering capacities with masculine trends — frequently they are latent or practicing homoscxuals — rally readily to the boy-girl's signals that caretaking is required. They prove to be highly attuned to both the allure and the needs of this kind of woman.

In the fairy tale, Snow White, the beautiful young daughter of a bad mother (stepmother, in fairy tales, equals bad mother) who actually banished her child from home and tried to have her destroyed, is a famous example of a young woman who survives through male protection. The seven dwarfs who give shelter to Snow White and take care of her are not real men. Much smaller than other males, they scurry around their home and pursue domestic chores much as womenfolk would.

The daughters of mothering fathers are in limbo. Having received inadequate mothering from the female parent but having enjoyed the benefits of a loving, attentive, caretaking, and companionable father, they can function well as working, creative, and playful persons. Yet the lack of a real mother leaves them narcissistic, fearful of heterosexual love, and only half complete as women. They often consider themselves physically and emotionally ill-equipped

to have children. If and when they eventually wed they are likely
to choose an incomplete male for a partner. A boy-girl often picks
a mate who does not desire a full-time home, parental responsibilities, and a meaningful heterosexual partnership.

Though the fixation on a mothering father remains consciously in
the foreground, and the longing for a mother appears much in the
background, yearning for a kindly, protective woman persists underneath a conscious suspicion and pessimism that such a person can
be encountered, as well as underneath an unconscious hostility
toward women. The boy-girl relates to males with a special sense of
familiarity that extends to an ease with male clothes, sports, and
masculine leisure activities. She is reluctant to participate in the
adult female world, and what females she favors have adolescent
ways about them.

> Tess, who began to act on the stage at the age of fifteen,
> achieved prominence after only a short while. She looks phy-
> sically like a boy-girl. She is very slender, talks with relatively
> little emotion (though her speech has an arresting quality),
> sits up straight with her legs spread apart like a boy or man.
> Tess came to treatment because of violent quarrels between
> herself and her husband. These quarrels, interspersed with
> physical wrestling between husband and wife, had the ring of
> fist fights between adolescent boys. After each militant encoun-
> ter Tess planned to leave her husband and the marriage in
> which she believed herself to be only lightly anchored. Invari-
> ably, the alternatives she envisaged involved living arrange-
> ments with some other man — usually an actor, dancer, or
> musician friend — who would be both pal and caretaker. The
> idea of settling down as a wife with a male partner, making a
> union last, assuming in a heterosexual relationship a basically
> different role from that of the male, and giving and receiving
> outright heterosexual love was for a while alien to Tess.
>
> The patient, as it turned out, was mainly her father's child.
> From the mother, who had been told at the age of eighteen by
> the family physician not to expect any offspring, she received
> what might be at best called a kind of occasional harsh care-
> taking. Tess remembers many illnesses and hospitalizations in
> the first twelve years of her life during which the father visited

her regularly while the mother put in only an occasional appearance. The patient, whose memories go back to the second year of her life, recalls that the mother bathed her mechanically, maladroitly, and carelessly, and that even as a very little girl she prevailed on her father to hold her and wash her in the tub. The girl's room was inadequately heated, she was not allowed the color schemes she wanted for it, nor the clothes she desired. Her mother read serious and supposedly enlightening literature to her to help improve her mind, but playtime and joy focused solely on the father.

Tess's male acting teachers took over her training and guidance when she was only twelve. They behaved as substitute parents who fed and housed her when she had quarrelled with her mother and did not want to go home, a home from which the father gradually absented himself more and more. Thus the patient turned to males — most of them homosexuals — for the kind of companionship and tutelage she had previously received from her male parent. The men to whose guidance she entrusted herself obliged, but cynically exacted a price. They usually demanded that she allow them to mastermind her activities, that she turn herself over to their guidance.

Like Tess, other girls subjected to a similar family constellation and feeling equally waif-like because of the desertion of the mother come to rely on sustenance from males and to learn how to elicit it. They know less about how to love than about how to arrange situations in which they can be taken care of. Should they form permanent attachments, as in the case of Tess, the situation eventually becomes bankrupt because the caretaking man, sensing the reversal and unnaturalness of roles, becomes irritated and demands return services from the female he shelters. He asks that she assume responsibility for tasks both typically female and typically male. Shaw's *Pygmalion*, the classic movie *Darling*, which showed a woman's shift from one caretaking man to another, and the tender scenes in the film *A Taste of Honey*, in which a pregnant girl, deserted by her callous mother, is sheltered by a homosexual male, these and other dramatizations illustrate the existence of tenderness as well as bargains between caretaking men and their female charges.

The fact that women who participate in the dynamic pattern

described are often found in the world of entertainment or art relates to the father's and daughter's fantasy world. The pretend dramas of parent and child which little girls play with their loving dads spill over later into the makebelieve world of entertainment and art.

In the treatment of Tess and others like her, the grave consequences of expecting that the husband will be the mother are persistently pointed out.

> Tess was asked to dwell on her husband's many lovable qualities and personal needs. Gradually, instead of reciting all the duties he had not performed, Tess started to pay attention to the needs he had and to the manifestations by which they were expressed. She refused to change the tires on their car, but she began to type letters for him and served finer food to his many friends. When, after a fight, she contemplated running to a male friend, she was able to anticipate the sequence of painful events her desertion would entail. She started to stick it out at home, at first for a few hours, eventually for a weekend, and finally for good. She herself assumed at first some and eventually a good many caretaking responsibilities.

Solutions

Many incidents indicate that the daughters of rejecting mothers become masochistic as a form of defense. They may then seek refuge in defensive, not innate, aggression and even sadism toward weak victims. In the despair of their loneliness and fear of abandonment they turn toward many figures whom they alternately indulge and desert. They may seek out men — many of them latently or overtly homosexual — who promise and deliver mothering, though at a price.

None of these solutions works in the long run. If the woman selects for a husband a man ready to shelter her more than he expects to be taken care of, the marriage inevitably will be imbued with sado-masochistic features. Inevitably, the woman who has chosen a partner who offers a good deal of mothering — all men are willing to offer some — confuses herself and her mate. She never fails wanting to eat her cake and have it too. As she encourages the mothering she gets, she weakens her husband and detracts from his image as a male. She ends up resenting his failure to be assertive, firm, and demanding because she has forgotten the bargain she struck.

The female's ready inclination toward masochism and concomitant rage and sadism is the outgrowth not only of her genital apparatus, as has been consistently claimed, nor of social discriminations, but primarily of her psychological destiny. It is determined by being the daughter of a mother who gravitates toward rejection of her female child. The highly complex defenses against the resulting masochism make many females power-driven, contradictory, labile, yet also imaginative.

Among all the ways out of the female dilemma only one works. It is to become a loving female rather than to remain a plaintiff, hell-bent on compensation for original deprivation. It is to be a care-taking and affectionate lover or wife, to become a mother capable of the understanding and guidance her small child needs, to be a perceptive and unselfish teacher. These and many other roles offer supreme opportunities for exercising the strength and know-how of the ego [16] and for taking the direction of giving love. Sophocles described one true and durable solution of the female dilemma when he made his Antigone say, "Not to hate with others, but to love with them do I exist."

3. Passive Men and Their Partners

If a man is to win a woman he considers desirable, what does this demand of his character structure? How do passive, dependent, and narcissistic leanings of long standing, invariably paralleled by covert or open hostility, obstruct a suitable choice of mate? How do these character traits hinder mutual sexual pleasure? What features of passivity interfere with sexuality? Are there specific therapeutic steps to clear out of the way or at least to reduce passivity of body and mind and let activeness come forth?

In marked contrast to ritualized societies in which the family arranges the marriages, our society expects and permits the individual to take the initiative. Hence two prime prerequisites are that the male be sociable enough to meet sufficiently many females to have a basis for choice and that he be free or become free of characterological conflicts and rigidities so that his choice may be deliberate and noncompulsive.

In the context of the activity-passivity continuum, it must be stressed that if the selection of a partner is determined by predominant narcissistic and dependency needs, the partnership is bound to go awry eventually. A male who consciously or, as is more frequently

This chapter is adapted from the article "Sex and the Passive Male," which originally appeared in the February 1970 issue of *Medical Aspects of Human Sexuality,* published by Clinical Communications, Inc., New York.

the case, unconsciously picks a girl to use her as an emotional crutch is bound to be disillusioned in the end. Such a relation is doomed, as is any attempt to satisfy narcissism and passivity through leaning, which in the long run is bound to create resentment in both the leaner and the one leaned on.

To enjoy the sexual act, to derive from it pleasure and relaxation as well as the gratified response of the partner, the man must be able to sustain and enjoy genital excitement for some length of time lest orgasms be premature and disappointing. The capacity to sustain genital excitement depends on the ability to deflect attention in some measure from the self and to focus it on the partner. Also a full and enjoyable sexual experience requires that a good measure of body turgor be tolerated, indeed relished.

To sum up: activism is an indispensable ingredient in the sexual functioning of the male. To take pleasure in female companionship and heterosexuality, the man needs to enjoy focusing energy and attention on the partner, to avoid self-preoccupation, and to be strong enough to endure pressures and distentions of the whole body as well as of the genitals. Passivity must be identified as a big troublemaker, not only in the evolvement of emotional functioning and well-being in general but in love and sexuality specifically.

Therapeutic techniques sensitive to the damages of passive inclinations and designed to build activism gradually in all life situations can do much to release the dynamism required for male sexual functioning. An active though not overpowering course of therapy is indicated. Awareness of the existence, range, origins, and effects of passivity is essential but does not suffice. In the course of treatment many components of genuine alertness have to be gradually awakened. To mention a few: the male patient's conviction — surprisingly often missing — that his rights to initiative are equal to the female's; the ability of self-expression and articulation of will and purpose; body awareness and body strength; the conquest of anxiety through new insights and approaches; * healthy visual curiosity about everything, including sexuality. To enjoy the female in and, especially, out of bed, the man cannot lean too much on her. But he can relish tangling with her in funny, gregarious, and enterprising ways.

* See chapter 4, "Mastering Danger and Anxiety."

The Passive Male Personality:
Two Profiles

Roughly speaking, passive males — and, for that matter, females too — can be divided into two categories: those who let their slackness show and those (whose number seems to be growing) who cover up passivity by hyperactivity.

The Overtly Passive Male. The passive man who displays his lack of initiative outright can be recognized by many body and personality characteristics. Very often his gait is dragging, his posture is poor, and when he slumps in a chair he gives the impression of a heap rather than of a structured organism with many integrated parts. His way of talking is slow and silences are frequent. Apologetic modifiers — "Maybe," "Well, well," "That's just the way I see it" — punctuate his sentences. He agrees to proposals advanced but resents his own quick acquiescence and thereafter often forgets or postpones commitments. He is oversolicitous of everyone, and particularly of women. He often can strike a stance of being a good listener, but in actuality, he is anything but tuned in. His thoughts drift off, and he is preoccupied with himself because his relationship to others is limited and cautious. Ideas are discussed, sometimes ad infinitum, but often turn out to be borrowed from other sources, hazy, or made up on the spur of the moment. In his relationship with his woman, the passive male tends first to overvalue his love and then to gravitate toward a gradual and always hostility-filled derogation of her strengths and joyousness. Quite often, sexual overtures either have to be initiated by the woman or are infrequent. One of the most frequent characteristics of the overtly passive male personality is the mixture of great need for and great anger toward the female partner.

> When Merton first met Mary, his wife-to-be, he thought that he had come across a goddess, and he immediately proposed marriage. At first sexuality was good between the couple. Gradually Merton tended to lean more and more on the financial resources and on the initiative of his attractive wife, who long before her marriage had started to adopt the role of a docile female. But Merton resented her to such a point that in his vivid dreams she appeared as huge as a female giant. When

Merton started treatment he was completely clear about his need/hatred feelings toward Mary, stating the case like this: "The one hour in the morning we spend together and the two hours around dinner time at night are like guerrilla warfare. She has laid down all the rules, and I seemingly follow them but in fact always boycott them. Everything that Mary asks of me I do backwards. I forget parts of her instructions. I am engaged in a nasty struggle with her, but to lose Mary would be doom."

The Disguised Passive Male. Hyperactivity is often employed to cover up lingering passivity, but it is basically made of different fiber than is straight activity.* Passive people, who hide behind a hectic defensive front, utilize a combination of muscles in such a way that their bodies are taut for long periods of time. The rhythm of their physical movements, their speech, and their ideation is accelerated, and this often leaves them fatigued rather than refreshed after an encounter. Exhaustion plagues not only the person who employs hyperactivity as a defense but also those exposed to it. Genuine activeness, on the other hand, permits others to feel invigorated and actually relaxed.

Hyperactivity is always characterized by a lack of integration and resembles the restless, chaotic behavior shown by small children when they are exposed to frustration. Body movements, thoughts, and emotions do not become integrated but hang together as though by glue. The picture resembles that of pseudoaggression, a well-known cover-up for timidity during spells of anxiety.[1] Men who hide their basic passivity under the more attractive facade of hyperactivity may be either courteous or provocatively and charmingly challenging. Whichever the case, they do hide the anger that exists. They, like their overtly passive confreres, accept proposals enthusiastically but are unlikely to follow through, since ego strength and tenacity are missing. With females they are alternately oversolicitous and quick-tempered. Again, like their openly passive counterparts, the hyperactive males tend to aggrandize females they courted and very quickly to dethrone the goddess they themselves created.[2] Certainly many men in this category get hold of sex on the sly. They may promiscuously hop from one woman to another or con-

* See chapter 1, "The Basic Need for Activeness."

sort with prostitutes or semi-prostitutes or even obtain a quick orgasm by rubbing against a pretty girl or a full-busted woman in the subway. Invariably the result of such sexual activities is deep shame and gnawing guilt, very reluctantly admitted.

Gil was brilliant and appealing both to his colleagues and to the women he courted. He loved rapid physical activity and played tennis almost every day, to the point of exhaustion. After every game he showered and dressed carefully, preoccupied with his looks. He talked so fast that it was difficult to keep up with him. Quips, humorous stories, and even practical jokes were prime components of his conversation.

What is interesting is that this patient, who appealed to every woman who met him, was not aware of his own attractiveness. Only at the end of the second year of analytic psychotherapy did he let on how ashamed he was of his indiscriminate sexual activities, which often involved women whom he considered unsavory and exploitative. He was also able to tell that he had spent three weeks in jail following a Fourth of July brawl in which he had molested several women. With his remarkable intuition Gil himself said that passivity was his prime obstacle. He reported that he often considered himself to be falling in love but had a difficult time following up on his infatuation. He either permitted his various female loves to dominate him or else burst into rages that nearly ruptured the relationships.

At one point Gil was attracted by a rather resourceful girl whom he all too rapidly elevated to the position of be-all and end-all. He discovered with shock that he gradually came to resent her beauty, poise, and social skills. In the wake of this relationship Gil lost both his professional initiative and his sexual power. He found that he was uninterested in, and indeed impotent with, the powerful woman he pursued, and he switched from her to other fast love affairs.

To be emphasized here is the fact that Gil's hyperactivity merely covered up a lingering dependency on strong females and strong people in general. Gil invariably resented these stronger people because he was a leaner but did not wish to look upon himself as one.

The promiscuity noted in such cases as Gil's is frequently dismissed by labeling it "acting-out behavior," but let us look more closely. The reason why Gil, like many others, turned from worthy but powerful women toward indiscriminate promiscuity is that this behavior, no matter what we label it, helped him to avoid acknowledging how much he relied on being pushed by strong females. Promiscuity, which represented a form of pseudoactivity or hyperactivity, was used to disavow his passive inclinations.

When hyperactivity involves many segments of behavior — such as ideation, work, and lovemaking — everything becomes fragmented. Ego disintegration is the frequent concomitant of hyperactive, hectic living. Anxiety, as a result, reaches a peak. The final way out is often a return of the original inactiveness that sent the patient into the spin of hyperactivity. We know that frequently after celebrations, travels, and complex human entanglements there occur letdowns. Sometimes they begin with drinking, followed by coma-like sleep. It is obvious how interrelated is the occurrence of hyperactivity on the one hand and inertia on the other. One is layered with the other. In the end, straight activity is the solution. Only the ability to be authentically active makes for a physiologically healthy, anxiety-free, subjectively gratifying existence. Once again activeness includes, of course, physical action, but its core is an active and creative mind.

Excess activity, alternating with apathy, is on the increase nowadays. The emergence of this pattern — which some therapists consider psychopathic and many laymen associate with disaffected young people — should make us aware not only of the dangers of passivity but also of parental neglects or offenses largely responsible for it. Overt passivity is very frequently the result of parental *overprotection*. Hyperactivity is often a consequence of parental *neglect* and parental absenteeism, which deprive the child of guidance and allow him to run wild. Consequently he grows into an adult who lacks a sufficiently delineated inner world to be steadily alert, productive and sexually stable.

Passivity and activity are two poles of human existence.[3,4,5] They represent two end points, with the life of each individual taking positions along the continuum between them. What most approximates the state we are used to calling normality is a rhythmic flow between an active and occasionally quiescent condition. Neither inertness nor excessive busyness do justice to the human body and mind. When the two states alternate abruptly, as they do in troubled hyperactive males, they pull the human being apart. But when an integration takes place, relationships in general, and relationships to the other sex in particular, make for gratifying interchange.

Blunders in the Choice of a Mate

Many males, whether they show their passivity outright or conceal it by hyperactivity, want to prove their potency by becoming involved with a series of females. Chances are high that they will seek out and attach themselves to women who are basically wrong partners for them. One of the chief sources of all passivity, and specifically male passivity, is an overprotective, controlling, all-powerful, and rule-making mother. The passive adult sons of such mothers gravitate quite often toward females who have the very personality that was the mother's prerogative. Explanations of this proclivity can be given in oedipal terms. Within an oedipal concept, the man simply wants to repeat the experience he once had. He is fixed on a determined female figure who shows him the way. As an adult male, he once again selects as a mate the kind of person who guided him as a child — namely, a strong and willful woman. Another explanation, and one that is particularly useful because the emphasis on ego adaptations is important, deals with the man's habits and defenses. Within this context the passive man can be viewed as selecting in adult life a strong and overwhelming female partner because that is exactly the woman he, on the one hand, knows how to cope with and, on the other hand, knows will be a complementary person. Welded early to a powerful mother, he knows how to appease, court favor with, and satisfy a woman who is on the lookout for prestige. Having leaned much too long as a child on a woman of this type, he lacks faculties and skills of ego to guide him through life, and he therefore selects a very strong woman in order to make up for his own deficiencies.

It is confusing to the adult male that many girls and women whose strength is really threatening make their own power appear in very attractive ways. They beguile men because they appear attractive, poised, witty, and vulnerable. This kind of woman is a danger to the passive male. She has intuitively adopted external manners of pliability and docility to hide a bossy nucleus. She appears to be quite naïve and in need of male support, but she is inwardly domineering and manipulative. Her soft-spokenness, amiability, and helplessness are merely artifacts designed to attract men, and often passive men in particular. Stripped of inner daring of their own, men who are deeply dependent, yet who do not wish to appear so, attach themselves to innocuous-seeming girls and women of this kind, unaware that these females are determined to go eventually for the driver's seat.

As companionship and sexual involvement develop, the woman eventually displays her true character, and the basically hesitant male is bound to feel rising resentment that the female has taken over the reins as the mother of his childhood once did. Emotional contacts, budding sexual attractions, and actual relationships are nipped by this frost. No matter what the woman's own motivations may be, the stage is set for the man's eventual erotic withdrawal and even for his sexual impotence. His feelings of rage at the woman who asserts her own strength, while she is both wanted and resented, take over and ban this woman from the sexual scene.

> Lytell was the son of a withdrawn and silent father and a voluble, overpowering, grossly overweight, and seductive mother. The mother played sexual games in bed with her boy whenever the father was away on a business trip. For years she arranged all details of her son's life. As a result, the patient developed a need for a guiding and seductive female figure. Lytell married a beautiful, witty, and efficient girl on whose initiative, social skills, and sexual overtures he relied very much. As the reliance on his wife increased, Lytell became more and more angry that he should be a mere tagalong, and eventually, modelling himself after his father, he became silent and withdrawn. He refused to answer his wife's and other people's questions, stayed in bed during the better part of many weekends, and became increasingly less potent. Indeed, Lytell was astounded to find that after only three years of marriage, rather than experiencing exaltation, he felt disgust

toward his beautiful wife, whom he had picked out to do him proud. No matter how hard he tried to live up to his marital obligations, his erections became fewer and limper. Eventually he experienced no sexual arousal whatsoever. Aware that his feelings toward his wife and his sexual relationship reflected his own problems more than hers, he at first berated himself fiercely. Eventually he entered therapy. But when he not only began to comprehend that he had yielded to passivity, but actually started to be more active, the situation changed profoundly. Lytell started to have relatively objective arguments with his wife. He discovered that many things about her were artificial and annoyed him. After some years he divorced her and formed a relationship with an equally strong but basically more sincere young woman.

When this patient, like those who characterologically resemble him, discovered that the depletion of his sexual drive was not due to organic damage, nor to a total inability to love, he breathed more easily. When he discovered that the emotional and erotic disharmony was the result of his own gravitation toward a second-row position, where the wife's power far outshone his, he started on a new road. Next came active and planned steps to assert initiative, strength, and independence. Lytell, like others, began to wonder what would happen if a husband said no to some of his wife's suggestions. What if he turned down a request for a vacation or extra expenditures that seemed nonessential? Why should the husband not insist on an active role in the rearing of children, the basic running of the home, and the shaping of a social and community life?

No reversal of faulty activity-passivity balance comes about overnight. Initial, and indeed encouraging, dents can be made quickly by pointing out serious disproportions in marital leadership and by showing how this disproportion relates to the gradual decline of sexual interest. The man begins to speak up more often and more insistently. Simultaneously, and indeed as part of the process, he gives up his seemingly neutral silence that simulates reticence and self-containment but actually expresses grave anger.

Males who are basically passive, and as a result have chosen partners too strong for them, gain nothing from hasty attempts to disprove their partial or total impotence by forced tries. It is the basic human relationship that has to be gradually changed, and specifically the activity-passivity balance between the two partners. Haste intensifies the humiliating notion that manhood has been impaired, that body energy has been undermined, that the female is competitive and overpowering. It does not make for the gradual and meaningful emotional and sexual breakthroughs that are truly needed.

Premature Ejaculations

If the man's emission is too hasty, both partners are deprived of pleasure and become tense. Especially if premature ejaculations occur repeatedly or regularly, the woman is frustrated and eventually resentful. The man, in turn, misses out on both the partner's exultation and his own pride and relaxation following satisfactory intercourse. Whether or not the man is fully or, as is more often the case, only hazily aware of it, passivity and its inevitable companion, excessive narcissistic preoccupation, are the common reasons for premature ejaculation.

As a state of body and mind, passivity never comes alone; it is always connected with both dependency and self-absorption. A weak man is both an angrily dependent and an uninterested man, who feels little mature love for his partner. He simultaneously relies on her for strength and resents her for having it. Since the partner is used for protection and possibly for sexual experimentation supposed to prove potency, it is small wonder that the love and sex emphasis of the weak man is on the self. Though less passionate than an adolescent, he is as self-preoccupied. During intercourse, both the resentment against the female and the self-preoccupation drain energy away from the sexual act. The main desire is to pull away from the intimacy, the closeness to the partner, to pull back into the shell of isolation. The premature emissions are but an expression of the wish to get it over with.

In such cases psychoanalytic therapy can bring a good deal of improvement. The sexually failing patient begins to understand how important it is that he become cognizant of all his feelings, including critical and negative ones, directed at the partner. The therapist's open-ended questions that allow him to pursue thoughts of his own stimulate activism. Queries about the degree to which feelings are focused on the female and her rising excitement and the degree to which they simply stay with the self will often be helpful. The first nuances of mutuality can thus be conjured up.

Many an unsuccessful lover is surprised to hear that sexual improvement can be expected from a greater allocation of attention to the partner and her excitement, while forced concentration on his own performance will fail to improve potency.

> Barry was a great Don Juan. He courted and won many beautiful women whose common characteristic, in addition to good grooming and fine looks, was their height. All were as tall as he or taller. As soon as he was fairly sure of a female conquest, he began to find faults with seemingly inoffensive details of looks and behavior he had not noticed before. As it turned out, the long limbs of Barry's women symbolized to him female strength and regal assuredness through which he felt protected, even though he resented these qualities, as the eventual criticisms showed. When, after a series of romantic disappointments and partings, largely due to premature ejaculation, Barry was advised to pay more attention to the girl while making love, he reported surprising results. Indeed, he had become more relaxed and more potent. "I always thought that sex infatuations just strike you and come about without design or will," he said. "But I find that I help myself by being an attentive lover. I can generate more interest than I thought I had in me. If I concentrate on my girl, I can make love longer."

While all kinds of problems of adult life aggravate and perpetuate passivity, there is little question that the seeds of passivity are sown in early childhood through damaging experiences. Boys who turn passive have not infrequently been toilet-trained too soon and too strictly. Training begun before a boy can control his sphincter muscles can cause an excessive early concern with the passage of urine. Boys who are bladder-trained too severely may develop a compulsion to pass small accumulations of urine — in other words, to urinate too often — a habit frequently perpetuated in adult life. If childhood wetting fears linger on, these fears quite commonly become associated with the passing of seminal fluid; then erections arouse in the adult ancient misgivings of incontinence and loss of control. Therefore, semen, much like urine, is quickly — indeed, far too soon — discharged.

Jonathan, a pedantic man raised by a very strict and excessively clean Scottish mother, anticipated sexual intercourse with trepidation for fear that he would ejaculate too fast. Asked about toilet habits, he reported that he always made sure to have an empty bladder, urinating ten times or more each day. (Urological tests proved this excessive urination to be only functional.) It is important to note additionally that after every urination this man was careful to wipe his penis several times to make sure that no fluid would stain his underwear. Asked in what way urine and semen were connected in his mind, Jonathan suggested that he might feel compelled to rid himself of semen as fast and fastidiously as of urine.

Not all men, we can see, look upon the accumulation of seminal fluid with pride. Nor can they let go of semen with pleasure and confidence. Whenever semen is considered by the man to be dirty because the boy was trained to feel disgust at what his body emitted or to regard all biological aspects of sex as sordid, the wish is to empty the body of seminal fluid rather than let it accumulate until it represents a powerful and pressing mass of manhood. The work of the therapist can do much to make it clear that all body products are the result of regulatory and indeed truly miraculous chemical metabolisms. The stigma attaching to anything that flows from the organs can be gradually extinguished.

Male Passivity and the Homosexual Orientation

Homosexuality, whether it is of the sort usually called latent or is open and practiced, is an emotional-sexual condition of great complexity. It may call for psychoanalytically oriented treatment. From the author's own experiences and findings reported by colleagues, however, comes the belief that the chances for the dissolution of the mechanisms that underlie the homosexual inclinations are better than sometimes reported in the literature.[6] In this book homosexuality is discussed because very specific aspects of passivity play a nuclear role in the development of male homosexual needs. Narcissistic and passive processes, with concomitant needs to lean on a nurturing person, are precursors of homosexual inclinations, whether these are merely fantasied (latent) or acted upon (overt). Narcissism, passivity, and the defenses against both are present among the important nucleii of the homosexual syndrome.

The male homosexual * is an identifier par excellence. His sense of specific personal adult identity is vague. The belief rules that the male is childlike, feeble, and powerless. Because of the notion, often based on actuality, that the self is weak, the homosexually inclined male is prey to anxiety. One way out is to find a male appendage who can be parented, thus permitting some sense of strength, however illusionary. Another escape consists of finding a supportive figure who is perceived as a powerful parent, usually the maternal figure, and whose strength is inferred very often on the basis of external and hence misleading assets. Healthy good looks and youthfulness, these are often taken as reassurance that the homosexual protégé or partner possesses inner strength. Also there is the idea that any adored mate will in turn lend his own assets to his homosexual benefactor or beneficiary.

All homosexually inclined men feel weak since they have not overcome narcissistic and symbiotic needs. As a rule their mothers overprotected and dominated them, and hence they failed to develop a strong, independent male ego structure.[7] Among the emotional currents of the homosexual male, cravings for protection and wishes to combat the danger of the moment through alliance with a firm member of the same sex play a large role. Unfortunately, the desire for alliance is not fulfilled through genuine companionship and exchange of emotions and ideas, but through surrender, appeasement, and clinging. The imperative of remaining a passive male child, albeit via some rather demonstrative detours, is always paramount.

Homosexual men, whether they express their desire for a partner of the same sex latently or overtly, are identifiers. They simply become their male partner, wholly or partially. Whether the coveted male is good-looking and younger, and hence an ego ideal in terms of appearance, or whether he is an older, supposedly benign, father figure, the homosexual's immersion in this person is quite conspicu-

---

* From here on, latent and overt homosexuality will be discussed jointly in terms of processes appearing in either situation.

ous. Such abandonment of one's own identity must be labeled as a particular type of passivity. Flirtation, subservience, craving for peculiar favors, these are attitudes of the homosexual male which always need to be corrected through psychoanalytic insights plus psychoanalytically based behavior change. In homosexual behavior the bid to be taken care of is always pronounced. The quest to possess — and thus to be — the other person is equally conspicuous. A homosexual patient on the verge of heterosexuality illustrated the prevailing mechanisms when he said this to a woman: "I like you the way I can like. I want to eat you up. When I hanker after men I want to imbibe them. Right now I sense that it is not only your breast I want but also your ebullience."

The roles of the nurturer and the nurtured are constantly being reversed in the male homosexual syndrome. Often the homosexual male is the nurturer because this gives him a feeling of strength and also reduces his subterranean hostility and guilt. At a later turn of events, the very same male may slip into the role of the one asking to be waited on by a confrere.

The narcissistic, passive, and dependent nucleii of homosexual lovemaking or wishes of lovemaking are quite clear. The male, usually scarred by early experiences with a powerful mother who did not permit the emergence of his identity, copies his overpowering parent, the mother, by identifying with her. Often, though not invariably, he walks and talks and behaves like a woman. Deprived of a clear-cut male identity, he is constantly at work trying to establish it by identification with another male. Whether occupied by latent or overtly expressed desires, he gravitates toward identification and nurture, two aspects of passivity. As always, such inclinations can be corrected and converted into activism, provided that the patient allows the therapist to take some time, and provided that the therapist convinces the patient that time and the development of strengths are of the utmost necessity.

How To Spot and Cure
Overt Male Passivity

Specific techniques, in addition to the psychoanalytic uncovering of the origins and functions of inertia, counteract and uproot passivity. Instead of dwelling at length on the male's ways of covering up his emotions and restraining energy with defenses that induce depression and passivity, the therapist can confront him quite soon (and more safely than is generally assumed) with his basic feelings, especially his massive resentment. A close and clear look at inner rage is invigorating and liberating. The claim that individuals might disintegrate if they face their angry and murderous impulses needs to be modified. It holds for relatively few cases. The uncovering of anger can be made safe if patients are very clearly told that conscious restraints of anger *must* be built and used in the place of unconscious, bewildering, and paralyzing defenses. At times the therapist needs to be a vociferous and active ally of conscious control.

Men engulfed in passivity and depression, whether these are cloaked by the mantle of hyperactivity or not, have little significant news to bring to treatment. Living on the arid diet of defensiveness, they have no access to vivid material to consider. Instead, they produce chitchat and repetitive complaints. In such cases some reeducation and elucidation are called for. What can be pointed out to depressed and passive males is the distinction between expression of relatively meaningless content (details and symptom complaints), on the one hand, and, on the other, concentration on and revelation of their own inner processes. The patients may first be irritated and plead confusion, but they do understand eventually. Relief sets in. It is effective to attune such individuals to the precious value of their own ideas and feelings, fleeting and sketchy as these may be. Eventually, what was previously misty and was therefore dismissed becomes more clearly defined and reported.

> Michael, having been asked early in treatment to pay attention to fleeting thoughts and especially to anger feelings, said in his tenth session, "As I walked into the street right after our last meeting I glimpsed the image of a raised fist. It was encapsulated, hardly belonging to me. But then I realized that I had wanted to hit you during the session. That is interesting because as I felt a surge of the anger I became invigorated and stimulated. Energy flowed into me."

Challenges from the therapist and, if the passive man is in a group, from other group members, are often activating. So are unexpected questions about what seem to be reasonable statements and what is called elsewhere in this book a lateral viewpoint.* Passive men — like all passive people — all too often look at their problems head on. They do not move around problems so as to get at new angles. For instance, I once asked a man who complained monotonously about his dreary fate and deprived existence, "What kind of a home do you want to own?" Startled and angered by what seemed to be a nonsequitur, the patient came to understand reasonably soon that his sense of frustration stemmed partly from a combination of his omnivorous cravings and partly from a sorry conviction that he must strive for nothing. At last he started to look at his old drab problems from fresh points of view, and feelings, desires, and doings became more comprehensible.

The important proviso in the use of challenge is that good will rather than hostility underlie it. If individual treatment is conducted by a well-trained therapist, he will be sufficiently attuned to his countertransference feelings to know whether a wish to challenge the patient stems from helpfulness or irritation. If groups work therapeutically, then hostile challenges are recognized as such by other members or the therapist and are counterbalanced by constructive comments.

Sulking, that easily missed communication of withheld rage, resentment, self-pity, and yearning for omnipotence which passive men favor, should not go unnoticed. It should become a focal point of treatment. A good many sulkers are not aware of their own moods or of the fact that they nurse them along carefully. When both the existence and purpose of sulking — that is, quiet retaliation through withholding — are pointed out, some sulkers begin to laugh at themselves.

Broad-range insight into the total passivity of the patient is always enlightening and necessary. Yet as a vehicle of change it constitutes only a first step. People usually do not start to come to life because they know that they are languishing and sad, or even because they have become familiar with their defenses. Rather, changes are accelerated by small steps of independent judgment, self-evaluation, and emotional expression, especially if these occur right in the therapeutic session and within the transference. For example, if a man declares

* See chapter 7, "Active Thinking."

repeatedly that he is worthless, a detailed account of any recent accomplishment, no matter how small, is called for. If the passive male asks questions, he should be encouraged to gather for himself all facts that can supply answers. However, this procedure does not exclude certain occasions when the therapist will furnish information to which the patient cannot have access. Not every question should be answered with a question in psychoanalytic work.

Vitality and participation in life do not usually return in massive fashion but rather bit by bit. Any latent initiative that becomes manifest in treatment, that is articulated and used for self-expression and genuine contact constitutes a building block in the slowly expanding structure of activeness, display of emotion, and exercise of the ego. With regard to passivity and depression, it is well worthwhile to shift the therapeutic focus. We go from broad insight to specific steps based on insight and leading to mental action. And these specific steps — for instance, new thought, fresh anticipations, or inventive reality-testing — make true insight possible.

Research findings show ever more clearly that the body and mind work together as a complex yet integrated unit. Hence, in the case of male inertia, it is essential that the body go into action along with the mind.

> Duncan, a small, lethargic, unsuccessful, almost mute young man who rarely sought intercourse because his sexual failures had been so frequent, took karate lessons upon the therapist's advice. The effects were remarkable. Posture, gait, gestures, and voice became more swinging, outgoing, faster in rhythm. The sexual life of this patient improved a great deal. This case shows that physical exercise, although it alone will hardly suffice to overcome psychologically caused passivity, often proves an important adjunct to psychological development.

4. Mastering Danger and Anxiety

Despite formidable accumulations of knowledge and an enormous supply of man-built tools and machines, human beings are relatively helpless in the face of danger. Frequently threatened by various perils, both internal and external, they lead precarious lives. And those who suffer from serious emotional disturbances face the manifold perils of human existence with a handicapped psyche. Their psychological confusions and shortcomings make fighting danger and anxiety an awesome chore. Only if disturbed people are helped to acquire psychological clarity and capability does life cease to be a deeply perturbing proposition and turn instead into an endurable and sometimes increasingly humorous tragicomedy.

The reasons for human fallibility in the presence of danger — and for actual mismanagement of danger, in the case of people with problems — are so comprehensive and as yet so sketchily understood that only some can be discussed here. In a general way it can be said that psychological disturbance interferes with a triad of techniques for dealing with danger: (1) danger-spotting, (2) danger diagnosis, (3) danger-fighting. An outstandingly intelligent yet equally vulnerable race, human beings as a whole do not have access to instinctive methods of danger fighting. Their native endowment does not include innate or, as we now say, "prefigured" [1] self-protections coded into the mind. Instead, many perils have to be fought off through deliberate thought and action, which, in people with marked psychological disturbances, often become twisted and tangled. Fight and flight reactions, which are among the most basic forms of self-protection, are not used discriminatingly when the psyche is mis-shapen in one way or another. For example, passivity and depend-ence, always among the nuclei of neurosis, breed two kinds of aberration, as it were. Either the disturbed person is deprived of healthy aggression, assertiveness, and reasonable mobility or else his tendencies to fight lead to furious attacks or precipitate desertions that in turn disrupt, at least temporarily, irreplaceable love relationships.

While the impact of civilization steers all human beings in the direction of some loyalty and peacefulness, weak and confused people, suffering from rigidity and life-distorting fantasies, lack discrimination. They cannot decide when aggression (which in itself is not the generalized human trait it has been proclaimed to be) [2] is out of place. Nor can they tell when the cause of love and devotion is truly lost and they should leave someone previ-ously beloved and take their loyalty elsewhere. Disturbed people, always falling back on the passivity and dependence that are the heritage of their misguided childhoods, are engulfed by confusion. They often mistake submission for devotion, clinging for love, and masochistic passivity for peacefulness. The skill of specific danger-spotting and diagnosis for which each kind of hazard calls is thwarted, and dangers are either ignored or else rashly judged to be catastrophes. Because of inner barrenness in the place of an abundance of ego skills, the selection of proper mental methods with which to master danger is narrowed to a limited choice.

The human psyche, always a delicate structure, is easily damaged. The effects of damage show up where the psyche sees problems as either excessively complex *or* excessively simple. Such malfunc-tioning makes it difficult for the psyche to make important distinctions between *external* dangers and *internal* threats. (The distinctions are not easy to make because, as a rule, in the presence of severe difficulties the internal dangers that abound entail, in turn, external hazards.) Because of defensive mechanisms such as repressions, projections, and so on, the perturbed mind becomes dense. Unauthentic emotions have been developed which do not serve as reliable road signs through the thicket of troubles. Threats and dangers from within are ignored, disguised, misjudged, or fought off with all too meager psychic equipment. Every type of internal danger grows rather than diminishes: self-deception interferes with the clear perception of reality, so important a safeguard of life;[3] contradictory identifications, total or partial, with past and present power figures fragment the self and make it feeble; unknown impulses — rage, for instance — push to the fore and demand release, thus swamping the psyche with fears of retaliation should its inner controls give way and the violent wishes be indeed acted upon. The list is veritably endless.

Is Anxiety a Help or a Hurdle?

Poorly protected against perils as disturbed people are — and in some measure the classification "disturbed people" includes at times all members of mankind — those who are seriously handicapped face yet another aggravation. They respond to danger with more intense and continuous anxiety than those whom we regard as stronger. When an individual is beset by emotional disturbances, anxiety experiences occur not as brief and mild interludes but as deeply perturbing and painful seizures that overwhelm and disintegrate the psychic system.

It was assumed originally by Freud that anxiety is a useful signal, briefing the individual about the imminence of some danger.[4] A later idea that appears more plausible — though it, too, leaves open many questions — is that anxiety, man's awesome emotional and mental endowment, is a signal not of danger but of psychological inadequacy in the face of danger. In this version, anxiety, rather than merely announcing the advance of danger, predicts that the mind, and in particular the ego, lacks the flexibility and facilities needed for the imminent confrontation with danger.[5] As soon as we look on anxiety as an announcement of insufficiency, it ceases to resemble a fire alarm warning a community that a conflagration has started. Rather, it is comparable to a more complex and subtle warning system that alerts the burghers to the poor condition of their fire-fighting equipment.

In the course of day-to-day life, all anxiety is unpleasant. But we can concede the possibility that a small dose of it can serve as a useful warning device. Big amounts of anxiety, on the other hand, are a different matter. Besieging many people who are deeply disturbed, massive anxiety paralyzes rather than helps. This finding brings us to the question of how to regard as functional and purposeful that medley of physiological sensations of which anxiety consists, such as stomach flutterings, shaking knees or hands, dizziness, and feelings that the very ground is trembling in earthquakelike fashion. How can these perturbing body sensations, all of them aroused in the autonomic nervous system and not under voluntary control, be considered SOS signals of a useful kind? Often, instead of serving a useful purpose, the anxiety that signals inadequacy gets out of hand through a vicious-circle effect. [6] The unpleasant physiological sensations of which anxiety consists arouse fear lest the body be ill or the mind feeble, and this fear in turn might beget a more intense sense of danger and inadequacy. Thus, what starts out as an announcement of probable inadequacy can actually heighten whatever deficiencies already exist.

There is yet another way, I believe, to look upon intense anxiety. Anxiety is each person's primarily physiological experience not of insufficiency but of danger itself. It is the highly subjective *body record* of danger, not some separate barometer that has only a measuring or signal function. Anxiety is not a rehearsal of inadequacy *before danger,* but is the individualized, immediate, primarily somatic experience *of a danger that already exists. It has no warning function and hampers rather than aids in preparations for coping with danger. Anxiety obstructs the clear awareness of what the danger is, and it intensifies already existing psychological shortcomings and deficits.* Most of the body sensations, which are like rivulets flowing into the mainstream of anxiety, constitute physical counterparts or reflections of the existing dangers.

Bodha became very anxious when she switched therapists. Her anxiety manifested itself physiologically in loose stools. Sensations that made her body feel like jelly upset her a great deal. All these symptoms interfered with her work and human relations. She felt an increased fuzziness as to who she was.

Both the description of the physiological anxiety sensations — all characterized by a quality of looseness — and the patient's fleeting thoughts and dreams pointed to the cause of the painful fear: the first therapist, a controlled and circumspect man, had made it possible for Bodha to feel a sense of containment through borrowing his ego boundaries. The second therapist, though aware of Bodha's great need for separateness and definition, was not an equally suitable model for self-restriction. When this young woman learned to set herself apart from others in her own ways, and when she began not to repress or curtail but to sort out the impulses that beset her, she gradually lost every trace of anxiety.

Anxieties disappear in proportion to emerging ego functioning. When patients learn to handle difficulties more ably, and hence are less exposed to peril, when they develop the ability both to spot danger and to draw on coping mechanisms [7] tailormade for the special pressures that exist, the contest is won and the anxiety that reflects it physically disappears.

A young physician, Eric, resented the graspingness, contempt, and flamboyance of his strong wife, yet he leaned on her in the false hope that her inflated power would rub off on him. Partly desiring a separation, but also continuing to be dependent, the patient lived in perpetual anxiety lest his wife evict him. Though he was aware of the transference of his emotions from his strong-willed mother to his wife, Eric did not get rid of anxiety by realizing the parallel between parent and mate.

Coming home one day, Eric saw his bags outside the door and found he was actually locked out. Two hours later, he arrived at a therapy group session physically shaken. His mouth was so dry that he could hardly mumble a few words. His palms were wet and his body trembled. Rather than dwelling on Eric's physiological display and repetitive descriptions of the felt anxiety, the therapist asked firmly that he tell the group how he planned to arrange his life during the next few days. Where did he plan to live? What was to be his next move? Just what books and furniture would he take out of the home from which he was now foreclosed?

The patient was taken aback by such practical questions and ridiculed them as out of keeping with the well-known psychoanalytic practice of dwelling on prior trauma. Yet gradually Eric could talk at increasing length about his plans.

He wished to write a paper, long-planned, and to take a trip to the West Coast. He also wanted to practice new dance steps, now that he no longer needed to respect his wife's objections.

After fifteen minutes of what the patient had considered superficial chitchat, he observed with astonishment that his anxiety and its physiological components had disappeared. The therapist explained that the exercise was not designed merely to distract him, as he had suspected. (That technique is one that many basically uninterested mothers use with their troubled children.) Rather, the aim was to help him review strengths that he possessed. The patient saw, with a feeling of relief, that passive lamentations do not reduce anxiety and that, instead, various forms of productivity are needed.

Willpower, long decried as useless in psychoanalytic contexts, [8] is an ally in the contest with stress. Will is a motivation. It stimulates the patient to grow, to refine and to expand mental tools with which to meet the inner and outer thrusts of fate.

To live up to the first task in the mastery of danger — namely, spotting and charting dangers realistically — the person in stress must proceed like a good scout or a surveyor of new territory. The terrain, which in most cases is psychological, must be viewed from every angle. A multidimensional outlook is needed to assess peril and to determine what ways of coping will work. Glimpses from the side, and even a back view, add significantly to closeups from the front. One of the many reasons why group psychotherapy has proved effective is its supply of multiple viewpoints available to anyone in trouble. The members of a working therapy group, all in many ways equipped with therapeutic potential, inspect their fellow-patient's problem from divergent angles. Spotting and sizing up problems is greatly facilitated by multilateral, often amazingly astute, views furnished by group participants.

While a limited number of articulated diagnoses of danger aid the mastery of anxiety, a profusion of demands, especially if they are contradictory, and a bombardment of stimuli aggravate anxiety. It grows in the muddy and overworked soil of confusion. If a patient is exposed to too many stimuli, if the ways out of a conflict are manifold and clash, if the individual life situation offers too many choices, and if too many other human beings are exercising demands, the result is not exhilaration, but uncertainty. Confusion is one nucleus of anxiety.

As we know, even the richly laden shelves of a supermarket throw some disturbed patients into anxiety. The profusion of available wares makes for indecision, a loosening of ego boundaries, and hence, an increased sense of inner dangers and anxiety. The over-abundance of psychological alternatives in other, more personal situations similarly stirs up anxiety. While human beings desire mobility, freedom of choice, and change, they also need containment and limitation.

The thought of existential philosophers who claim that the absence of bonds and curtailments, though desired, leads to a certain "dizziness of freedom" [9] is closely related to the issue raised here. So is the idea that anxiety arises when many vistas of "being" [10] or of identity stretch before the inward eye of the disturbed individual who can not yet set limits. The wider the range of possibilities, the greater the choice, the higher are the confusion and uncertainty of the disturbed person.

Though the existential idea that anxiety stems partly from too many possibilities of being is extremely interesting, the approach to anxiety taken in this book is rooted in psychoanalysis. This approach sees as one important factor in anxiety the existence of too much stimulation and of too many conflicting tugs and needs.

When patients first emerge from the state of psychic depletion created either by passive self-paralysis or by more actively imposed rigidities, they often feel overwhelmed by the multiplicity of inputs, needs, and solutions that now descend on them. Anxiety experiences characterized by the patient's sensation of being engulfed in a vortex are the frequent result. Once some of the needs and choices are assigned a secondary role and the basic outlines of desire and potentiality are clarified, the experience of the whirlpool lessens and anxiety gradually wanes.

Bodha, a self-paralyzing and self-limiting patient, improved through analytic psychotherapy and faced previously non-existent possibilities of success. She was about to obtain a diploma from a professional school she had intelligently and conscientiously attended; her weight had gone down and her hair had become lustrous; she and her interesting, even though difficult, husband had started to get along and her frigidity had made way for orgasms. In the midst of such new-found plenty, Bodha, like many others who begin to face success, once again became anxious. Among the many causes of felt danger the one most clearly registered was the possibility that this unusually talented girl, suddenly faced with success, would be pushed into unmanageably many situations.[11]

In another kind of situation anxiety is felt by passive and dependent patients when they lose someone previously relied upon (even though referred to largely in unspoken language). The reasons for the patients' fear in these cases are largely internal. For one, a person who has served as an important focal point toward which feelings and thoughts could be directed leaves a void when he or she disappears or is discarded. As a result, unless therapeutic help is effective, the patient, passive and dependent, is bereft of a target toward which to direct experiences and is swamped by impressions, needs, and feelings. These now swarm unformed within the psyche and create disturbing fuzziness. A second reason is that disturbed persons feel that the figures they love, but on whom they actually lean, are endowed with magical powers to cure ills and to supply strength. [12] When such supposedly magical helpers disappear, either because they are alienated or simply because of external circumstances, the dependent patient feels empty-handed, unshielded, exposed to the dangers of the world, and hence anxious.

The road to cure in such instances goes via various way stations. Patients must realize that the persons they endowed with magic powers are fallible and human. What is even more important, patients need to find out that the only reliable power for making new contacts and for securing protection lies within the self.

When a male friend, the fifth in a row of exuberant and very young men, left Maria, the divorced mother of little twin daughters, she became very anxious. She was much amazed to find that an illness that kept both her children in bed actually acted as a relief. The reason soon became clear, and Maria said, "I like it when my daughters are sick. When they are tied down in bed I know that they won't leave me.

I also realize they won't make too many demands. Their presence makes me feel protected — they are neither too far away nor too near. But what an ungroovy mother I am to think that two little girls can do something for me. I need my own strength and a real man to put me into this world." With new insight and strength gained in therapy Maria managed to master her disquieting feelings. To her own surprise she discovered that, with the young man in her life gone, she could make different and supportive contacts with female friends and married couples.

When anxiety has taken hold, psychoanalytic help derives from many therapeutic steps among which the development of insights into the nature of the patient's conflicts certainly plays a prime role. Much emphasis has been given elsewhere in the psychoanalytic literature to the role of insight and to techniques that facilitate it. Therefore, in this context let us stress *additional steps that are not meant to be substitutes*. The measures that will be mentioned have an importance beyond their contribution to self-understanding. They help to strengthen the weak or warped ego and thus to shore up the personality. No attempt is made here to diminish the importance of psychoanalytically produced self-understanding. But the stress is on ways of following up insight with psychological action.

The aim of the therapeutic steps discussed is to increase alert perspicacity, vigorous conduct, the affirmative possibilities of the personality. Special techniques are needed to dispense with passivity and dependence, or their cover-up of hyperactivity. [13]

1. Usually it is during the first clash with danger that a patient's existing capacities to size up what has gone wrong fragment. To rescue the patient from such fragmentation it is helpful to advocate *pausing* and, in its wake, *restructuring*. The skill to initiate a short break between threat and reaction can be learned where it does not exist.

2. Related to this prescription of pausing is the fact that whereas strong personalities achieve unprecedented clarity of perception and thought during stress, many troubled people experience a blurring of senses and thoughts. Conscious and unconscious hyper-

activity, hectic movements, and the premature use of many defenses add to the encroaching mental fuzziness. All this confused response to stress must be slowly but deliberately undone through psycho-therapy that achieves *a change of focus.* Many patients become hypnotically riveted to danger situations past the point of precise danger-spotting. As though hypnotized, they stare at oncoming peril rather than casting about for appropriate escape routes or coping mechanisms. The often-found preference of those in therapy for discussing symptoms rather than investigating deep methods of relief illustrates this paralyzing tendency and documents the need for therapists to teach patients how to make an about-face. Danger-inspection must be accompanied by *a creative preoccupation with means of rescue.*

3. Indecision in choosing between divergent means of danger-fighting is conspicuous in neurotic personalities. Hence, psycho-therapy can help by stressing the need for the patient to make choices on the basis of deliberate preferences. The inability to decide whether to take flight or to stay put, doubts as to which detour to select, questions about which figures to trust, these and more make for indecision, uncertainty, and a subjective experience of con-fusion and whirl. This kind of experience is often found to be a prime ingredient of severe anxiety. The way out is *the selection of basic lines to pursue,* in keeping with healthy predilections and individual personality structure.

5. It is difficult properly to pinpoint the location of danger. It is hard to differentiate between the threats of inner danger — twinges of conscience, thrusting impulses — and outer perils — a likely loss of job, the malicious intent of a close person. But the psychothera-pist can help the patient to become his own diagnostician, *recog-nizing the true location of danger.*

6. Like Alice in Wonderland, patients are given to the percep-tion of strange sizes. Frequently, dangers are overrated, and there-fore hasty solutions are desperately snatched at. Coincidental with such overrating of danger's size is an underestimation of the self, despite a covering grandiosity. As when dangers are underrated, proper functioning is warped, and anxiety invades every pore of the being. *Realistic size evaluations* can be acquired by learning to understand the mechanisms that affect danger-enhancement or danger-denial.

The Useful Pause
Between Alert and Action

At the onset of danger a disturbed person responds with either initial paralysis or hyperactivity, neither of which is a satisfactory response. Hence remedial pauses are called for. When people learn (through psychotherapy or through their own experience) to put the brakes on when they collide with trouble, they give the mind a chance to prepare capabilities tailored for the particular threat. A pause allows the self which has been battered to reassemble, to pull itself together and make itself felt. For many people, the cigarette mediates the pause, but there is really no reason why we cannot use other deliberate slowdown patterns, mediated by self-control, to substitute for props that threaten physical health.

> A well-known professional woman, Audrey spoke at many meetings and made frequent television appearances. But her anxiety spells became increasingly frequent, and she entered psychotherapy to alleviate her misgivings.
> It became clear that Audrey lost her sense of self whenever she felt threatened. In particular, she felt as though she moved in alien land when she faced a crowd. Gradually this patient discovered that slowing down her reactions, movements, and contacts created a much needed sense of familiarity with the audience. When she talked more hesitantly, and hence naturally, the ensuing little interludes allowed human contacts to coalesce rather than being either ignored or scattered. This kind of pausing put Audrey in touch with both her audience and her own self. It made what she had to say authentic.

In emphasizing the effect of the pause upon the perception of threat and the onset of anxiety, it must be specified that timing matters. The duration of a pause is right if it creates a short intermission rather than a lasting prelude of aimless, fumbling, and passive hesitations.

Experiments in the psychology of learning have shown that memory can be improved by interspersing mental effort with properly timed pauses. It seems likely that physiological and mental intermissions facilitate neurological restructuring which in turn furthers such mental skills as memory. Similarly, intermediate pauses, neither too long nor too short, which vary with the individual, make possible the careful scanning of the self and of currents underlying danger situations.

A pause strengthens the threatened individual's waning belief in many kinds of strength actually possessed. And a halt helps at least in some measure to correct paranoid distortions that perceived threats are the outcome of major designs meant to destroy. Especially when helped additionally by psychotherapy, many disturbed people come to realize that stresses are mere by-products of other, more basic, happenings and occur without evil intention on the part of either fate or other people.

One of the first things, then, that a threatened person can learn to do is to make sure that the mind takes a break when a danger signal is sighted. This pause is the equivalent of the ready-set-go conditioning that coaches teach to athletes. The difference is that instead of preparing body muscles for a physical contest, the patient prepares his psychic equipment for an emotional contest.

> When Beverly was in the company of more than one person, she usually turned taciturn. At the root of her subjectively embarrassing silence was the expectation that other people would act like her perfectionist and excessively ambitious parents, demanding of her great pronouncements, finely articulated. Yet though the patient unearthed the essence of the social dangers she anticipated and the anxiety she felt, she still remained mute in company. A breakthrough occurred in a therapy group when she was assured that she could wait as long as she wished until she ventured into articulate speech. Pauses helped Beverly to make contact with her often jumbled and chunk-like feelings which turned into gems of experience once she allowed herself to take her own time.

When animals sense the threat of danger they fall back on reflex reactions that delay immediate and impulsive responses. The tiger who sights a hunter narrows his eyes temporarily, both to focus more precisely and to delay further reaction. Sensing danger, the dog grimaces, growls, and casts about with his eyes and ears before he sounds the final, sharp, full-fledged barks. Human beings, who do not possess such built-in delaying reflexes — for children scream immediately when they experience fright or sense danger — must acquire and develop habits and customs that force the mind into a brief wait before it goes into action. We have to learn not to push the panic button right away. Adjusting a tie or dress, putting on more lipstick, these are small social rituals not only born of the narcissistic wish to make a favorable impression but also arising out of need for a useful stalling device before going into action in new and hence threatening situations.

As the result of the hyperactivity that frequently comes with danger, details of perception, thought, and emotion often fuse into a blur. In addition — surprisingly enough, since hyperactivity is often considered as an enlargement of the personality — the field of awareness narrows instead of expanding. Rather than covering extensive territory, the perceptions, thoughts, and emotions stay confined to a limited sector. Clues likely to lead to solutions are hence missed. Like lost objects that are usually found not at the place where they were thought to be dropped but off-center, the significant clues nestle not in the core but in the remote corners of awareness.

> Examples of blurring and narrowing the mental field under the impact of danger occurred in the treatment of Helen, a forty-nine-year-old patient. One day, when this woman expected a piece of bad news concerning her much-loved only son, she found herself adopting puzzling reading habits. A research worker who customarily studied newspapers and announcements with precision, Helen became oddly inaccurate. For instance, as she later discovered, when going over the invitation to a greatly anticipated lecture series, Helen missed the reference to a speaker she had expected to appear. An hour later, on rereading the previously studied announcement, Helen found she had missed a large-print line at the bottom of the page that stressed the lecture this same man was to give. Interested though she was, in her anxiety Helen had not studied, or even read, the entire prospectus and had narrowed down her area of attention.

People who are unaware of the blurring and narrowing of perception that interfere with proper danger-spotting and with danger relief often do not recognize the deprivations they undergo, much less the origins of these deprivations. It is when they feel themselves bereft of the presence of protective, helpful, and even magically endowed partners, friends and therapeutic allies that they collapse and give in to fragmentation, blurring, and constricted awareness. Once they can recognize the existence of either present helpers or their own ability to find such personalities in the future, they recover strength and broadened vision.

The apathy following danger and deprivation has been studied in some degree. But the ill-effects of hyperactivity, mental blurring, and narrowing of the mental field have not been followed with equal concern. We are but insufficiently aware that euphoria, a protracted state that often accompanies trouble, also interferes with mastery of danger. Euphoria, like apathy, blinds human beings to both danger and the possibilities for coping with it and must be recognized as a sign not of strength but of disease.

Change of Focus:
From Fixation on Danger to Rescue

Besieged by feelings of stress and anxiety, many patients insist on focusing too long on crisis and danger. They believe that if they discuss their problems and fears over and over again, every difficulty will vanish. They are not aware that what is sinister does not give way simply because it is reviewed, any more than a thorn in the thumb will disappear when merely subjected to scrutiny. No amount of obsessive inspection will remove either the thorn or the anxiety. Only proper countermoves are effective.

Often people speak in symbolic forms of anxiety or of dangers they anticipate. Afraid, for instance, of inner eruptions, they talk or dream of atomic explosions. It then behooves the therapist to enable the patient to read and understand the special self-created language and, after that has been accomplished, *to move on.*

The formerly popular idea that talk relieves anxiety because it produces catharsis — a notion that has encouraged repeated ventilation of trauma, stress, and anxiety — holds true in only a limited way. It is a fact that the delineation and articulation of a feeling or an impulse helps to master what goes on inside, for all experience, in order to be contained, must be tied to some formed symbols. However, beyond that, articulation is not the totally effective process it has been at times considered.

Many people who keep narrating the sad stories of their grievances and anxieties hurt rather than help themselves. Without interventions by the therapist too much time can be spent on satisfying masochistic needs, particularly the desire to elicit sympathy and love by a display of suffering. Instead of being glued to old or new problems and the created anxieties, patients must learn, without the use of denial or other mechanisms that act merely as blinders, to look in the opposite direction. Once dangers have been spotted and sized up, the routes of extrication through ego activity must be sought and pursued.

Any preoccupation with crisis or threat that exceeds the time necessary to size up the nature and the proportions of danger and the needed escape route is a waste of energy. It prolongs and might even reinforce suffering and anxiety. Who would not get upset if he returned over and over again to the burned ruins of a house he lost? Wouldn't he do better, after a time of mourning and thought, to give his energies to building another home? The notion of the repetition compulsion, Freud's idea that we master trauma by repeating in an active way the frightening events that befell us passively, is only partially true. To go beyond trauma, one must go beyond reenactment and create new activity.

The expectation in psychoanalytic psychotherapy is that the patient is to be his or her own diagnostician. A variety of benefits is to accrue from tracing back into childhood the occurrence of early traumata — for instance, hurtful relationships that have led to the warping of the personality from which the adult individual still suffers. And indeed there is much to be said for such retracing of the past: life is viewed as the coherent continuum it is; past traumata, when revisited by the searching adult mind of the grown-up patient, are drained of their emotional impact; the adult comes to see that, with his present psychological capacities, he can deal with the memories of old difficulties and with the actuality of similar new pangs in novel ways; and discoveries are made that lingering rages, underestimations of the self, fears, and so on are based on the invalid expectation that what happened once will necessarily occur again. In the wake of such discoveries made in retracing the past, many subterranean and unconscious processes come to light and, moreover, get dismissed because, in the light of individual modernity, they appear ludicrous.

Though in many instances it is useful if the therapist confronts the patient directly with that which is feared, the patient's own search for the meaning of some of his absurdly anxious acts is useful since, to mention just one factor, it assigns initiative to the patient. But sometimes individuals abandon themselves too long to the bittersweet memories of the past. This happens whenever the repetitiveness of the search is not recognized as resistance to change, which it in fact represents. In such instances, passive, primitive, masochistic danger-courting rather than danger-fighting tendencies are encouraged. The patient is allowed to dwell on trouble rather than to take the next step and consider self-made rescue operations. Passive dwelling on trouble is confused with genuine discovery. Squelched, slowed down, and misled by the preoccupation with danger, the adult ego, infinitely capable of evolving novel adaptations to situations and personalities that appear threatening in the present, remains inactive.

Bodha had become aware of her selfishness and the threat her manipulations presented to her husband. She also realized that to retaliate he might leave, and this idea terrified her. This gifted woman was sensitive, dependent, and filled with guilt. At each treatment session she asked for just a few minutes to discuss her most recent anxieties and the latest episodes of insult inflicted upon her by her husband, Gregory, who was also seen by the therapist.

Yet gradually, as Bodha became convinced that dwelling on her anxieties and on her husband's genuine offenses made her only more narcissistic and dependent on him, thus aggravating rather than relieving anxiety, she shifted ground. She began to see the route of liberation, namely, that she had to obtain more self-differentiation, that she needed to give more attention to others and their needs, and that she had to shore up her own resources. She started to work harder and with more dedication. She got a bicycle to move around town and eventually learned to drive, a difficult step for her. This switch from tenacious self-preoccupation, from repetitive narrations of outer dangers (the husband's counterprovocations) to absorption in other events and people and to a building up of new skills brought Bodha and her mate closer.

New directions are always refreshing and strengthening, in life, in art, in the explorations of nature. The mere involvement with events and persons not implicated in existing or imminent stresses brings the ego to active functioning. When this is achieved, specific ego capacities will be envisaged, tried out, and acquired to assure escape from the acknowledged danger. Anxiety disappears. When faced with a crisis, many patients rally if they become *genuinely* steeped — as distinguished from falling prey to artificial diversionary maneuvers — in matters that are unrelated to the crisis but that command attention and require constructive thought. As a result of excursions into neighboring fields, the mind approaches imminent crises more capably. Thought processes that had been paralyzed by the immediate crisis become activated by contact with unrelated, hence relatively danger-free, situations. The stage for ego activities, previously cluttered by the monotonous review of the crisis, is now cleared.

We must, therefore, in therapy shift our emphasis from what is wrong to how it can be set right. We must go from id to ego. We must build up the ego — through expansion, enhanced selectivity, learning, or loosening — so that where there has been a wild reign of passions there emerges instead a balance between desires and controls.

The number of reviews made of crises furnishes one of the criteria that make possible the evaluation of relative passivity or activity, of anxiety or confidence. Nonexploratory, reiterative, exclusively backward-looking mental stock-taking of problems and symptoms suggests considerable passivity. On the other hand, a patient who, under the pressure of perceived danger, talks with interest of other topics, not in flight but because his mental span is broad enough to touch on an array of different events, very likely possesses access to activity, mental alertness, and preparedness. The makings of the ready-set-go attitude, like that preparing an athlete for stress, are there. Comparisons with athletic behavior suggest themselves with good reason. Athletic performances, like the skill of the gifted surgeon, are not determined by physiological training and physical readiness alone.

The mind, the ego, is largely responsible for the high level of motor performance.

As has been mentioned, actual dangers, though not always of a mental-emotional kind, are often obscured, both by the insistence on sticking to narrations of symptoms and by repeating symbolic formulations without trying to understand their significance. Cover-up situations that are not the patient's real concern are like the stand-in who takes the place of the real star in the motion picture and, again like the stand-in, are often overrehearsed. Work with psychotics shows that patients appreciate and use early deciphering of their symbolism. They give a sigh of relief when the real dangers are pointed out. We see this quite often in group therapy when members, unaware of the existence of and reasons for another member's defenses and resistances, come quickly and incisively to the point.

Marian, a schizophrenic girl who had just been brought to a day-care center, approached a breakdown rapidly. In her morning therapy group she told the therapist and other members that she felt cold like ice, was near death, and ought to be taken to the state hospital. Her intense rage toward her mother was quite obvious as she explained living arrangements and conditions at home. During the treatment session she begged to touch the arm of the therapist who was young, rightly cautious, and fearful lest such physical contact might precipitate the already far-reaching crisis. After the meeting, the patient approached another, more experienced male therapist present and asked to be held. The therapist recognized that this wish was prompted by the patient's fear of death. Wishing to kill her mother with a knife, as she had said she wanted to do, she had turned her impulse inward and had begun to act as though she were near death. Clearly, the more Marian lost the distinction between inside and outside, the more likely was her collapse. The therapist told her firmly, "Yes, hold me and I will tell you when you have to be yourself again, the old, clear Marian." The patient clutched at the therapist and held him tightly. When the therapist told Marian that now they must sit down as two people — to make the experience of distinction very clear to the patient and also to reinforce in her the idea that with her own controls vanishing the therapist would serve as a temporary check — she took a chair. She was told very firmly, "Marian, you can think bad things, but you can not do them. You can think you want to kill your mother, but you must never do it." When the therapist, wishing to make the control more visible, asked Marian if she wanted to write these words down, she nodded affirmatively. She kept the slip of paper on which she had noted down the therapist's injunctions in her pocketbook. Meeting the therapist in the corridor later, she pointed smilingly to her pocketbook, signaling that she knew what to do. She improved within days and then left the day-care center much more hopeful and in control. The plunge the therapist had taken into a rapid delineation of the partly unconscious problems had helped and not hurt.

Passive patients implore their therapists to let them talk of their problems "just once more" and often disguise their crisis reviews as free associations. If we examine the nature of the mental content of their behavior, a prominent element stands out: "If I think of 'it,' then 'it' will go away."

The advocated shift from concentrating on danger to concentrating on other images and goals, as a means of getting out of a danger situation, differs from distraction. Distraction is a trick used by the parent, teacher, or orator who introduces into the field of awareness an object or an idea that takes eye or mind away from reality, pain, and anxiety. By contrast, the method of shifting focus discussed here consists of awakening the insight that nothing further can be gained by continued fixation on a target and that attention must span other areas. Danger must not be repressed or ignored, but must rather be put aside temporarily in order for mental resilience to emerge.

In the more primitive stages of childhood the mind fixes on the target of danger because in this way the child's attention is maintained and the temptation to think away, to deny, existing threats is reduced. Keeping the mental processes focused on the target represents a valid form of rallying strength at that point of development. But the method can turn into a liability if it is continued indiscriminately during later phases of life.

Later on, in anticipation of pressure — for instance, in the form of inner needs — the healthy child's mind develops the capacity for scanning the environment and exploring the possibilities for satisfaction or relief. Thus attention to the danger target is succeeded by attention to environmental means of escape, rescue, and satisfaction. Where this development lags, it must be initiated in psychotherapy.

Observation shows us that the prolonged fixation on danger, partly functional as it may have been in childhood, precipitates a passive state such as occurs in hypnosis. A person about to be hypnotized fixates an object to the point at which his ego becomes so passive that it recedes and makes room for the will of the hypnotist. In working with anxiety and one of its prime causes, passivity, therapists must enable patients to make distinctions between ego submission, in which the mind no longer works out the proper means of rescue and abandons the individual to enfeebling anxiety, and constructive preoccupation with hazard for the purpose of mapping out the causes and nature of danger.

The Way Out of Confusion

Among the many-branched causes of anxiety, confusion stands out as a prime factor. Confusion, as the term is used here, means a greater abundance of psychic events than the ego can cope with. An excess of input or of interior currents can create a mental and emotional deluge that cannot be channeled. Artists abandoning themselves to creative eruptions and people who reach "peak" experiences because they have thrown off inner fetters, because it is spring, or because they give in to their senses are often seized by anxiety. If the level of conflicting pressures rises while the ego stays too weak to sort out those that are most important and to forge them into a whole, confusion and anxiety are again ready results. Particularly where two or more solutions to a conflict have relatively equal pull a confusing perplexity is inevitable.

Every medley of mental events that exceeds the individual's capacity to bring divergent expressions, feelings, or needs under one harmonious roof and thus to make choices creates confusion. Invariably, the experience of such confusion is paralleled by sensations of physiological dizziness and whirling, familiar to those to whom they signify anxiety. Ambivalence, such as the sensation of feeling two

ways about a person or a project, is but one relatively simple instance of confusion. Its contribution to anxiety feelings has been
underrated.

One way of mastering confusion is to compartmentalize, though
not necessarily as blindly, tightly, or perpetually as obsessive-compulsive people do. Compartmentalization and other order-creating
devices, such as a mental list of priorities of need or the discipline
of taking up problems one by one, reduce anxiety created by confusion. The development of structure through reliance on inner or
outer directions and controls reduces the peril of being swamped
and fragmented by too many and too divergent impressions and
pulls.

> Anthony, an executive, summed up the value of such devices
> well: "When I work in my New York office, I think about East
> Coast problems from 9:00 to 11:30. Then for two hours there
> is time for social contacts, many for business and some for fun.
> The early afternoon goes to thoughts about my Detroit outfit,
> and at about 6 o'clock I start to feel pleasant about my kids
> and home. It's the only way I can keep from getting dizzy, and
> it does not make me a cold and calculating guy. Some notion
> that my wife and the family are around exists always, but I
> have to keep it dim. I have to keep things, in their place be-
> cause before treatment I was in a muddle and always felt weak
> and anxious." This patient had not become obsessive-compul-
> sive, but he *deliberately* used some compartmentalizations that
> disturbed patients are *compelled* to fall back on. He resorted
> to pigeonholes not to separate permanently events that be-
> longed together but to create temporary order and structure.

As we have seen, too much is as threatening as too little. Many
people, when they have too many opportunities for work, for love
and play, become as anxious as when they are forced onto too
narrow a path. Similarly in treatment, if patients make more discoveries than can be digested, anxiety sets in. What is necessary is
not only that feelings be freed but also that primacy be assigned to
some, that others be put aside momentarily, and that discoveries be
absorbed by going over them repeatedly and viewing them from
different angles.

Almost every conflict has not merely two but several solutions that are at variance. Treatment helps the patient to look at these divergent ways out and make choices that bring happiness instead of self-destruction. Facing these choices among clashing solutions can create deep confusion and intense anxiety. Particularly perturbing is the indecision a patient feels when confronted by three kinds of possible settlement: If he feels endangered by someone who is close to him, should he flee, fight, or stay put? If treatment is effective, the patient invariably finds out that the safest way out is none of these three, but is instead a new way that has not been formerly contemplated, that did not, in fact, formerly exist within his reach. For example, the exercise of firmness and healthy self-assertion vis-à-vis other human beings who do harm is one of the best solutions.

When neurotic personalities are confronted with messages of rejection — whether these are unavoidable or provoked is another issue — they feel the three tugs mentioned above. They want to run (flight), to destroy (fight), and to stay put (masochistic clinging). The physiological whirling sensations that are bound to emerge, together with an emotional mixture of rage and helplessness, send the patient into an anxious spin.

Orvin, a long-married forty-six-year-old patient, was perplexed that he stayed longer and longer in bed and close to his wife, toward whom he felt a great deal of rage much of the time. His claims that his wife ridiculed him and held him in contempt seemed partially substantiated, partially exaggerated. His complaints were also in a way unwarranted, since this provoking patient saw to it that his wife played the role of the offender whom he, in turn, could hate. However, the issue here is that Orvin turned more and more passive as he kept himself increasingly tied to the home. He was anxious for the better part of each day, and insomnia increased. Perhaps the most intolerable symptom was tingling sensations in the legs which mystified Orvin and convinced him that he had lost mastery over his body. "Something," he said, "is at war in my legs."

Gradually Orvin reported that though he walked about less the feeling inside was that he was compelled to move *and* stand still *at the same time.* The therapist concluded that contradictory nervous innervations were at the root of the distressing tingling sensations: unconscious impulses to run, to flee his home, clashed with contradictory impulses to remain close to the seemingly powerful wife to whom Orvin clung masochistically. The patient's trouble was the hysterical clash between innervation and inhibition of the leg muscles.

In this case, the results of the flight wishes were unusually pronounced because Orvin, an action-prone man who flew his own plane, did not stop at just the idea of getting away. He actually flexed the muscles of his legs, started to get out of his chair, and raised his hand many a time to telephone for a plane. *The wish to leave did not remain a thought but entered the beginning phase of action.* Similarly with Orvin's fight wishes. Many fleeting thoughts showed that the patient came close to pushing his wife down two flights of stairs. But being a man with considerable self-control, he was quick to inhibit his arms and shoulders so strongly that the muscular contractions led to cramps and spasms.

The muscular tangle between innervations and inhibitions which resulted in the standstill of growing inertia was paralleled in the ego. Orvin not only left for his office later and later but eventually stopped work altogether and for a while could not support his family. At the same time, obsessive preoccupation with work increased. But the patient, like others similar to him, was more disturbed by the tingling sensations in his legs and the spasms in his back than by his growing apathy. The latter had always existed as a nuclear character trait, side by side with a gift for initiative and action.

In this case, as in similar ones, the therapist quickly had to make distinct contact with the patient, who had already established a dangerous narcissistic distance from the world. The therapist pointed out quite soon the wavering between fight, flight, and staying-put reactions and made it clear that all three had many disadvantages. The patient then made sense of the dizziness, whirling sensations, and tingling feelings in the legs and comprehended that these were the physiological counterparts of his catastrophic inner state. The mere conviction that body sensations, previously deemed mysterious and seemingly coming from nowhere, had a meaning was reassuring. Many attempts were made to strengthen this man who had allowed himself to become so dependent and enfeebled. After several months Orvin's ability to assert himself vis-à-vis his wife emerged, and his own provocations diminished. Though flight was not encouraged in treatment, the desire to get away was clearly delineated, and the patient examined his wish to leave and his intent to do away with his wife without intense anxiety. Not surprisingly, he soon decided that neither flight nor fight nor clinging was the best method of coping with his anxiety. Instead he enjoyed the strength with which he could challenge his wife constructively and the forcefulness with which he once more made a living for his family.

All clingers have inherent, though unused, strength. After they have taken the first step — that is, have gained insight into the discrepancy between fight, flight, and staying-put wishes — they start on step two, practicing ego growth. Sometimes it helps to "go into reverse" as it were. Specifically, persons who cling to the very figure they wish to desert and destroy must, after they have understood the nature of their confusion, make deliberate efforts to move away from rather than toward the real or imagined antagonist. Instead of dwelling on the mate, boss, parent, or employer who is at once feared and followed, these patients need to refer to people less central and more clearly well-disposed toward them. Instead of physically remaining near the object of clinging, they need to steer into opposite directions, not in angry flight but in the sincere effort to become independent, to stay out of the orbit of whoever is seen as the rejecting or threatening potentate. The addiction to the telephone which clingers use to stay in touch with the one they hate and fear and depend on can be reduced and curbed. In short, the discovery that the very person about whom the patient hovers is resented and feared calls for the development of new, and indeed opposite, modes of relating.

In our society, the suspicion of the younger generation toward the older generation which claims to know what is best is notably great. But submission is no longer the prime method of dealing with the enemy of the older generation. Instead, apartness and defiance, which are the other side of the coin, are favored. Also, at the same time that nearly every moral standard and practice of the older group is treated with distance and opposition (psychological methods probably less dangerous than clinging), a new love-seeking is introduced through the back door. Within loose settings of peer groups, indiscriminate and often undeserved and unappreciated sheltering and assistance are given. Though this offering of love does not quite equal submission, it once more produces a variation on the theme of passive acceptance, of leaning over backward, when exploitation occurs.

Despite the ominous presence of nuclear weapons, widespread poverty, and warring nations, we live in a fairly safe world. We are surrounded by comforts and medical advances that assure a better-than-ever life. But with at least some forms of physical danger lessened, new psychological confusions arise, born of young people's new efforts at self-protection such as go on forever in this ingenious world. The psychologist, sociologist, and wise political leader — and all people of goodwill — must help in the work of cleaning up these new confusions.

Pinpointing Danger

Psychotherapy is a special kind of fact-finding expedition. Before the patient enters into the psychological search and starts to see himself and the world more clearly, he is satisfied either to let things slide or to explain psychological events with untried, unfactual pseudo-theories. When he senses the vague physiological manifestations of anxiety, he fails, on account of his understandable ignorance, to make some important connections. He or she neither realizes that the anxiety, frequently disabling, is a physical equivalent of imminent danger nor knows that a distinction must be made between the dangers located outside the self and those lodged inside. To spot danger is a useful antidote to anxiety and a first step in combating it.

Like two mates, each of whom feels sure it is the other partner whose shortcomings disturb what would otherwise be a peaceful household, neurotic persons habitually assign the reason for trouble to someone or something external. Psychological amateurs, they cannot and do not want to pinpoint with objectivity the location of stress. The reason a patient is afraid of thunder, so he or she thinks, is that a thunderstorm is so dangerous, not that the self is so angry that any outer explosion sets off a fear of internal eruption. The psychoanalytic literature has shown that in most instances it is the impulses, emotions, and thoughts *inside* that are the most powerful determinants of anxiety. Although this idea has been claimed to be a more comprehensive explanation than it in fact is, since many times it is indeed an outside force that makes us cower, the proposition has much validity. As patients learn to pinpoint danger correctly and no longer need to shield their vanity, they can admit it when the real cause of trouble lies inside. As a result, they become firmer, clearer, and stronger. Now they have finally found that to combat anxiety they can fortify their own mental strength and capacities and draw on them for self-protection.

The fraility of the natural human equipment in the face of danger suggests the necessity of adopting promising techniques to help ourselves. One useful outlook upon which many people stumble instinctively is to link some new dangers with some old perils. In coping with danger and anxiety it is helpful to fit new dangers into a familiar frame of reference.[14] If new hurdles, when first encountered, are connected with old ones that were conquered, the chances of initial paralysis and apathy are reduced. Once such helpful links have been made, the ego can go into action and do some custom tailoring. It can devise novel and appropriate ideas, concepts, and skills for making headway in difficult situations.

Illustrating how progress toward objective pinpointing can be made, especially the shift from outside to inside, is the case of Barbara, a twenty-one-year-old psychotic patient who was treated in a hospital. Barbara lived with her parents and had been lured by her mother into a symbiotic relationship. One of the functions of the symbiosis was that the mother, who was paranoid and always aggrieved by injuries supposedly inflicted on her, possessed in Barbara a fairly helpless target at whom she could hurl her anger.

When Barbara entered the hospital, she had the delusion that an aunt (representing in this case the mother herself) was going to kill two neighbor boys. Barbara's mother was envisaged as a saint who was protecting Barbara and the children next door against the aunt's evil intentions. Thus danger was clearly located outside, in the aunt who was a cover-up for the mother. Originally apathetic, Barbara became increasingly active and articulate during treatment. When her anger became more sharply delineated, the sense of bewildering confusion of which she had always complained was gradually lifted. The patient said that she began to know what was outside and what was inside herself. As Barbara lost the fear of expressing her anger she mumbled swear words behind the backs of doctors and nurses, and eventually confronted them openly with complaints, some of them bizarre but many realistic.

As the patient improved markedly, she made perspicacious remarks. She would say, on occasions when she felt anger welling up, "I think it's a dog barking crazy" (locating danger outside). "No, that's a lot of nonsense, it's that dirty thing in me kicking up" (locating danger, namely her anger, inside herself). One Monday when Barbara was distressed, as always, by the long weekend at home, she beamed because she had managed to make a "tie-up." She had overcome an incipient panic by connecting a quarrel at home with something that had happened at the hospital. "Mama started on a new tack on Sunday," Barbara said, "and I was scared that she would cut off all my hair. Then it occurred to me that that old lady in the hospital had wanted to cut her daughter's hair and put her daughter's little dog away. Suddenly Mama's plot seemed funny. It wasn't anything unique. It stopped feeling like an earthquake. I got some handles to take hold of it."

After only five months of treatment, Barbara appeared greatly improved. The external enemy, her mother, was still a fierce one. But Barbara had made more than a nodding acquaintance with the enemy or the danger inside, her rages. Having feared previously that she would not be able to control them and hence would actually harm her mother, she now felt clear and could anticipate when inner controls were needed. She had started to be on speaking terms with her inner self whence so many dangers had come.

The inability, especially marked in disturbed individuals, to distinguish what occurs within the body and mind from what happens in the external world goes far back. Small infants, so psychoanalysts have reconstructed,[15,16] hang on to an elusive peace of mind, as it were, by fantasying that pains inside the body really belong outside.

We don't know yet just how the baby manages to turn the world inside out, but we do have many confirmations that "projective identifications," to use one proposed term, or just plain "projections" are formed in very early childhood so as to preserve the fantasy that the self is pleasurable and in this way to hang on to hope. Without such illusions the child becomes pessimistic and apathetic.

If such childhood projective identifications or projections persist later in life, havoc is wrought in the adult. A confused world image prevails, leaving it unclear just what troubles originate in the self and which ones are caused by others. Unfortunately, few obscurities caused by early methods of defense are as tenacious and as resistant to therapeutic intervention as the misinterpretation or illusion that what is bad comes from outside.

Correcting Size Distortions

Unusual perceptions of size and preferences for either oversized or miniature objects are the frequent experience of small children, psychotics, excessive drinkers, many homosexuals, and people overcome by shock or fear. Fairy tales owe much of their popularity to the giants, dwarfs, and tiny or gigantic objects in them. The same goes for *Gulliver's Travels,* in which the hero discovers two extreme worlds, one of giants and one of miniature people. Such size distortions, which on first and rational glance seem to have little or no bearing on normal everyday experience, make contact with more hidden, less openly admitted emotional and mental currents and hence exert both an appeal and a threat of unreality.

Gifted cartoonists and other artists, whose intuition tells them what games are played on the public, use this proclivity for size distortions. Such artists show us dangerous people, things, or ideas as gigantic, and the frightened nonhero or supposed victim as tiny. And the viewer looking at these representations feels relieved when his perceptual secrets are shared by the professional illustrator who sets down the exaggerations that frightened egos commonly perform. The viewer, while remaining anonymous, is no longer isolated, for such funny treatments of perceptual confusions show that his are not crazy, idiosyncratic processes after all, but are shared by others.

Dangerous settings and occurrences increase misperceptions of size to which both the normal and, to a higher degree, the troubled person are subjected. Upon immediate impact all aspects of danger seem to be large. Therefore the phrase "danger looms." Simultaneously the disturbed self, together with physiological properties and meager store of know-how, is felt to shrink and become small.

Don Quixote, the courageous protagonist who appears somewhat ludicrous upon first glance and has all the characteristics of a neurotic or psychotic challenger, touches us because we recognize in him some tendencies within ourselves that have been hidden from self-inspection and the searching glances of others. He, like the anxious and disturbed self, perceives small occurrences as larger-than-life dangers. When he mistakes a windmill for a giant he proceeds like the disturbed man who fears that a shadow in the corner is the reflection of a powerful intruder or that a routine remark of an annoyed neighbor will have portentous consequences.

Patients cope poorly with danger and hence generate anxiety too readily when the first, brief, and unnoticed — since unconscious — perceptions exaggerate the expected impact of the feared encounter. While such perceivers feel their bodies to be shrinking, the field of the mind narrows and resources become depleted. As a result of this discrepancy between the perceived size of the threat and that of the self, a weakened and shrunken body and psyche are seen as confronting a magnified threat.

> Gregory, Bodha's husband, was invited to write a paper for a forthcoming convention in Europe. The paper was merely to summarize the literature already published about the topic in question plus his own findings, which had already been published in various journals. Shortly after the invitation, Gregory became depressed, complained of numbing headaches, and reported that he had asked his wife to drive the car. It turned out after some questioning that this ambitious patient, whose work had been praised as pioneering and who had reason to feel that he might make a breakthrough in the field of glandular research, perceived the request for his paper as a job requiring a year's preparation. Simultaneously he felt that his tall frame had shrunk. He had refused to drive himself to work because he felt his hands were too feeble to control the car.

No wonder that with such immediate, often physiological, responses to danger, the psyche manufactures and marshals powerful defenses: denial, forgetting that which hurts; imagined omnipotence which boosts strengths and powers at first underrated. But quick as these defenses are to take over, they are actually a sequel to the foremost and even swifter response which aggrandizes threat and diminishes self.

The imagined large size and devastating consequences of anticipated dangers and the correspondingly small dimensions of self and resourcefulness can be gleaned from patients' associations and images which we can perceive if we manage to delay later rational correction. Few people, and especially few who are disturbed, expect to be knocked down by insignificant and ordinary strangers. To the person with fear the stage is always set for a tragic drama; comedies are not in the repertory of expectations.

> Helen, as we have seen, was a good self-observer and was quick to notice what threats did to her perceptions. When an inner conflict upset her or when she felt unsafe for practical reasons — for instance if she planned to make a visit in a dangerous neighborhood — shadows on walls appeared magnified. When her husband was in a bad mood his large hands seemed huge. By the same token, she felt small and weak and started wondering how she had ever managed to settle anything.

> It helped Helen to become alert to these self-initiated distortions. As she gradually changed her perceptual habits, she got hold of her specific, real, well-practiced potentials. She started to know what she was and whether things would turn out well or badly.

Patients can learn to shift. In some measure, psychoanalytic psychotherapy is a learning theory and paves the way for learning experiences. Exaggeration on the end of the spectrum and underestimation on the other, with reality the central point, are the lookout posts that have to be examined for size and reality before we climb up on them to take a look at the world. Children, neurotics, schizophrenics, and others can be gradually taught to beware of extreme positions and to find out where the midpoint of reality is.

Locating reality properly has important social implications. In a population whose childlike and infantile propensities are fanned, the midpoint of reality, the ordinary proportions of both living and inanimate things, may appear uninteresting, and the large headlines may promise to spell the real truths. Demagogues and rabblerousers take advantage of the absence of size distinctions in a population that feels itself in danger. [17]

Partly for this reason we need ways to make what is real more luminous and more interesting, and to prove that reality is one of the great remedies, desired, nay, craved by all, a stepping stone toward freedom from anxiety. [18] Poorly taught, prematurely stimulated, or discouraged egos *can* be taught to make shifts and to seek out the reassuring specifics and less impressive proportions of reality, and in this way can be set free from the burdens imposed by unneeded exaggeration.

5. Active Loving

One of the prime human fears is that the individual will be exposed to desertion. Hence the human ego, which is the developer of relations with others, narcissistically fears above all the injury of abandonment. For this reason it is far less perilous to offer love than to insist on receiving it.

Even the state of being-in-love, that condition which we associate all too romantically with exclusively tender emotions and with unlimited supplies of devotion, is anything but a guarantee that the lover is safe and shielded against abandonment. Indeed, a person who is in love is particularly vulnerable and very likely to buckle if the beloved threatens rejection and desertion, either temporary or permanent. The ego of the enamored person is no longer held together by tight boundaries, such as contain it during more neutral periods. Quite to the contrary, the boundaries of a person in love are loose. They have opened up and taken in much larger-than-usual portions of the world, for every lover is loving not only toward his beloved but toward nearly everyone. Infatuation makes the person expansive, renders him or her trusting and rather defenseless. The state of receptivity is all-pervasive. Preoccupation with the store of images that represent the beloved in his or her absence is nearly complete.[1] Hence lovers are poorly prepared for anticipating and coping with abandonment.

With the ego in a relatively precarious state during the height of passion, and with the role of the passive recipient of love intensifying rather than reducing the lover's hazardous condition, it is safer to love actively than to remain merely the recipient of affectionate or passionate favors. But no calculating expectation of personal advantage can suffice as a basis for initiating active loving. Self-concern is not adequate to determine the genuinely outward-directed emotions; to be ready to extend love rather than to focus exclusively on getting it, a good deal of ego strength has to be available. To bestow love, to extend concern, attention and energy without exacting a return, the adult ego must have completed much orderly growth. An able lover draws strength from the residues of an infancy and childhood that were filled with the love of parental caretakers and that allowed the baby and child to store up healthy self-love (self-cathexis). Love is first borrowed from others until the self is, so to speak, enriched enough to beam love in the direction of others.[2] The able lover, more preoccupied with loving than with being loved (although the two are far from exclusive), was able, at the right stage of development, to burst the cocoon of narcissistic isolation, leaning, and dependency. He emerged into independence because he had had his fill of comfortable guidance and love and hence could move ahead to the next step, independence from parental nurture. Individuals who have not gone through the normal and necessary stages of narcissistic gratification, dependency, and self-emancipation — all begun in childhood and completed toward the end of adolescence — can, through psychotherapy, belatedly make up for what they missed out on. If they are genuinely helped, it will become unnecessary for them to insist on adult compensations for childhood deprivations. No longer will it be necessary to perpetuate demands for love, piling it up rather than dispensing it. Unhealthy determination to hover around the passive pole of receiving can, through therapeutic interventions, give way to a conviction that mutuality and reciprocity, by which passion is both obtained and bestowed, represent love.

Norris, a thirty-eight-year-old patient, was convinced when he entered treatment that the only way to relieve himself of the constant fear that Marcia, his handsome and energetic wife, would leave him was to get out of the marriage. He was also convinced that she shortchanged him by not offering enough love and concern. In the beginning of therapy his contributions as a patient consisted of perpetual complaints. Marcia asked for too much domestic help from him, she did not allow him the fun of building a little summer house in Virginia, and so on.

Fairly soon Norris comprehended that his behavior was childlike because he always watched how much he got, depended so much on his wife that he spoke more of her than of himself, and complained about rather than aided his family. The patient admitted that references to his wife, whom he mentioned in every second sentence, revealed how little independence he had achieved from a central female. He ceased to examine Marcia and began to look at himself and develop his potential for ego activity, thus establishing the first core of independence which, in turn, made it possible for him to give love to Marcia and the couple's two little boys. Norris also saw that he actually contributed very little to the domestic life, for instead of doing, he merely promised and reassured, substituting verbiage for action. As this man became less plaintive and demanding he actually got more good-humored love from his wife. As he absorbed the affection he now received he could emancipate himself from his previous narcissistic confines, which were responsible for his insistence on getting rather than giving so as to make up for a deficit incurred in childhood.

Adults who remain insatiable and demanding children at heart look upon love as a measurable quantity that can, for example, be gauged by the number of hours spent with the beloved. The size of gifts or the frequency of practical help is similarly regarded as a measure of the other person's dedication. In short, many a disturbed adult looks upon love as a pie and counts the number and size of the pieces allocated to him or her. In order to love truly and actively, such a childlike and literal perspective on loving has to be abandoned.

There exist many more interferences with generous grown-up love: preoccupations with retaliation, when the partner is considered too stingy with affection, obstruct love; excessive worries about the extension of the ego boundaries — that is, concern with self-containment — defeat loving relations; avoiding the intrusion of the partner's needs, which are experienced as a threat rather than a worthy challenge, makes for one-sided, selfish, and ungiving love and eventually brings about retaliatory abandonment. Equally harmful to love are communications expressed in a language all one's own. Communications of this kind occur when the person who thinks he or she is loving is still bound by narcissism and passivity which have not been washed away by the tides and waves of human contact. Lovers who speak only a language all their own are cut off from true reciprocity since the tongue of others has been neither heard nor learned. In addition, stagnation in the bog of narcissistic self-preoccupation and passivity makes it impossible for a lover to make distinct observations of the needs and mental-emotional makeup of the beloved. As a result, affectionate, appropriate, and pleasing acts meant to satisfy the beloved are rarely forthcoming.

Mutuality and Reciprocity Defined

To give love and not to concentrate on receiving it, to weave with others the fine fabric of mutuality are aims with which all schools of psychotherapy agree. Our common goal is unnarcissistic, active love and mutuality, exchanges in which neither giving nor receiving is exclusively insisted on, relationships in which differences not only are tolerated but become a takeoff point for individual development, since they are perceived not as intrusions but as stimulants. What we have neither unity nor clarity about, however, are pathways to take, the processes required to get to the destination, for not all roads lead to Rome. How then do we travel, what psychic baggage do we take along to reach the goal?

Many passive and narcissistic people harbor exaggerated love expectations. Hoping to achieve relief from anonymity, they over-dramatize their loves. Such infatuations are actually a means of self-aggrandizement as well as a residue of infantile omnipotence. Even relatively undisturbed people, who have found their way to maturity and have pretty well parted with narcissism in everyday life, harbor the secret hope that perhaps through the ways of love they can recapture the illusion of omnipotence. Maybe a love can be found and held tightly which will guarantee that one is loved above everyone else, regardless of conduct, exquisitely and forever.

The disturbed individual who by definition still demands impetuously to be loved, even though his actual demeanor is mild, and who is so passive that protective shelter remains a necessity is even much more obsessed with love. Perceiving obtained love as the last island of safety, such persons, in the insistent quest to be loved without limits, flit from partner to partner. They demand with the fierceness of a temper tantrum that the mate of their choice give total love or offer an equivalent modus vivendi that guarantees safety.

Clinicians and psychologists can make explicit the distinct process required of an adult who desires to live in a relationship of mutuality. For example, progressive psychosexual development, such as Freud charted, and continuing ego development, as it is now being mapped out, are the wherewithal of active love. Should the movement have been stopped and should fixations have occurred, should there be gaps in the ego, then the one who seeks mutuality is too preoccupied with outdated needs and weaknesses to extend himself or herself. For example, if oral needs for nurture and protection or omnipotent wishes were left unfulfilled in the process of development, then the person bent on "love" in the abstract will cast about cleverly for chances to make up the deficit. This person rallies hastily to seeming opportunities to get what has been withheld. In this activity, the awareness of genuine love and the readiness to bestow love actively get lost.

To achieve mutuality, then, undue intrusions on the emotional and love reserves of a partner have to be avoided. Only if the transition from dependence to independence either exists or is accomplished belatedly through psychotherapy will this be the case. An essentially dependent partner cannot sustain his or her own life and safety by relying on inside resources. Love, as a result, becomes less than a state of caring. It turns into a pursuit of rewards, an exploitation, with those who are close as the immediate victims. The less the individual is aware of his dependency claims, and the more they are disguised and expressed in nonverbal acts, the more harm is done to the relationship. In the long run, the exploited partner is bound to want out and desertion looms as the exploiter's ultimate reward.

In the absence of mental independence, "foreign aid" remains a perpetual necessity and is paid for with a diminution of self-esteem [3] and concomitant rage reactions toward those who have been leaned on to prop such self-esteem up. "Impasse" [4] occurs when the environment — in this case, the partner — refuses further mental, emotional, and practical help. Hence the process of becoming and remaining independent is a cornerstone of reciprocity, whose achievement is worth a lifetime of ever new efforts. Going beyond the enjoyment of friendships and intimacy, independence calls for the perpetual development and exercise of new strength and new ego skills appropriate to the adult's specific life situation. Every period of mature life has a quality all its own and makes particular demands. Life is in flux not only for the child but for the fully grown person as well. The absence of dependency is a large order required of the lover, since love tempts us to lean and borrow, habits that preempt mutuality.

Another essential of mutuality, of the "live and let live" state, is the maintenance of identity and self-differentiation. Such maintenance presupposes that there are no fixations on another phase of childhood development as outlined by Freud. In order to sustain identity within the tightly knit compound of a joint life and in order to accept and enjoy rather than resent and oppose the different needs and opinions of the other,[5] the struggle for autonomy which starts in childhood must have been reasonably completed. If the adult still is absorbed in it because it was thwarted in childhood, then active love and mutuality are once more shut out. The adult individual still deeply concerned about achieving independence strays from the paths of love. Loving contacts are regarded by him as yet another occasion on which to defend his autonomy. As a result, differences of opinion, of rhythm, of need, and so on, are perceived as hurtful intrusions rather than interesting encounters with a personal world that is different.

Active love, with its necessary setting of mutuality, comes about purposefully, by using the psychological bricks and mortar that are either at hand or else acquired belatedly through psychotherapy.

There is a side to putting together the building blocks of active and independent relationships which interests the ego psychologist. Many an excessively dependent, narcissistic, and passive person with inadequate identity matures by moving along the direct route of behaving differently. Rather than depending first on understanding his self-indulgent and passive confinement and then taking the steps that lead out of it into a dynamic life, many patients go about their self-liberation in the reverse way. Provided that along the route they gain insight, they are indeed well advised to move toward loving interest and caring actions through active step-by-step practice.

The decision to reach out toward active love by going straight toward the goal deserves trial. The processes of active love can be acquired first through an effort of will. Repeated attempts to be a giver, consciously undertaken, do disperse narcissism and passivity and may well contribute to identity. In fact, the final dispersion of narcissism and passivity always occurs in the wake of concerned and enterprising behavior on behalf of others. If the purpose of the actual practice of giving is not a sly glance at the possible safety which active love promises to bestow, but a genuine wish to correct psychological deficiencies, the quality of love will be improved. The new approach to love is not reserved for erotic love of an adult partner but often becomes a genuine part of the self, employed with parents, offspring, and friends.

Noah, the father of three sons, declared himself responsible for the behavior problems of his two older boys, whom he had neglected. For example, he had always shooed them away from his office because their visits intruded upon his narcissistic nirvana-like retreat. He had tried to compensate with money for the inadequacy of paternal care. Noticing that his youngest son had begun to go the way of the two older brothers — he was picked up for shoplifting, for instance — Noah decided to make a deliberate try at being a caring father. He forced himself to listen to his son's tales. He invited him to come to the office to proofread manuscripts. He studied his son's needs and met them as much as possible. And noticing how fuzzy the child's sense of his father's identity was, the father made an effort to define himself and to articulate his thoughts and feelings clearly. In the process, the son improved and the father's narcissistic concerns and passive self-indulgence wore thinner. While he failed, in the whole, to delineate his assets, he managed to articulate his shortcomings with humor and without much masochistic emphasis. In short, both parent and son matured.

Protection Against Abandonment

The fear of abandonment, inevitably present when anxiety and infantile needs for dependence and omnipotence still hold sway, muddies the waters of human relations. It disrupts potential stabilities and compels false rather than naturally ripening loyalties. A dramatic show of loyalty may be one of the means by which an anxious person tries to stave off the always expected blow of desertion. Having by definition received in early youth a bigger share of abandonment — in one form or another — than could be handled by the psyche, the disturbed person tends to perpetuate in adulthood his early instilled fear. Absorbed with possibilities of recurring abandonments, the individual misses his many chances to live safely in the present. Desertions are actually invited. Discoveries about new adult ways of love that lead out of the mire are lost.

Yet unfettered by the ignorance that is the lot of the child and not driven by the necessity to seek refuge in quick submission, the adult has a choice of counteracting possible desertion in various ways. Without being fickle and excessively casual (foregoing object constancy), he can make substitutions, and a lost love object can be replaced by a new one. Instead of dwelling more than briefly on the retaliatory anger and the confusing self-devastation which are the immediate reactions to having been left, the adult can gradually activate himself to shift from preoccupation with experienced danger and damage to new interests and opportunities for love. Instead of remaining preoccupied with possibilities of desertion or mourning for a lost love object, instead of combating fear with passivity, he can proceed in the opposite direction. The proviso is that awareness predominate, so that the individual searches knowingly and calmly for new loves to replace losses, rather than proceeding hectically and indiscriminately, simply propelled by depression and longing. Moreover, the pain of abandonment has to be acknowledged and some mourning has to take place after the loss of the partner before one can cast about for a replacement without guilt.

Launching new relationships, rather than counting up how much and how often love is received, serves many functions and satisfies many needs. It allows for self-activation, and it banishes the fear of abandonment quite naturally. When one can love, one is sure not to introduce into basic relationships an untoward emphasis on possibilities of desertion. Those adults who approach present-day attachments with fears of desertion and insistent demands to be reassured against that dreaded eventuality succeed in the end in making abandonment an actuality. They talk of it and defend against it to such an extent that it becomes a reference point in any relationship and is eventually acted upon by one party or the other.

Of course, it is the original trauma of repeated parental neglect (usually a real neglect rather than a fancied one) that is responsible for continued adult absorption with questions of when and how the old pangs might again be inflicted. Patients who lacked the good fortune of mothers in tune with their needs, who did not grow up in a family that upheld and sustained the child — a good "holding environment," as it has been called [6] — become obsessed with desertion. Their minds and emotions have to be redirected. They need to discover that instead of passively waiting for the blow to fall they can move actively, not by dishing out desertion but by caring. Instead of the emotions of hopelessness and pessimism they can gradually acquire confident and optimistic feelings.

Many patients functioning with precision and judgment in intact areas of the personality still do not comprehend that, in love, variety is possible. Ceaselessly circling around the spot of the old desertion trauma, like airplanes caught in endless holding patterns, these patients do not notice their predicament until it is pointed out. Once the mind has discerned that its concern with eventualities of desertion is pathological, the next step is to comprehend that the adult has a range of choices. Perhaps it is not immediately possible to find a permanent sexual partner, but there are chances to move toward other people who will appreciate love that is given. The prime goal is to realize that new relationships can be initiated *actively,* rather than to dwell on the fearful assumption that what occurred before will once more happen. This is not to disregard the usually unconscious pathological motivations that produce intense separation anxiety. The purpose here is to bring one facet of the patient's situation into the sharpest possible focus.

Dwelling on past trauma is dwelling on the threat of danger rather than on the means of rescue.* Setting up repetitions of leav-

* See chapter 4, "Mastering Danger and Anxiety."

ing and being left, observed often in psychotherapy, is often falsely attributed to the repetition compulsion. Actually, in many instances we are faced not with evidence of the repetition compulsion but rather with a phenomenon that might be called *repetition through anticipation*.

It is the function of the repetition compulsion, as it was defined by Freud, to ameliorate the aftereffects of trauma. By repeating actively incidents suffered passively, a mastery over fate is attained. By contrast, repetition through anticipation does not serve the function of mastery but instead perpetuates passive suffering. Unlike the repetition compulsion, repetition through anticipation stems in part from a cognitive error. Smarting under the memory of the pain of desertion, the patient continues along the dimension of abandonment and his fear of it. He suffers from a cognitive gap, a particular form of stagnation that limits his concerns and his perception of existing possibilities. This cognitive gap induces paralysis. Potentially strong adults who consciously or unconsciously are preoccupied with past pangs fail to acquire new ways to deal with the trauma of desertion, should it occur again. Instead of finding out what kind of partners will be loyal, instead of developing better judgments of trustworthy people, and instead of proceeding to new efforts toward the preservation and continuation of love, they preempt chances for love stability. The likelihood of yet another desertion is heightened if the mind dwells on past trauma and the usually primitive defenses against it, such as counter-desertion or self-induced indifference. At the root of preoccupations with the past lies a cognitive error, too long ignored, but recently stressed by Fairbairn [7] and others. These clinicians and theoreticians are right when they claim that the automatic assumption that future injuries will resemble the past derives from faulty cognition.

People steeped in repetition through anticipation resemble underprivileged persons who, for instance, never having eaten anything but a rice diet, expect that wherever they dwell rice will be the dish placed before them. They are in a stage of torpidity from which they must be awakened.

The repetition compulsion suggests escape from trauma and hence eventual optimism and initiative. Repetition through anticipation inaugurates fatalism and passivity. Many who have suffered in infancy the trauma of desertion, say, come to expect that this is the way things are. Taking desertion for granted, they speak it, expect it, and suggest it to others, actually setting others up to leave them eventually.

Adults who are the offspring of mothers with one foot always out the domestic door frequently forestall active love. They set themselves up for desertion and stifle their potential for active love. Adults who as children feared maternal desertion dwell more on old desertions, in anticipatory repetition, than on new opportunities to love and be loved. They endow new figures who emerge lovingly in their adult life with the old habits of a rejecting mother and thus unwittingly plant the first seedling notions of desertion in the minds of their partners. Always looking backward rather than forward, the adult who as a child was subjected to desertions that were never overcome expects that the fragility of the link between the deserter and the deserted will once more occur in new love relations.

The young actress Tess, as a baby, was not wanted by her mother, who neglected her in extreme and unusual ways. Once, for instance, she refused even to take care of her sick and feverish daughter. Nevertheless, there existed between the harsh mother and her child one important contact. Though sometimes used for purposes of punishment, it left Tess with the feeling that in one respect she was loved. Her mother grasped Tess's moods and needs without any words on the part of her daughter, an empathy at times used to devise particularly smarting chastisements. Though the mother concerned herself not at all with sharing or relieving Tess's moods and needs, the child nevertheless took the mother's immediate comprehension of her state of mind to be a sign of love.

When the patient left home in a huff at the age of seventeen, with the intention never to return and thus to punish her negligent mother, she took with her a spiritual and mental inheritance that thwarted her capacity to love actively for many years and accounted for many experiences of rejection. Upon close scrutiny, these experiences seem to have been invoked by Tess herself.

A beautiful girl whom narcissistic men wished to be seen

with, Tess was avidly courted. But once she had established even tentative contact, she started to think, speak, and act desertion. Either she walked away from an admirer who did not show understanding, or she exhausted him with long explanations of how she had been hurt and neglected by a friend, or she demanded to know just how serious his intentions were, while she teased him mercilessly to show that she did not care whether he felt anything for her or not. In any event, the living presence of desertion was always introduced to such an extent that eventually nearly everyone glided along the tracks Tess set up and left her.

With a tenacity of which she was quite conscious, Tess demanded that men who showed her attention be in tune with her unarticulated and often purposely veiled feelings. This attunement, to her, was the ultimate proof of love since it was a repetition of the only way in which her mother had been in tune. Tess minimized or ignored many other shows of love. Addicted to but one kind of emotional nourishment, she insisted on receiving it alone. This greatly limited the number of available partners for her to love actively, since few people were able to read her mind with the subliminal empathy that the patient's very disturbed mother had possessed.

Using psychotherapy quickly, the patient not only gained insight into her major problems, but also altered her approach to love. Seeing that it was invariably she who steered relationships toward the destiny of desertion, because of her obsession with this trauma, she stopped worrying and began in small ways to demonstrate her own concern. Her growing habit of bringing little gifts to friends — clippings, addresses, pamphlets, or books — pleased her as much as the recipients. No longer insisting on receiving love in just the one form in which her mother had given it, immediate empathic understanding, Tess became willing to be touched by other demonstrations. She fell in love with a man whose prime ways of conveying affection were gifts, good spirits, and physical warmth. Her scope of love objects widened as she intentionally tried to move beyond old tastes.

Disturbed, primitive, neurotic functioning predisposes toward quid pro quo expectations and reactions. You give back what you get, you do as is done to you. If deserted, respond by deserting, if ridiculed, snap back with sarcasm, and if gratified, return the favor. On the other hand, the flexibility, competence, and richness of the ego are much expanded by the discovery that a modality of action or feeling displayed by someone else need not elicit a response along the same dimension, either by following suit or by reacting in the opposite way. Independence means that the self can choose any one of a score of affects and conducts, uninfluenced by what was handed out. A response is the more genuinely creative and active the more it stems from a realm of experience entirely of the individual's own making. We need not take our cues from others, but have the freedom to choose them uninfluenced. From this outlook, which can be set up in therapy, can come the decision to turn a former trauma of desertion around by being considerate and caring. A firm protection against abandonment is the resolve and awareness that a call into the forest need not evoke an echo but can summon up hitherto unheard sounds. Such swivelling around through therapy seems to have been contemplated by Ferenczi when he spoke of the use of active treatment methods which, if used carefully and without turning into wild analysis, can disrupt ingrained static continuity, redistribute energy, and evoke novelty.[8, 9] It is primitive and pathological functioning that prompts human beings to become immobile and passive, continually inspecting their wounds and dwelling on their symptoms. Higher-level behavior, which can be profitably pointed out in treatment, initiates movement and activity.

Love is a necessity. The presence of an affectionate and attentive partner permits the opportunity to articulate inner processes. Communication prevents the wordless confusion and, in extreme cases, even the chaos that leads to anxiety, bewilderment, and ego diffusion. Some assurance as to the availability of love is necessary not only to the child but also to the adult who needs to be able to predict the mental and emotional climate of tomorrow, if not of the next year, in order to retain his stability. Yet, to assure love, it is more important to anchor in the self the ability to love than to try to make certain that the partner will inevitably be present, desirable though the other's loyalty is. The only human guarantee that love is accessible lies in the capacity to love actively.

Integrating Two Poles:
Self-Differentiation and Closeness

Far from providing the bland cure-all for anguish which romanticists have assigned to them, the human involvements of love and passion are the seeds not only of joy but also of potential problems. Prolonged togetherness threatens identity and self-differentiation, each of which is a sine qua non of a clear-headed existence. To avoid stifling, excessive closeness and to preserve a mutuality that is strengthening rather than depleting, each partner in love must recognize and accept the need for healthy apartness and individuation and must know that these needs do not preempt attachment, loyalty, and passion. Distinct singleness, despite love ties, and the acceptance of individual separateness and identity after sexual and emotional union are signs of health and not evidence of neglect or mixed affections.

Healthy adults admit and pursue their desire to hold on to the inner nucleus, and they insist, without a sense of guilt, on apartness and on objective disagreements. They even enjoy light physical tussles. All these experiences, provided they come naturally and are not forced, sustain identity. But some disturbed individuals lack the awareness that, in order to maintain individuation, one need not leave or threaten or destroy a partner. For such individuals, any stand made on one's own is experienced as a guilty abandonment because independence is confused with desertion. Early symbiotic and fusion experiences with a mother or with both parents are the models and determine the need for remaining sealed to a partner rather than healthily linked. The psychic flexibility to alternate between healthy apartness and loving conflux is absent and needs to be developed if tolerable and nonengulfing mutuality is to emerge.

Yet other disturbed individuals go by the all-or-nothing principle. They cannot move toward independence except by taking the extreme position of lacerating fights, quarrels, and physical violence They have had no precursory experiences of nondestructive and calm abstinence and self-differentiation; therefore they either create jarring breaks in a relationship or else suffer the misgiving that should they venture apartness it would degenerate into an unbridgeable gulf. Once more it is the childhood past that accounts for the distinction between annihilating fighting and total desertion, on the one hand, and moderate self-containment on the other. Parents who opposed their child's healthy attempts to attain independence and autonomy implanted early the notion that there exist only two alternatives: either to remain caught in confining ties that are, of course, deeply resented or else to cut these ties with such fierceness that relationships become battered and bitter.

Where the psyche has no knowledge of the tactics of calm apartness, destructive methods are used to maintain or regain that measure of self-differentiation without which the individual suffocates in a love relationship. Lack of interest, sulky withdrawals, wishes not just to be alone periodically but to run off entirely, slashing quarrels, bitter sparring, and, in the final event, reactions of hatred and disgust, these are some of the unhealthy means by which identity is is established.

Timothy, a divorced thirty-three-year-old patient, was guilty over the breakup of his marriage, since he felt that he had contributed in sure, though as yet undefinable, ways to the rupture. During treatment, this man, who suffered from premature ejaculation among many other symptoms, fell in love with a woman who possessed nearly all qualities he desired. She was warm, she shared his intellectual life, which mattered a great deal to him, and her face and figure aroused his sensuality. Two months of almost uninterrupted togetherness — the girl had moved in with Timothy — followed, with Timothy enjoying new-found potency. To Timothy's surprise, however, he began to pick fights soon after he had become accustomed to his little paradise. He returned home from work later and later and became more and more silent and sulking. When the patient finally found himself repelled by the beautiful breasts of his girl, he was totally bewildered, for he realized that his revulsion had no basis in reality. He berated himself as a madman, a total egotist, and he said he was convinced that for the rest of his life he was doomed to live as a hermit.

Gradually it was possible for Timothy to understand more fully something that, in fact, he already knew but could do nothing with. He detected that he had permitted, as in the case of his first marriage, an intolerable engulfment to overwhelm him. An isolated and withdrawn man, he had exerted himself beyond the point of his endurance when he attached himself so closely to his girl for two months. He had forfeited his fragile identity which he maintained primarily by isolation and standoffishness. Since Timothy could not yet manage to pull apart from his new relationship in a healthy way, he eventually stumbled on quarrels, on sulking withdrawal, and, in the final event, on disgust reactions to cut the unhealthy ties he and his girl had mistakenly established with one another in place of a freer, less engulfing love. As this patient concentrated more knowingly on his own identity and found ways to pursue his need without hurting his girl, the atmosphere became brisk, sunny, and clean. The disgust vanished.

Revulsion as one means of pulling away from the allure of dangerous attractions which for one reason or another threaten the self is a primitive process. Its inevitable sequel is guilt, self-disdain, and the vague experience that the disgust reactions are alien to the grown-up self. Aversion and revulsion, especially toward a nice object, do not fit in with the usual experiences of adults, and the archaic disgust experiences hence tend to engender some sense of self-estrangement. When previously loving mates begin to be repelled, it is well worth looking into the possibility that closeness has become devouring and has destroyed self-differentiation, with revulsion finally emerging as a last-ditch protection against the dangerous loss of identity.

Very disturbed people who lack the conviction that the shoring-up of identity in love is a precious individual right turn to even more bizarre and destructive ways of obtaining some sense of identity. Fearful of their impulses to obtain separation by violent destruction of intruders, and anticipating retaliation for contemplated annihilations of love or of the marital partners themselves, such people often enact clash and separation within the self. Intrapsychic methods are used instead of interpsychic ones. As in the case of other people with problems, quarrels are used to capture a sense of self-differentiation, but the field on which the antagonists meet is the self. One part of the psyche or the ego advances one idea or wish and, assuming the place of a sparring partner, another part of the ego takes an adverse and contradictory position. The result of such inner sparring is exhaustion, for nothing advances or achieves completion.

When one sector of the ego is set up against another sector, similarities with other inner conflicts abound. The struggle between the "I" and the "I" resembles the tug-of-war between the ego and the superego when the ego proposes one motion and the superego vetoes it. There are parallels with conflicts due to, say, the demands of one parent figure who has been internalized and another one who pushes in different directions, and on it goes. In this context, however, the aim of the self-contained struggle is the emergence of an identity, and the strategy is to avert dangerous intrusion of alien ideas that threaten a fragile identity. When the disturbed person eventually leaves a lover or mate, the fierceness of the inner struggle frequently diminishes, but nevertheless, the only satisfactory solution is not separation or divorce but the acquisition of the power of self-assertion and self-affirmation.

Lee, married for twelve years to a serious man with whom she basically disagreed on everything, did not dare to reveal even to herself her marital discontent and sexual frustrations. Rather, the disdain with which she regarded her kind and hard-working husband filled her with guilt and the conviction that she must hold in her fierce criticism of her mate. Lee spent many hours each day in an empty and dark room where she carried on angry dialogues with herself. As she brought such self-contained arguments to treatment, it became clear that one body of ideas stemmed from Lee's own convictions while the counter-ideas were quite characteristic of positions taken by her husband.

Nostalgically Lee recalled and discussed two earlier love affairs with unreliable, exploitative, and otherwise inferior men. With them she had been able alternately to merge in passion and to carry on violent quarrels that shortcircuited fusion experiences and represented the very methods she was used to in her earlier wild fights for identity vis-à-vis parents and teachers. While Lee called her love affairs and the passion and fights that were part of them "crazy ways of being myself," she knew well that she enjoyed the extramarital relationships because they avoided dangerous intrusions and served the purpose of maintaining identity.

In psychotherapy, Lee reached at least a modicum of self-differentiation via several pathways. Major gains accrued when the patient, perhaps encouraged not by the therapist's words but rather by her behavior, allowed herself to attack her, at first whimsically, then derisively, and finally outright. Professing and probably expecting that provocations would produce anger in the therapist, the patient was relieved when there were no evident consequences. Another aid to her progress was a temporary separation from her husband which Lee, in desperation, arranged. While she stayed away from the man from whom she needed to distance herself healthily so as not to be totally submerged, the patient started to speak, think, and feel in consonance with herself. Relieved, as though infused with new blood, the patient rejoiced in the remission of self-laceration. She saw in her change evidence that she could live together with her husband safely only if she voiced felt opposition and created in other ways a much-needed and unhostile separateness.

Active love and reciprocity call for the mutual sharing of differing views and personal developments that need not be parallel in the two partners. It is as exciting to observe a partner's mental and emotional movement as it is to share his or her bed. People who carry on identity struggles and other conflicts by setting up one part of the self against another deprive real love relations of the spice and zest of articulate challenge. They live parallel with yet apart from the partner. Interior splits such as those described are not confined to schizophrenics, but can be found among passive-hostile, obsessive-compulsive, and borderline patients.*

Two simultaneous needs confuse and disturb such people. On the one hand, they crave the partner's encouragement and love that help to draw them out of their shell. On the other hand, in order to achieve a genuine identity [10] and to avoid backsliding into narcissism and passivity, self-assertion and opposition are a necessity. But disturbed people do not readily grasp that gratitude, loyalty, and love, as well as disagreement and self-assertion, can be expressed simultaneously toward the same person. A kind of splitting is more often considered the chief way out of the felt dilemma. The mate who made possible the first cracks in the narcissistic, passive walls

---

* This behavior illustrates the continuation from neurotic to much schizophrenic symptomatology.

remains as a recipient of submissive love. But simultaneously the disturbed lover casts about for other and frequently less lovable partners to serve as a target for hostility and opposition.

Invariably, patients who cannot feel free both to love and to oppose the same person live their dilemma out in the transference situation. Because of their isolation, they may need some display of concern and warmth on the part of the therapist who cannot then practice the rule of total emotional abstinence, much as it has been recommended.[11] When the need for self-assertion and opposition emerges in treatment — often symbolized by travel to foreign lands as well as by fighting — and when the patient, still desiring to continue oral embeddedness,[12] gets ready to attempt independence, anxiety results. In treatment as in real life, the wish is expressed to leave the once-loved figure of the therapist and to try out tussle and protest with someone else. Explanations that an actual change of cast is not necessary to develop from overdependence to healthy opposition usually prevent the withdrawal that the patient contemplates.

Sima, a physician, entered psychotherapy to escape a lengthening cycle of depressions which ensued whenever she abandoned men interested in her. The offspring of a beautiful and narcissistic mother and an autocratic, self-absorbed father and reared by a nurse who did not speak English, the adult Sima was hardly used to articulate her thoughts. She was caught in a web of blurred narcissism. Lacking a delineated identity, she found every encounter with a man was a threat, since she had no way of differentiating herself from a partner. Instead, she was dangerously immersed within minutes after initial introductions in a beau's opinions, expectations, and needs. Sexual relations invariably came to naught, not only because Sima had oedipal problems but, on an ego level, because at the point of sexual union the patient's identity receded so much that anxiety overcame her.

Sima improved gradually, aided by the belief that the therapist cared. But when she then started to challenge and disagree, she was convinced that she must leave treatment, for the idea that both affection and challenge could be directed toward one and the same person was alien. A sense of humor, which was a saver of identity and of integration, together with therapeutic interpretations, helped to save the day. Though this patient never became a fighter, she learned how to hold her own with charming humor and no longer felt she had to leave those from whom out of necessity she dissented in a healthy way.

Masochistic submission, always coupled with reproach, and paranoid attack, always a plea for love, are interconnected.[13] Fusing and forfeiting identity, which are the masochist's practice, alternate with opposition and hatred designed both to attain individual distinction and to force love.[14,15] If a person is submerged in only one of these related phases or if the submersion precludes all healthy cooperation and vigorously objective dissent, professional help is needed. Only through a true and genuine progression from fusion to self-differentiating opposition to self-assertive cooperation can mutuality and reasonable, undisturbed love become possible.

Like children who fear that declarations of their opinions and intentions will be construed as insurgence by unattuned parents, many grown-ups, themselves the victims of unfortunate childhood experiences, sit still lest they be attacked for challenging. Hesitating to engage in the fencing that is a prerequisite for sustained independence, they turn away from active love and give in to the passive standstill. They ignore the truth that whoever loves, fights. They ignore the value of fearless interaction that guarantees active love and mutuality, settling instead for appeasement, consensus, or withdrawal.

Patients who as children had their healthy feelings of contrariness and opposition stifled turn to body sensations both as sanctuary and as symbol and expression of opposition. Conversion symptoms of a kind emerge, though the repressed and physiologically expressed energy consists not of libido, but of hate and of challenge. Pains in the legs and the small of the back can express fierce antagonism and disagreement. Some patients, whenever honest disagreement is forced underground by their fears, feel like the victims of some Gulliver-like situation. They may report that whenever in outside life or therapy they wish to register protest but fail, they have the sensation of being pulled by many strings, like a marionette. Discovering the often hazily registered existence and meaning of such sensations or images, patients help themselves to get wise to their experiences.

To establish identity and ensure its continuing existence, a turn from passivity to activity is required. The identifications that are the essence of early relationships call for little activity, but higher levels of relating make initiative a matter of necessity. An exhaustive catalog of processes that yield adult relations would be a fat one. Among the processes are these: up-to-date realities have to be looked in the eye, and the yearning for a return of nurture has to be put aside through genuine growth; the needs of others, even those not always admitted by them, must be gathered from various clues; self-interest and concern for others have to be balanced in varying proportions; and joint encounters as well as the pressures of the world have to be met with manifold skills, appropriately timed and coordinated; and on it goes.

The turbulent young people who, in order to distance themselves from identifications with their parents, engage in belligerent opposition become captives of excessive closeness with their peers whose company they crave to escape harsh confrontations with complex life situations. Acknowledging and often carrying to excess the stand against their elders in order to achieve identity, they allow their selfhood to drown in mass experiences, in the excessive closeness induced by drugs, or in premature and protracted intimacy.

Especially talented personalities — Goethe, Michelangelo, and Leonardo da Vinci have been mentioned [16] — may be able to reach their potential through symbiotic unions. But ordinary life situations demand that those who want love and mutuality to continue avoid engulfment by setting one another free through brief spells of being apart and through contests, both physical and intellectual. The linkage that love produces can be gratifying only if the personalities to be united are separate entities before and after love periods and sexual fusion. It is healthy to pursue separate though not antagonistic paths.

A Bulletin Is Not an Interaction

Interchanges with others remain short of mutuality if they abound with self-references. True interchanges are different from monologues and bulletins about personal woe or welfare. They become genuine vehicles of concern when they spearhead some entry into the personal territory of others. The people whom the clinician characterizes as narcissistic, passive, and dependent favor communications that tell how they themselves feel, although they may delude themselves and, for a short while, others by some vocal intonation of sympathy and interest. Even less aware of the narcissistic nature of their communications than of their environment, and ignorant of how replete their messages are with descriptions of their own feelings, they are puzzled. Why is there so little reaction to what they say, and why are silences the frequent sequel to their long narrations? The explanation is that reports on feelings, no matter how sympathetic, and on physical sensations, regardless how joyous or pathetic, lack the mutuality of two-way communications. They rarely reach others, and they squelch rather than kindle a loving reaction.

Authors who want to caricature binding and narcissistic mothers and wives — men are less often so described — show these females immersed in monologue. Oblivious of questions directed at them and of responses made, they are aware chiefly and often exclusively of the feelings that the approach of others arouses in the self. They are equally oblivious of the feelings they arouse in others. The comments of offspring, companions, mates, or lovers serve mainly as takeoff points for monologues about narcissistic sensations and thoughts. Mutual communication and exchange are nipped in the bud.

Since long and blatantly self-preoccupied monologues are readily identified as manifestations of self-love, as interruptions of mutuality, and since their essence is readily perceived, they do relatively little harm. The listener to, though rarely the originator of, what amounts to a filibuster is usually aware of what is being done to him and others. Growing irritation with the monopolizer is hardly likely to evoke self-reproach in the listener. The crescendo of verbiage may conceal the existence of disconnectedness from the monopolizing person, but those who are with him know what gives.

But other narcissistic, one-sided messages that interfere with mutuality and give-and-take of love are more subtle, more elusive, and more likely to instill guilt in the listener. Clad in the mantle of verbal kindliness, these communications are often difficult to identify. The finesse and cordiality with which they are advanced beclouds their narcissistic and hence one-sided nature and confuses both communicator and listener. For instance, many people, receiving messages of this disguised narcissistic kind, are puzzled as to why they experience so little interest and concern for their seemingly affectionate company. And the senders of the narcissistic reports, stunned by frequently shown lack of interest, benefit when they find out in psychotherapy what is wrong with their communications.

When narcissism, passivity, and dependency prevail, people are more in touch with their lower than with their higher senses. The lower senses, such as awareness of body temperature and of body conditions, tell them how they feel, while the higher senses of sound and sight, which normally enable us to be in touch with the world around us, are less frequently tapped.[17] The sense of being closely wound up in the self and enjoying some magical protection predominates. In the absence of sophisticated and rapid access to the higher senses and of developed emotions and thoughts, communication with others rarely reaches mutuality. It seems to suffice when the narcissistic individual conveys how he feels or, sometimes, how he thinks. Exchanges are static, settling on the self of the isolated person, and veer away from reaching the core of others. The listeners do not get involved, they are not stimulated, no new vistas are opened up for them, nor are any gates of the world flung open.

Many beautiful women and handsome men who are deeply narcissistic will be picked out in a crowd, impulsively courted, but then soon deserted. Their inability to establish interaction and mutuality is the frequent reason for the suffered abandonments. When this is explained in psychotherapy, excruciating pain on the part of the patient is the frequent result.

> Cynthia suffered episodes of narcissistic isolation. She discovered gradually that the frequent and obvious irritation of her husband reflected his dissatisfaction with her behavior, but she could not tell what was wrong. When Cynthia, disillusioned with her marriage, became temporarily involved in a love affair with a neighbor, she was sure that she had recaptured something she had lost in marriage. She felt more attractive; she conversed more animatedly with her lover, her husband, and her acquaintances; and her spirits rose. When the therapist eventually remarked that the new relationship bore a mere resemblance to love, and that Cynthia and her neighbor acted out the *folie à deux* of a mutual narcissistic

admiration society, the patient became understandably angry. Yet when Cynthia found out that, despite her increased communicativeness, her acquaintances and colleagues listened only half-heartedly and passed her by like ships in the night, she became less resistant to the notion that, once more, it was a renewal of narcissism that had raised her spirits and heightened interaction.

A major breakthrough occurred when, on a sunny spring day, the patient entered the office and described her enjoyment of the weather, the freshness of her spirits, and her happiness. When the therapist said, "You speak about yourself, but rarely address me," Cynthia was stunned. She grasped the point when it was explained that her statements were more in the nature of bulletins than interactive communications. What she talked of were her own body feelings, her kindly emotions, and her thoughts as aroused by someone's remarks. Rarely was there an involvement with the other person, since Cynthia responded almost exclusively by referring to what was evoked within herself.

Saying that reports about body sensations or feelings about the self disrupt contact does not imply that attention to physiological sensations is misplaced in psychotherapy. Quite to the contrary, the language of the body often tells both patient and therapist more about unconscious feelings than do verbal descriptions. Physiological clues are valuable in therapy and in life as part and parcel of enhanced awareness of what goes on in the mind. They are signals to be observed and heeded. Yet when two or more people get together, body signals, bulletins, and self-absorbed revelations do not facilitate mutuality. Instead of conveying stimulating messages and displays of affectionate concern, they halt the back-and-forth flow of emotion and thought. In the long run, the frequently unconscious use of bulletins makes others feel excluded from contact. The fact that many individuals resembling Cynthia discuss friendly rather than resentful feelings centered on the self and say "That makes me feel good" or "I sense a warmth toward you" does not alter the essential effect, namely, the disruption of mutuality.

Perpetual "yessers," who respond to suggestions, observations, and stated thoughts with a curt "Yes" or a "Yes, I see what you mean," also disrupt the threads of contact developing between themselves and others. Repeated yes statements are not necessarily affirmations of another person. When used profusely, yes answers rarely promote mutual engagements and do not further the challenge of involvement or create a constructive interest, needed if two-way bonds are to be developed. Sure enough, as in the case of the benign bulletins, the yes message has the appearance of goodwill. Even at worst it is a harmless statement elevating the other's vanity. Hence it is difficult to discover what is wrong. Why does some one who says yes readily become an eventual burden? Why does interest in him begin to lag? And why is there the creeping feeling that nothing goes on between two people if one of them is a yesser? The answer is that a mere yes or its equivalent is not a mental exchange and does not keep mutuality alive.

Beverly was confused, when she started treatment, by the discrepancy between men's initial interest and their eventually lagging attention. She then fell in love with a widower in whose company newly found insights, strengths, and previously buried emotions unfolded. The patient, aware of her previous passivity, still found herself often tempted to fall into the soft lap of an encompassing inertness. One day, Beverly remarked that she considered herself a drag. "Why," she said, "do I always say, 'Of course' and 'if you think so,' when Twain suggests a plan for the two of us? This isn't relating. This is not making a twosome. It's lazy lack of interest, that's all. From now on, if he tells me something, I'll get a feel of my own position, look for my ideas, and spill them out. Then we'll have a tangle, a tumble, a love play, a real touching."

Beverly was right. Many a yes is a message of a lack of interest so total that the sender does not even want to spend energy on articulating more than this monosyllabic, seemingly safe, conflict-exterminating communication. Sequences of yes answers undermine mutuality as surely as they appear innocent, and in both the short and long run prove to be just what they are — nothingness. Let us by all means say yes when we mean to agree whole-heartedly, but let us not take refuge in yes answers which prevent daring participation in the gambits offered by others.

Escaping the Narcissistic Cocoon

Narcissism is not a good bedfellow for active love. Only in the sense that narcissism is a hunger for appreciation does it keep people in touch with others. But contacts sought by love-starved persons are often designed to reap not love but applause and the enhancement of shaky self-esteem. Indeed, the narcissistically entrenched person resembles the love-starved child who, obtaining but morsels of attention or mere substitutes for it from parents, is bent on making up deficits of affection.

The gulf between the isolated and self-absorbed self and the rest of the world is spanned when patients cease to measure the stature of others by the size and shape of the self. A powerful reason for immobility in treatment is the riveting of attention on old ways. Narrowness of perception and observation hold back forward movement much as does the continuation of old and unconscious needs. As long as patients do not view problems from new angles, as long as novel confrontations are omitted or are not expressed in words that make the patient listen with a fresh ear, dawdling is likely. What is alien and old remains the individual's law rather than what is alive and meaningful.

Systematic observations of other people can be learned. The practice of such observations leads away from narcissistic and faded reviews of people and situations, but without attacking relationships. Human beings who are eager to acquire some know-how of active love will do well to become amateur scientists who observe knowledgeably. The human world, when surveyed from many angles and with alert eyes and minds, ceases to be a neutral field and becomes novel territory that evokes interest and eventually affection. As bird watchers love the winged creatures they observe, so human beings who have trained themselves to be observers develop new sympathy for the mankind they study with objectivity. Far from being dull and detached, systematic observation amounts to an exciting enterprise that invariably uproots the self-preoccupation and self-needs that are the core of narcissism.

Some prerequisites of objective and orderly observations can be specified and, if heeded, will help people to love the world that they have come to know vividly by dint of imaginative study.

Attention should be turned on the giveaways of nonverbal behavior, and completed actions should be given more importance than declared intentions. People who wish to shed their narcissism must study completed deeds rather than enticing promises, just as conscientious voters give more emphasis to the record of candidates than to their campaign speeches. Long periods of surveillance bring better results than sporadic moments of inquiry. Also, it should be recognized that just how a person reacts to divergent stresses is a good index of what he or she is really like. Though neurotic observers, because of their need for certainty and for getting unfinished business over with, and because of their dislike of cognitive discrepancies,[18] tend to ignore variations in conduct on different occasions, it is just such observed disparities that yield the most worthwhile clues.

Narcissism diminishes slowly, and the therapeutic steps which induce the eventual dispersal of self-preoccupation, isolation, and self-love come from many differing approaches to the patient's pathology.

The pressure of inner and unconscious needs contributes largely to the acceptance and, indeed, promotion of inadequate observations and perceptions which, in turn, solidify the narcissistic position. For instance, a person who can obtain a sense of identity only if he hates those on whom he is compulsively dependent will give in to the urge to distort his environment. He needs to justify the aversion and hostility on which he leans for the sake of self-differentiation, and he looks for suitable targets of hate. Yet, as indicated on many other occasions in this context, becoming healthy, strong, and effective requires a double-barreled approach. First, the patient is gradually, and in a variety of ways, confronted with and made aware of the outdated nature of his needs in the hope that they will be discarded. Second, there exists every reason to proceed from the positive side of the ego as well and to cultivate personal growth by encouraging the development of specific ego functions such as objective and alert observation. This second approach can be used to make a decisive breach in the narcissistic cocoon. When narcissistic patients go against the grain of perceptual intolerance and impatience and expend more effort on observing, the outcome is richly rewarding and does not preclude simultaneous emergence of insight into destructive inner forces. Often the two approaches supplement one another and form complex and constructive patterns rather than paranoid distortions. The acquisition of objective observations is a major tool in the struggle against narcissism.

Nat, a narcissistic paranoid patient seen in both individual and group treatment, often, though not invariably, misconstrued the expressions of the therapist. He insisted that she favored other group members, accused her of switching from friendly to indifferent behavior, and claimed that she wished to see him remain weak and a victim of her whims. Nat's shift from objective perceptions of the therapist's intent — which was to awaken his strength and gifts — to protestations that he was neglected and held back suggested more capacity for observation than he wished to utilize. He distorted so as to justify reproaches, temper tantrums, and self-pity. Judging that the patient had enough strength to dispense with many masochistic satisfactions, and that he had sufficient trust in the therapeutic procedure to accept a restriction of need without paranoid retaliation, the therapist asked Nat firmly to stop distorting. The result was a gradual emergence of extraordinary judgment, so reliable indeed that the patient became a conspicuously successful businessman.

The approach from the "outside in," [19] used in combination with the inquiry that befits psychoanalytic psychotherapy, worked in this as in other cases. The patient's observation and a new emphasis on objectivity, at least with regard to certain people and situations, diminished the narcissism of this highly talented, very curious, and scientifically oriented man.

Lovers and neurotics, like children, rarely heed the rule of prudent observation. It is when they have the gravest doubt about whether their feelings are reciprocated that they ask direct questions about the beloved's intentions. What such doubters fail to watch are concrete actions. Attuned, often, to nonverbal messages of disloyalty and thus unconsciously suspecting the devotion and love of the person they subject to inquiry, their courtroom-like interrogations are designed to extract assurances from people whose deception and neglect is perceived on an unconscious level. In the effort to render the ego of the dependent narcissist more competent, psychotherapists achieve some measure of success if they sensitize patients to the importance of deeds over words and nonverbal messages over explicit statements. Without distracting from other valuable approaches, it should be said that many a narcissistic, dependent, and masochistically clinging patient improves as word-centered attention to others is given less weight and comparisons are made between episodes of behavior exhibited by the person who is the object of the love-queries. The fetters of narcissism and dependency are shaken off when realistic touchdowns are made in the world.

David, a narcissistic homosexual patient who abhorred his passivity, met, after nine months of treatment, a beautiful woman who reminded him of his seductive mother and beautiful sisters. Yet the only thing he could report about Deirdre was that she was well groomed. Gradually he added that she had traveled a good deal through South America and had taken her dogs with her. The patient, a product of the three-pronged entity of narcissism, passivity, and dependency, relied totally on Deirdre for information about her feelings toward him. Her repeated, charmingly expressed, yet impersonal assurances that she found David attractive were his primary clue that she felt love. It can be added parenthetically that, when David entered therapy, he had three homosexual friends whom he could not distinguish one from the other. In the beginning, he equated their ages and loyalties, though eventually he discerned clearly that the youngest was the only trustworthy friend.

One day after a picnic with Deirdre, David returned home feeling very anxious. It turned out that Deirdre, having promised to bring the lunch, turned up with exactly the kind of refreshments that David disliked. Also, when the usually passive patient wanted to drive away for beer, to tie a hammock between two trees, and to search for a pond in which to swim, Deirdre stopped him at every point. Later, in David's apartment, she was considerably more preoccupied with waste, spots, and furniture than with her would-be lover. Though she made many declarations of love, David began to feel uneasy.

In this case, two conflicting levels of awareness existed together, and their clash produced some of the anxiety. The verbal protestations did not fit the *acts* of the girl, and the picnic episodes, as well as Deirdre's lagging attention later in the day, contrasted sharply with her behavior a day before when David had bought her a trinket.

When prompted by narcissism and pressing needs, observers see what they wish to discover. The deeper the pathology, the greater the compulsion to view others as means to gain one's ends, destructive or not. Even the sample on the basis of which opinions are formed becomes weighted. For instance, after frustrations have been suffered at the hands of someone else, those words and acts of that person that are unpleasant are the ones remembered, and even distasteful acts committed long in the past pop back into the judgment-forming section of the mind. Given these conditions, resentment and rage seem justified and can be given full vent.

Although many such needs are regarded as irresistible and not susceptible to change by direct intervention, corrections in group or individual psychotherapy can prove helpful if their timing is right and they are not offered too early. A misperceiver cannot always bear the onslaught of a dissenting group or therapist who claim that his observations are distorted and unfounded. In many instances it is imperative to turn the tables and to ask the clamoring group members what moves them so intensely to oppose the claims made. And in individual treatment, decisions as to where to start — with the narcissistic needs that distort the world or with the capacity for more precise observation — must be made constantly. Usually it is in the middle and end phases of therapy that the objectification of observations has the greatest impact on the patient's view of the world and on his narcissistic position. Recognizing the short-lived safety of distorted views and fed up with their own narcissism, many patients are willing to refine and rectify their observations as a means of spinning the cables that will support the bridge extending from the territory of narcissistic self-absorption into the territory of the living and true world. It never pays to underrate the ego's urgent push to go into action.

6. Creative Human Contacts: The Case of Marriage

A renaissance in the manifestation and solution of human problems is under way. This has become clear slowly but convincingly in the mental health profession. No longer are the people who come for help plagued primarily, as was formerly true, by the distinct distress of clear-cut neurotic symptoms which, like obstructive intruders, block the passageways to well-being and activity. Nor is it the vague wish to "adjust" to situations considered unalterable and hence acceptable that engenders the would-be patient's desire to change.

True, symptoms such as phobias, obsessions, and somatic ills still harass a goodly number of people in the Western world,* but the frequency and range of clear-cut and demonstrable symptoms afflicting the mind like a physical illness have diminished. The exceptions are anxiety states, which have become, if anything, more frequent.

As the symptom neurosis has dwindled, there has come a wider realization that instead of the symptom the personality as a whole can be the signal and expression of problems. Fears, inhibitions, and defenses are ever more frequently embedded in character traits. Hence it is the total personality, or large sections thereof, that has become the object of study and modification. In the place of the previous pervasive concern with adjustment, we find almost the

---

* In countries with different customs and mores, such as India and Nepal, to take two examples, severe symptom neuroses are widespread, and hysterical paralysis, for instance, is quite common.

opposite inclination. The general and specific aims of both patient and therapist are to alter situations rather than occupy a prepared niche and to discover new avenues of self-expression rather than subdue interests, ambitions, and drives.

It is broadly understood today that psychological well-being, independence, flexibility, and productivity — the foremost present-day ideals — can be restricted as grievously by character rigidity, by pervasive masochistic self-subjugation, and by encompassing negativism as by the sharply contoured symptoms that are known to interfere in more readily demonstrable ways with an unharassed and creative life. Personal habits, the total outlook on life, and such basic human orientations as passivity and narcissism can mar relationships, disrupt attention, and deplete energy and imagination to a point at which individual performance becomes third-rate. Whatever the specific nature and form of psychotherapy, the ultimate goal, as a rule, is to enrich the personality with new psychological skills, to build bridges between diverse parts of the self, and to put the sectors together in new ways.

Instead of achieving meek adjustments, the emerging idea is to move away from old attachments and life situations, to develop fresh and previously untried ways to take charge of, rather than accommodate to, new situations. Whether eliminating specific symptoms or rebuilding the whole personality is aspired to, a common aim of therapy is to get rid of an overgrowth of stale, routine, and pre chewed patterns. In this affluent and mobile society — psychologically both enlightened and confused — the cry is for vitality. Our desires lead us in these directions: to probe the depth of the self; to unearth the precious ore that is now known to lie buried below the surface of polite, blustering, or timid personal behavior; to let the mind canter rather than plod over pathways and fields that have been cleared through technology; to fill human relationships with surprise, flexibility, and creativity characterized by freshly coined words, concepts, and debates. A wider participation in public affairs and art * is considered no longer the privilege of the few but a self-evident right of the many.

To experience a life of heightened human adventure it is not necessary to organize expensive safaris, to climb mountains, or to

* Many artists, dramatists, and critics stress that modern art can be enjoyed only by a public that "does a lot with it."

either make or collect acknowledged art. The world at large, and every human contact specifically, offers an occasion, if we so want, to experiment with creativity. Nor is it merely the restricted areas of the metropolis or the Eastern and Western seaboards that offer opportunity for greater honesty and more give-and-take in human relations. The country-wide emergence of new ideas about marriage, child-rearing, and political reorganization is evidence of the ongoing fermentation.

Many of the goals that are in the air appear not only new but also elating. But certain means used to pursue them deserve concern. Drugs and the acceptance of wide personality swings and instabilities must lead to harm and merely short-lived exultation.

Maria was a young woman who tried urgently and through harmful means to achieve a richer personal life for herself after she had been abandoned without warning by her rigid, critical, and money-oriented husband, who left her abruptly to marry an older woman. Following a six-months' depression, Maria took up with the first of what was to be a series of penurious and footloose young lovers. All but one moved into the relatively crowded quarters where Maria lived with her twin daughters. The lovers, all on drugs, initiated the patient into drug-taking and, for half a year, she took many drug-induced "trips," returning sometimes elated and sometimes depressed and visibly shaken.

Maria, who considered herself old at the age of twenty-eight, obviously wished to burst the shackles of her rigid character, the product of imprints left by both parents. They had demanded that she be well-mannered on every occasion, brilliant beyond her capacities, and grown-up before her time, so as to mother the mother and to be a young mate to the father who was infatuated with his bright and fine-boned girl.

Maria emerged from the depression caused by the sudden and enforced separation from her husband with a ravenous appetite for erotic adventure, dramatic clothes, body exposure, experimentation with new writing (she was a poet), entertaining, and foods. She became indiscriminate and promiscuous in every way: not only lovers were chosen and abandoned impulsively; so were baby sitters, women friends, physicians, and pieces of furniture.

The major aim of Maria's new life — namely, to savor more experiences — appeared by and large valid for this young woman, though it seemed indicated to help her acquire more loyalty and constancy toward others [1] and to sift out mimicry from self-chosen goals. It was Maria's *means* of attaining her goals which were destructive of herself.

In summary, after one and a half years of treatment which Maria enjoyed and to which she came with the eagerness that she showed in all her enterprises, the patient stopped taking the potent and most harmful drugs. She became what her children called a "groovy" mother who spent time and thought on their upbringing. Instead of remaining alternately a rebel against and an appendage of her parents, she took the initiative in introducing them to new plays, walks, and more spontaneous interchanges with her. To her own amazement, Maria started to read instead of remaining inert on her bed chewing gum or eating candy. She did more work, and above all she enjoyed her more frequent and more vivid contacts with others as she stopped picking up their cues and instead introduced her own ideas.

Marriage, which we shall study as a particular form of togetherness, has the drawbacks of every stabilized relationship. In smaller or larger measure it interferes with the art of building with the mate fresh, churning, and creative acts of human contact that stay clear of the tracks of much-trodden routine. To understand some of the obstacles, let us put marriage beneath a microscope.

One of the causes of difficulty is the need to maintain in marriage — as in other institutionalized relations — continuity and stability. If the mates are to achieve interdependence,[2] if each is to give up in some degree other sources of direct erotic gratification and primary emotional support, if the images of other people are to be dimmed sufficiently to allow the personality profile (object representation) [3] of the partner to become prominent, if the two mates are to abandon certain internal defenses and instead rely to some extent on one another for protection against anxiety,[4] if this and more are to happen, then a good degree of continuity in the relationship is guaranteed.

But continuity is a flag that is white on one side and red on the other. It offers opportunities and dangers. When a ménage proceeds without end in sight, as it does if two people get married, then processes that destroy initiative can easily get started. Mates, regardless of sex, are readily assigned mothering functions, because of the enticement of ever-present closeness. Identifications between mates are bound to crop up and interfere with individual expression. Whoever lives with another person experiences friction and resentment and usually settles either, at least partially, through submission, pacification, and emulation. The capacity for attention and observation, an ego skill that guarantees that the world will be accurately surveyed before danger hits, starts to flag whenever surroundings become familiar. This explains why many people who live together do not even notice new developments in the mate when they set in.

All the mentioned mechanisms and more explain why the stability of the marital setting tends to corrode individuality, creativity, and alertness. To give the marital relationship a chance to be continually rejuvenated, the mates must be aware of the special dangers and also know how to get away from stifling routine. Rejuvenation of the self and of its creative capacity need not come from fresh conquests, but can be had for the price of surveying accustomed human territory from fresh perspectives.

Probably the exaggerated respect of American society for the romantic basis of marriage stems from the false hope that independent mate-choice and initial passion will stop the decay of love and the emergence of boredom. But examination shows that what preserves spontaneity is not some preexisting suitability — though there should be some degree of that, to begin with — but the know-hows of maintaining and protecting activity, initiative, independence, and creativity from corrosion.

Combining Commitment With Freedom

Marital life not only offers emotional support but also engenders certain anxieties. To cope with inner fear, most husbands and wives, tempted by the continued presence of a mate who to some degree is obliged to stay put, develop a measure of symbiosis. They fall back on modes of intimate closeness and, indeed, entanglement that are known from the earliest period of life when the mother, to aid the survival of her helpless child, makes herself a part of the offspring. To some degree even marriages between very mature and independent people detract from the exercise of freedom, ingenuity, activeness, and inventiveness because the temptation to become one with the mate is never totally resisted.[5, 6]

The infractions of individual freedom are proportionate to each partner's degree and form of disturbance as well as to the balance of marital trouble that emerges between the two people. When symbiotic holdovers are marked in either one mate or both, then regression to a symbiotic, enmeshed, dependent existence will be frequent, long, and deep. One or both mates will exploit the marital union. If mothering was inadequate, because the maternal figure either did not give her child its symbiotic fill or prolonged the intimate ties too long (or was guilty on both counts), then the adult will use marriage to make up for the deficit or to prolong a symbiotic addiction or both.

The more arrested the personal development, the greater is the craving for a symbiotic way of life that does not belong in an adult setting. The less complete the individuation, the weaker the ego, and the fewer and more warped the ego skills, the greater is the need to lean, to hover over the mate, and to borrow strengths and skills which the self has not evolved.

When mates first live together, leanings toward symbiosis tend to manifest themselves in ways such as these: frequent sexual unions prompted less by desire than by the need to prove togetherness; telephone calls, often spaced only hours apart, with each partner actually having little to tell the other except words affirming the mutual ties; the sharing of activities not because one partner is truly involved in particular doings or hobbies of the other but because once more reiterated demonstrations of closeness need to be given in compulsory fashion.

Then, however, when the marital confinement becomes too tight because of the symbiotic pressures, each mate makes attempts to regain freedom. Men might proceed differently from their mates and claim the demands of their work to avoid the domestic scene. Women, who are often tied closer to home, may try to escape their fixed position through daydreams. Whatever the method, it will not work unless the bacilli that infect the air are discovered.

Symbiotic practices grow like weeds and take light and soil away from mutual stimulation, creative interchanges, and the fun that people can have because they have the other's company. When, instead of living independently and interdependently, two people hover over each other and foster a cloying immobility, then they become submerged in what feels like a pond of treacle and stop bathing in the invigorating sunniness of company that can stimulate growth and initiative.

Radin was the son of a widowed mother who had to leave her boy prematurely to make a living. She was indirectly and erratically domineering so that her son was at a loss to tell when he obeyed because he was enticed by subliminal maternal directions and when he followed his own choices. Highly eccentric, the adult Radin often pursued strange interests to make up for what he lacked in genuine, well-seasoned development as an individual.

When Radin, still filled with symbiotic longings, formed a sexual relationship, he soon submerged himself in it. In giving in to his passivity, he expressed his yearning to make up through sex and courtship for the premature interruption of closeness to the mother. But in the end he always resented excessive involvements with girl friends. To help himself get out, he teased, deceived, and humiliated his partners and kept the avenues of promiscuity open.

After Radin had improved to some extent through psychotherapy, he fell in love with Elise, who was more open, kinder, and intellectually more stimulating and demanding than her predecessors. Wishing to marry Elise, Radin determined to resist his habitual demands for indulgence and to guard against both clinging and deceptiveness.

Out of the wish for greater honesty, Radin offered Elise more truthful accounts of his whereabouts, thoughts, and doings. And he watched carefully lest he slip into the easy routine of small expectations that would induce dependence and the ensuing inevitable routine and dullness. One Sunday afternoon, as Radin lay next to Elise, he was about to ask her for a book when he stopped himself astutely, realizing that he was about to start a small leakage that might admit a flood of demands. He got up and fetched the book himself, not because he felt the request to be an imposition but because he properly diagnosed it as the advance wave of what could readily become a gargantuan stream of pressure on the beloved.

Partners can abstain from extorting small gestures of indulgence, which in turn easily call for repayment. Even if demands for indulgence are made only from time to time, stasis [7] appears tempting. Then one or both partners begin to stand still instead of moving ahead to new forms of contact, new metamorphoses, fresh inspirations. The status quo becomes the desirable mode of life, and rituals take the place of innovations.

Because of the anxieties that marriage is bound to evoke (even where mates are healthy, but more pronouncedly in cases of psychological arrestations and disturbances), the grandly ambitious design of living together alertly on a monogamous basis often miscarries. What prevails instead are wishes to come to a halt, to maintain an immobile balance, and to invoke repetitiveness, sameness, and ritualized conduct. Though blustering may cover up their weakness, those who are disturbed often do not look on the wedded state as a chance to grow and unfold personal creativity. It becomes a pensioned existence in which small amounts of guaranteed supplies are served at psychic mealtimes.

If the ego, that important terrain of psychological skills, is too weak and too narrowly construed, then in its attempts to help itself it adopts methods of behavior that render life dull and empty. Besides the symbiotic leanings toward perpetuation of the status quo, there is a sterile repetition of formulas, ideas, and acts. The adult who is paralyzed by his or her own weak ego proceeds like the inexperienced and clumsy child who in an effort to learn how to swim or to ride a bicycle repeats a few fragmentary motions. With attention riveted on danger rather than on possibility,* the child fails to pause and then to try out new ways. In sterile, auto-

---

* See chapter 4, "Mastering Danger and Anxiety."

matic fashion the same motions are repeated. The faculty of attention
lags, new things cannot be grasped, the mind cannot wander from
one way station to another that is more highly elevated. Development, forward movement — in short, much that goes into the making
of creativity — are waylaid if the ego is weak and if symbiosis,
invited by the marital closeness, is used as a crutch. Rather than
exploring life in the pleasure of marital company the mates are stuck
in stagnant repetitions.

> Riva, married to Ernest for thirty years, had freed herself
> through several therapeutic treatments to pursue a productive
> and socially interesting life. Yet in her relationship to her
> detached and arrogant husband she still permitted herself to
> fall back into childlike and primitive habits. If Ernest, who
> never left but often threatened to, insinuated desertion or if
> he became fiercely critical and derisive, then his wife began
> to resemble the person she had been as a teen-ager, ceasing
> to be the remarkable woman she had become. She hovered
> symbiotically near her husband, pleaded for a good word,
> uttered repeated childish demands, and even found herself
> using manual gestures that she thought she had long since
> given up. What fun, zest, and initiative Riva had been able to
> introduce in the marital relationship vanished.
>
> Improvements occurred when this generally adult woman,
> too frequently pushed backward by upsets in her marriage,
> turned away from her husband in her search for encourage-
> ment and contact and looked to good friends instead. As she
> inched away from her rigid insistence that the offending
> husband himself heal the wounds inflicted by him, the dan-
> gerous entanglement lifted and fresh behavior emerged.

Artists are in part doctors. They cure many a psychological ill,
though not necessarily with intent. In creating new visions and
experiences, they insist that old modes of vision, of listening, and
of speaking be sacrificed for new ones. The weak and symbiotically
inclined person needs not only to understand the pitfalls of the
psyche but also to search out fresh forms of human contact. Let
art be one of the guides.

When one or both partners become dependent, symbiotic, and
enmeshed in sterile repetitiveness, what matters primarily is not

the discovery of how all these mishaps were caused. Rather, what counts is that the old ways be dismissed, that the roots that keep them nourished be eradicated, and that new behavior be sparked.

When the dramatic developments of infancy, childhood, and puberty, which launch the cycle of life like a rocket to the moon, are completed, then new spurts of growth must come from within the largely, though never totally, completed psyche. The older the person gets, the greater his need for creativity and rotation from within. In the adult, growth is no longer represented by startling biological events and historically determined psychological developments but by self-initiated movement and creativity. In a way, whoever settles for leaning and standstill falls ill.

The Delight of the Surprise Response

People who live closely together — and what people live more closely than two who are married? — tend to take on each other's coloration. In psychoanalytic lingo, they identify with one another. The more primitively the personality functions, the more will it use early relationship models, among which identification, the deeply anchored and compelling need to *be* the very person who is central, takes first place. The more disturbed a mate is, the less is it possible for him in adult life to stop imitating close associates. His emotional disturbance represents the present-day hangovers from harsh parental rejections. Perhaps lingering identifications present a continued effort to get close to the figures who formerly practiced dismissal and neglect. Perhaps imitation is an attempt to replace these figures or tempt them into loving gestures by appealing to their narcissism through copying them.

When the inevitable differences and frictions that are the result of joint living crop up, it is often through the device of identification that a mate, particularly a weak one, tries to pacify an indignant and resentful partner. Indeed, sometimes the weak partner's sense of self is so thoroughly renounced by the mimicry of identification that the nucleus of the self is dissolved, inducing new anxiety feelings because of the excessive loss of identity.

When people cease to be free and lose initiative, either they become stooges or, should they manage to preserve some incomplete selfhood, they turn into counterpunchers. As a protective technique, counterpunching is ineffective. Whoever is resigned to merely hitting back fails to initiate the time, the aim, and the strength of blows. These are left to the opponent, whom the counterpuncher follows in too docile a manner. Psychological counterpunchers, followers in their meek ways, give serial reactions. When the opponent calls out "A," the follower passively gives back "B." Never is an "M" or a "Z" forthcoming. To repeat: the more primitive the relations to others, and the closer the following of the first model of identification, and the higher and more permanent the level of hostility which identifications are designed to allay, then the deeper are the identification muddles into which marital partners sink. It is a sign of improvement and of the recapture of initiative when predictable and automatic reaction sequences are punctured by a surprise response, such as humor.

> Timothy was well over the hump in his treatment when he revisited an old girl friend with whom he used to have a suffocating relationship. He had hardly put his coat into her closet when he heard Susy ask whether he would visit again soon. To the patient's delight he found himself not merely replying but speaking up with effervescence: "When I go home today after this trial visit, will you cut me some of those roses in your garden? I like the pink ones." Timothy enjoyed his words because instead of turning out an automatic reply he had ventured out on his own. He had neither responded to the unwelcome and inappropriate question affirmatively nor bristled with opposition. Instead of settling for the dull, humiliating, and familiar role of counterpunching he had struck out on his own.

To differ with others who are close takes stamina which the weak must develop. But the rewards are great. In the stead of warmed-up imitations, copied gestures, and rigidified affects there appear in time individually shaped activities, unaccustomed words, and a rich stream of varied affects that flow from the innermost self. A new lease is taken on life, and the vitality that wells forth is rejuvenating and well worth the expenditure of insight, effort, and practice.

Molly, a young women whose strong erotic appeal to men was largely due to her whimsical ways of agreeing with their pace and preferences, gradually realized that she resented the mimicry which ever since a supposedly happy childhood in a family of four sons she had forced upon herself out of fear of being separate and different. As one day she walked briskly beside her latest boy friend, she noticed that he had turned grouchy and that his walk had begun to falter. Without blinking an eye, Molly continued her own brisk pace. With surprise she found that, after a while, her companion, in turn, changed and picked up her good humor and quick walk. She said laughingly: "What a pity you didn't keep it up longer. I want to practice. I like it and it's good for me." What Molly, of course, meant was that she enjoyed and wished to reinforce her new-found power to take strides on her own without imitating her companion.

This is by no means to suggest that the healthy way for mates to live together, to avoid dependency, and to retain initiative is to ignore each other's feelings and acts or even, as a matter of principle, to go against each other's grain or to defy. The emphasis in this context is not on opposition — though on one level disagreements do often strengthen individuality — but on the importance of becoming self-started, on taking the cues from oneself, on listening to one's own inner rhythm. We remain fecund not by picking up rules that others either supply or defy, but by self-examination and the deliberate selection of possible laws of conduct.

Unencumbered, happy lovers — rare as they are, if we look at the bitter truth — must know the secret. To remain together in good spirits they have to safeguard apartness and avoid the temptation of suffering together like Romeo and Juliet, who are not enviable models, and of relying for buoyancy exclusively on one another. To stay disentangled in a healthy fashion each must often go his own merry way, hoping that the other will join up voluntarily and offer companionship.

Beverly, who was a charming but meek and uninteresting lover to the enterprising Twain, learned some useful lessons in psychotherapy. One day, as she was about to admire her lover's beautiful eyes and jaw-line, which he examined in the

mirror, she changed her mind. Why should she take her cues
from him, she decided. Instead, she asked a question so funny
that it broke the two lovers up in a welcome interlude. "Shall
we call our two sons 'Irrepressibility' and 'Sockless'?" Beverly
asked, referring to her lover's undaunted spirits and his careless
disregard for his socks, which were usually missing when he
got ready to dress. The answer of Twain was more frivolous
and funny than customary, undoubtedly because he enjoyed
Beverly's less adoring and exuberant spirit. "I'll tell you what,"
he said, "let's call the first boy 'Irrepressibility' and not worry
about the second. He won't be around for quite a while
anyway." This was Twain's way of letting Beverly know that
he wasn't yet ready to contemplate a second child since father-
hood was anyway a perturbing prospect.

Beverly's departure from customary feelings of anxiety,
clinging, masochistic submission, and sad regrets that she was
still a girlfriend and not yet a wife, introduced a new experience and with it eventually an entire series of innovations.
Helped by psychoanalytic psychotherapy, the patient suffered
and exhibited far less dependency and, taking off on her own,
built new connections between herself and her lover, at the
same time turning around the prevailing mood. She became a
master of surprise questions and answers and with this an
innovator.

To live together in animation, mates need to guard autonomy
and not only understand but welcome each other's differences. Destructive as hostile and paranoid reactions are if they are perpetual
and totally indiscriminate (as are encompassing and ever-present
negativism and opposition), some aspects of opposition and negation
have an advantage if a certain judiciousness can be retained. Fair,
elegant, and timely dissent helps to keep people and mates separate,
just as the "No" and "I won't" of the little child are the spearheads
of due separation from parents whom he perceives at times as engulfing.[8] As patients comprehend the presence of masochism and
identification routines, they sense instinctively that the first steps
toward independence and genuine reactions are aided by opposition.
A moderate and "healthy" paranoia can be an aid in inching away
from entrapment. It helps to challenge others, to set oneself apart,

to get a sense of one's own body feelings, to glimpse neighboring vistas through individualized perspectives, and to gain the ability to stand on one's head even while one's tired mate falls into bed.

One of the many reasons why humorous remarks have such broad appeal is the surprise produced by true wit, which is partly, but not entirely, the same as the sudden emergence of unconscious ideas and wishes. People love surprises because they break chain reactions and make dents in confining rigidities. Tired mates are refreshed and their initiative is restored when the partner presents a delightful surprise of conduct and words which puncture the established molds. Provided the scene stays basically sane and clean, innovation is welcome in the setting of tranquility. When a mate gets things rolling in new directions, when clues supplied by one mate cease to be the prime eliciting agents of the behavior of the other, when the traces of a tit-for-tat pattern vanish and when humor is a source of new beginnings, the welcome for surprise is usually there.

All the world loves not only the lover but also the adventurer. It is he — or she — who shows the way to exploration and inventiveness. To remain elastic instead of going stale, the partners of a marriage need to elicit from each other and from themselves new ideas. Even *enfant terrible* manners are sometimes happily greeted. The unexpected surprise, not so much in the form of a gift as in the form of an invention of the mind and soul, is a supreme delight.

Shifting From "What" to "Why"

Marital life, like other mergers that aim at permanence, diminishes the capacity for *alert attention*. If, once the starring roles have been cast, the performers remain the same (and are not recast through promiscuous adventure), the partners become used to one another. They are less viligant and less attuned to changes of mood and appearance. At the same time, they are less perceptive about the world at large.

Attention, an important protective function, performs the duties of a personal sentinel. It alerts us to signs and signals of approaching danger. Being vigilant, we spot about-to-happen events before they actually take place.[9,10]

Settings that lack surprise, suspense, and innovation foster the status quo and reduce attentiveness. If attention is practiced but little, it atrophies like functions of organs not put to use. Marriages diminish mental agility for more reasons than can be named. Many people, once they have made a love conquest, cease to remain observant since the prime reason for their initial attention was the fear of losing the beloved or the desire to conquer. Partners who copy each other lose sight of the mate's individuality. Two persons who are determined to avoid arguments, as many married mates are, will blunt the edge of acuity. If loyalty is confused with cloying and clinging, free companionship gets lost, and so does the faculty of amiable scrutiny.

When attention flags, many important messages go unnoticed: perils are overlooked both at home and outside; the nuances of feelings and words are disregarded or misunderstood; above all, the genuine intention of a mate remains unnoticed while the focus is on seemingly large but actually unimportant details. In the lingo of the psychotherapist, the mates begin to focus on content instead of on process. The real questions remain unasked: "Why is he (she) acting this way?" "What is he (she) aiming at?" "What is the goal?" Instead, a static emphasis is put on the string of words used.

Acts that look different are often similar because between them exists an important and meaningful link. The great explorers of science know this truth and use it to detect relationships between seemingly unconnected phenomena. For instance, the botanist Linnaeus grouped plants meaningfully when he pointed out that not the shape of a leaf or the color of a bud but less obvious characteristics, such as the root system, should serve as the criteria for classification.

Mates who preserve their alert attention and sensitivity to process become and remain attuned to the essence of marital communication. They hear the intention that hides behind the spoken word; they recognize identities underneath dissimilarities and thus become ever more attuned to process. Content still matters, but is of secondary importance.

Let us take a hypothetical example of a husband who, during a weekend, raises various and apparently contradictory objections: he tells his wife that she spends too much money at the beauty parlor; when she puts before him a bowl of mock turtle soup he throws it into the sink and complains that he does not like to eat from a can; and when a neighborhood child whom the wife favors appears at the front door the husband shooes him away, announcing that he does not want to be bothered.

To the unattuned mind of many a wife, such instances would appear different. Yet once we look for intention and process, we notice constants in each encounter. The husband is prompted by anger because he feels that his needs are not sufficiently respected. The anger is directed outward and not against the self. The level of energy is high. The language lacks finesse and is blunt, obviously to leak the underlying message and to underline the husband's intention to get even with his mate.

Of course, the content of communications, such as the words used in a loving greeting or in a quarrel, is not negligible. But unless the process, the intention, the significance of the words exchanged is grasped, understanding is lacking. Attention has proved counterfeit and insufficient.

Jim and Therese, two intelligent and likable people who were married during a passionate love affair, became disappointed and exhausted by continuous strife. The quarrels always seemed to be about nothing, as long as mere content was considered. Asked what a recent fight was about, Jim explained, after some hesitation, that Therese exploded when he dawdled in the kitchen. She also lost her temper when he marketed "upside down," buying the frozen items on the shopping list first and the staples last.

Therese, in turn, complained with a wry smile designed to reveal her martyr life that Jim did not bathe their son on time. He also left his clothing all over the house for her to pick up, though she stressed her need for rest on account of her ulcerative colitis. Further, he wore the wrong clothes when the couple went out to visit.

Separately and together each of these two people fought a battle to pursue and express individual needs and to protest against the mate's obliviousness of these. But the fight was waged in the shadow arena of a "kitchen-household-child-rearing neurosis." The real issues, the essential intentions, remained obscured as long as both mates focused on *content*.

When *processes* were clarified in the course of psychotherapy, acuity picked up. Alert attention was directed toward the targets of purpose and meaning. New perspectives were gleaned when lateral * vistas were opened up and when looks were cast in fresh directions.

What Jim intended to state through his lassitude and disorder was an objection to being pushed around by Therese. Strewing his clothes all over the house, he wanted to convey emphatically that he was not about to give up his deserved possession of the marital domicile or his previously unimpeded access to Therese's time and attention.

Therese's somatic complaints were designed to charge the atmosphere with heaviness in which her masochistic inclinations flourished like flowers in a hothouse. Insisting that her husband bathe the child "on time," she tried to signal that she desired voraciously to be indulged and that she meant to hang on to her rigid control of home and mate. As Jim, a would-be painter, pushed for a more casual way of life, Therese, a punctilious chemist and the only daughter of a wealthy lawyer, publicized her claims for tidiness and regularity.

The mates, to be sure, were reluctant to admit the intentions and truths that underlay the symbolic domestic messages. But not to be minimized was their real inability to decipher the significance of behavior, once they had become immersed in one another. The speed with which understanding improved and attitudes changed once therapeutic help was sought showed that ignorance matched reluctance to perceive.

A variety of reasons account for the inability of one mate to get attuned to the conveyed intentions of the other. Like parents, like patients in treatment, like everybody, two married people become deaf to the inherent verity of communications because of resistance — that is, the determination to keep that which is hidden, hidden. "Let sleeping dogs lie" is a principle that carries much weight in human communications. Self-isolation and self-confinement must not be underrated. People, including married people, submerge themselves in their own system of information-gathering, listening, and self-expression. So far can such isolation go that the individual

* See chapter 7, "Active Thinking."

remains unaware of any message not presented in the terms to which he has become used. Only communications that are related to his own daily fare — the specialty of the house, as it were — are heard.

In rigidified marriages even visual acumen, which is but little dependent on personal needs, is easily lost. Plastic surgeons can tell stories of cosmetic surgery on wives which remains unnoticed by husbands.

Activity, initiative, and reciprocity, without which marriage becomes a sham, can be restored through the personal experience of psychotherapy which teaches the patient(s) to pick up process rather than remain fixed on content. Crises, surprises, quarrels, exposures to science and art, and deliberate attempts to capture new vistas are other means toward the worthwhile goal.

7. Active Thinking

A prime concern of psychotherapy is the training and liberation of the individual's thinking. For one to live affirmatively, vibrantly, and without much anxiety, one's thoughts have to be searching and imaginative, and to this end they often have to be remodeled. Starchy old ideas are not an admission ticket to an exuberant and successful game in the ball park of life. Psychotherapeutic treatment should enable a person to order and reorder his thoughts, to make new cause-and-effect connections, to search for valid clues — in short, to think inventive and provocative thoughts. Thoughts such as these are usually accompanied by feelings of moderate elation, sure signals that thinking soars.

To steer one's life, one must make specific and valid rather than stale and routine connections. Repeated failures have to be correlated with existing gaps in one's psychological makeup. When mental concepts — the pigeonholes invented to bring order out of chaos — have lost their usefulness and have turned into dusty shells, their rigid confinement must be cracked open. Ideas have to be rearranged according to new criteria. The concepts and hypotheses we hold can be likened to a commercial enterprise. The well-functioning mind is like a well-managed department store that keeps its numerous types of merchandise in different sections. To do justice to new products and to avoid stale displays, the arrangement and location of sections can be changed from time to time. This flexibility may irritate the more rigid customers, but their irritation will be more than offset by the interest the change arouses in the alert shoppers.

Active "thought search" is required to solve daily problems; passive rumination must and can be avoided. To understand personal failures and disappointments in family and friends, we must steer away from the simplistic and usually irrational habit of pinning the blame on others. If we look at our own self-deceptions we discover that many supposedly natural and inevitable ways of doing things really represent personal deficits and empty spaces. As the body's muscles and tissues have to be kept flexible and resilient, so must the currents of the mind, a goal that can be made delightful through "thought games."

Thought games are voluntary engagements of the mind, undertaken without pressing need or immediate purpose. Although best initiated for their own sake and not for any practical reason, thought games do yield their own advantages. They enrich the mind, and they structure time.[1] Solving crossword puzzles, reading between the lines of newspaper articles, engaging in witty discussions, studying some subject that promises intellectual or esthetic rather than immediate financial or other tangible rewards, these are examples of thought games. They give the mind a good run for no other purpose than to refresh and enrich and to maintain mental agility.

Thoughts are only rehearsals for action,[2] a truth that escapes many neurotics and psychotics who believe that what they have in mind is tantamount to a plan already carried out — a plan, furthermore, that is improper if not outright punishable. Actually, thoughts, resembling theatrical rehearsals, are provisional, not final, and hence can be taken much more lightly than can the real full-dress performance. Anticipatory thoughts make for a safety that is most precious. Every imagined possibility can still be explored, emotions likely to accompany action be pretested, and consequences be weighed in the mind beforehand.

Of course, to stall indefinitely on action is neither satisfying nor practical. Only those who think "in good faith" — who think in preparation for the best decision rather than indulging in daydreams — are enriched by anticipatory thought. Anticipation that is mere delay creates a sense of futility, but forethought that is the first important step toward concrete behavior greatly bolsters personal pride.

Emery, who had gradually overcome his obsessive traits, thereby also relinquished his tiring preoccupation with minutiae and, to his growing surprise, began to act. It was a joy to see how this man, freed from previous fears and invigorated by energy, announced what he was to do. *"I have decided* to go to Italy for a year of study," he stated proudly, aware that he would indeed follow through. His words and attitude reflected how much he relished his new-found ability to combine thoughts with initiative where previously he had only been able to run through the empty labyrinth of a mind separated from the flow of energy.

That thoughts must be active and searching in order to steer rather than sidetrack life is well illustrated by many reading and writing blocks.[3] To a large extent, unless organic brain disturbances interfere with intelligence, those who gain nothing or very little from the literature they read and those who make no headway with their writing approach their task inertly and in a fumbling manner. Minds that are on silent strike because they resist pressure stand still before the written word. They fight it or abdicate before it, but do not tangle with it.

To her surprise, Lee, the highly gifted woman we have encountered before, noticed that while she easily remembered poetry, especially by Asian authors, other reading passed her by unremembered and unenjoyed. Lee discovered that what made the difference was the amount of her active involvement. She noticed that when she made her own selections she reformulated what she was reading, argued with lines and passages, and scribbled comments in the margins. Subject matter treated this way stayed with her. As soon as a teacher or a lover or, eventually, her husband asked her to read something, Lee's tenacious passivity resisted it as intrusion into her mental life, and her memory of what she read vanished since she did not engage with the printed word.

Ideas, explanations, and concepts that fail to touch essential connections lead into a blind alley. They may arouse emotions, but those emotions will quickly evaporate. By contrast, linkings that have validity for the individual introduce a moderate affective elation. This can be noted in psychotherapy itself. If the patient says that he understands "intellectually but not in his guts," he usually does not understand at all. The reason is often not just ingrained resistance but real lack of comprehension. The only connections that stir the mental waters are those that spring from idiosyncratic cause-and-effect understanding. When novel links are made between events, because formulas are no longer rigidly applied and past and present life data are freshly and carefully connected, there follows fuller *understanding,* always eventually leading to desirable *change:* lengthened attention spans, greater personal involvement, a larger display of affective activity, and deeper stirrings of inquiring activity.

Some people claim that they are terrified by even short separations from a meaningful person because they are still enmeshed in the trauma of infantile abandonment. Of course, nobody can quarrel with this statement, but with its value and pertinence one can indeed take issue. An explanatory concept of this sort is usually too narrow and rigid to open the gates of self-understanding. The reason why even temporary loss paralyzes and terrifies many people is not merely that their loneliness may recall a childhood trauma. Much more is at stake in terms of ongoing, present-day processes that undermine functioning. The adult who is left behind experiences an increase of passivity and a concomitant loss of self-esteem, for to be left rather than to be leaving limits self-determination. Not only is loneliness hard to bear in itself, but it also greatly reduces the person's chances to delineate and externalize images and thoughts, since the customary human recipient of one's formulated notions is missing.

When such specific process connections are made, and when the patient is further encouraged to look for appropriate temporary substitutes to make established functioning once more possible, the childhood-trauma explanation is not discarded: the explanation is merely divested of its rigid character as a closed formula. The formula is thereby made effervescent, and concrete ways that lead *out* of the repetitious separation-must-lead-to-panic syndrome are now seen to exist. To the extent that comprehension is widened, more links to life are established and more affect-charged interests come into play.

Most neurotics are repeaters. From one failure they slide into another that is similar or nearly identical. Yet the deduction, often drawn too readily and too fast, that this is due to a *repetition compulsion* that forces the individual to reenact an old trauma may again overlook pertinent truth.

Among the potent reasons for what the patient regards as his repeated misfortunes is not the repetition compulsion, with its emphasis on active reinstatement of passively suffered pain. More significantly, the ever new suffering is caused by definable human shortcomings. True enough, these shortcomings were caused by previous deprivations. Yet what matters is that, like weeds, the shortcomings have strong roots and continue to grow and indeed to spread unless removed. When people are shown that their emotional and mental stock is both sparse and out-of-date, and when the development of psychic and intellectual skills is encouraged, old problems disappear. The scripts of the individual's life drama get a different and happier ending.

Before Slim married, she was often deserted by suitors who had initially approached her with ardor. The masochistic and enraged patient told herself, falsely as she found out, that desertion was her destiny. Her own selfish and cold mother had tormented her with corporal punishment, ridicule, and frequent long absences. Men, similarly, were bad, selfish, and abandoning.

This insistence on fatality did not help Slim, herself a cynical and selfish young woman, little aware of what she brought to her love relationships. But when she looked searchingly at the series of desertions, Slim made more valid connections between her fate and its causes. She discovered that out of familiarity, as it were, she gravitated toward men who had a detached personality, and that she actually precipitated their desertions by exhibiting only the harsh and critical side of herself, while hiding her need and capacity for love and protection.

To be sure, Slim's suspicious and selfish ways had been intuitively devised in childhood to make the little girl a match for the harsh, fickle, and vituperative mother. But now she had to become aware of the difference between her cloud-shadowed old world and her bright new one. In her adult life the stale manners of long ago were out-of-date. If she were to avoid further painful desertions she could not afford to claim sulkily that the jinx of the past still ruled her fate. To give the new figures in her grown-up world a fair shake, she had not only to form but honestly to use more open and encouraging attitudes.

In life, in study, in science, and in psychotherapy, exclusive retrospection fails to lead to discovery. To the evaluation of the past we must add searches for the possibilities of the present and future. Thoughts have to be pioneering if they are to serve man well. Thus all retrospection must be combined with exploration of new territory.

Fresh ventures and the reshaping of thought into new molds demand not only talent but effort.[4] Many people with problems know neither that they have to make fresh starts nor how to go about the hunt for the new. Where are the launching pads? How does one make life relevant? How is a person to develop that mysterious thing of which the psychologists speak, the cognitive map, or the thought schema? [5]

Stumbling about for a while is good for a start, because it promises entry into new fields. Later on, the bewildering clichés, the fuzzy and borrowed notions that do not fit, the obsolete blueprints have to be discarded and new ways of thought have to be learned. The procedure for the therapist is not to sermonize but to approach with questions, perhaps with kindly teasing as developed by the paradigmatic technique, and with a slow guidance toward the first independent steps. Psychotherapy, contrary to frequent claims,[6] does not merely occupy itself with the rechanneling of sexuality and aggression. Indeed, it can work only if the very instruments with which the fresh life is to be built are retooled. Thinking can and must be rejuvenated through therapeutic experience.

The Blank and the Bright Mind

Many people who think that they think actually play hooky. They do not apply their minds productively, but squander their talents. Letting the mind lie fallow is part of every psychological disturbance, and the first step toward health is to notice that nonthinking prevails. When people confuse dawdling with pondering, when "busy" thought and "busy" talk goes on and fragmented ideas are

muttered without aim, when the individual gives in to passive rumination instead of getting the mind to work and sending out thought
shoots, when awareness is low and the ideas that pass through the
head are merely accepted rather than deliberately chosen, when
that which emerges is drained of affect rather than filled with
elation, when these and other laissez-faire habits prevail, then
chances are high that the mind is not coming to grips with anything.
It is certainly not engaged in imaginative thought search or thought
games. What goes on can instead be described as mental vacu-
ousness, half-thought, and blankness.

The mood of a ruminator, who often thinks in circles, is flat; his
face and body lack expressiveness. By contrast, orderly, prognostica-
ting, plan-forging, and imaginative thinking is accompanied by some
elation of mood and a bodily sense of alertness.

Thought search requires that we reach out. The understanding of
people and problems and the planning of projects are approached
along pathways that have a destination, though the entire route is
not yet discovered. There is a sense of trying out, of testing and of
weighing different approaches. Let it be repeated in this context
that active thinking, though pleasurable and frequently exhilarating,
must be *invited* into the home of the mind. It calls for effort. It
demands a readiness to spend energy, as when we get ready to play
tennis, climb mountains, or practice music. Lazy and blank thinking,
in turn, is designed to let the individual off the hook, so he can take
it easy once more. Thought fragments are discharged but not assem-
bled, and the bin of ideas is emptied and not filled. Images pass
through the mind, but they do not excite through their shape and
rhythm; they are rather like tired and faceless troops that give a
mechanical salute in a routine parade.

Chant-like repetition of key phrases is a signal that the speaker is
not truly engrossed in them. The message, easily deciphered, that
is to be conveyed through repetition of words and phrases is a
longing for protected dependency.

When Bodha was loved and successful, she sized up the
world wisely and wittily like a young guru or psychological
diagnostician. But when, especially in the early phases of
treatment, she suffered setbacks, she became apathetic. Her
mind caved in, so to speak. She would then slump into a chair,

either in front of the television set, for which she had no respect, or in front of a window, staring into space, intent on
nothing. A good self-observer even in bad moments, she was
able to report the little chants that ran rhythmically through
her mind: "A woo wave," "Loving waters," "Give me," "I want
my daddy," "Maybe, maybe." These recurrent chants revealed
her overwhelming desire to attach herself to something or,
better, someone who would take care of her.

Bodha readily recognized her craving to be a baby. But she
had to learn that to get out of the quagmire she needed to
apply some effort and seek direction. She found an exit, for
instance, if she thrust forth ideas, read or made poems, and
stopped pouting or thumb-sucking — a frequent habit in these
circumstances — to take up some plan.

The passivity-activity pendulum swung towards self-activation when this young woman, who loved not only to read but
to write poetry, put together some imaginative ideas and words,
went to her music, or began to outline a project.

The self-indulgence that is the companion of rumination and the
low energy level it requires will cease to be pleasing when patients
discover that the stings of their failures and the pangs of their
anxieties are related to taking it easy for too long. Aimless thinking
proves to be an excessively costly luxury because it extorts an exorbi-
tant human price.

Clive described his slackness with an honesty that had
been hard to come by for this man steeped in fantasy. "I think
that I could do worthwhile things or have worthwhile ideas,
as my friends tell me. But how is this possible if I do all the
woolgathering that I indulge in? Constructing a past that
never was instead of getting to the crises that mushroom
around me takes me to hundreds of dead ends. Dull images
that spring up from nowhere predominate when I daydream.
I'm not really putting my imagination to work. I squander
an hour when I don't have ten minutes to spare, while I kid
myself into thinking that I think."

Clive waxed very angry and accused the therapist of banal-
ity when it was carefully explained to him that what he offered
as free associations were evasions. Yet he gradually gave men-

tal effort a try. To his surprise, his ideas became richer. His grandiosity and search for magic protection slowly dissolved; he started to apply small solutions to big problems. One of his first ideas was to turn the tables on his boss. Instead of being inwardly angry at, but outwardly deferential toward, the older, more experienced superior, Clive would ask him surprising questions, thus seizing initiative. Eventually there emerged a rip-roaring wit, whose poignancy — and this always distinguishes the likable wit from the underhandedly aggressive jester — sprang from roots of truth rather than from self-indulgent and neurotic concealment. Ultimately, Clive decided to find both problems and fun in real rather than fantasy life. Broad improvement, both physical and mental, had been much assisted by thought discipline.

"Thought contamination" occurs when desires bend a person's logic and lead to wishful thinking. This, however, is not the only or even the main type of fallacious reasoning caused by emotional problems. "Thought arrestation" — not to be confused with the thought retardation of the brain-injured — interferes with initiative, so that the entire arrested thinking process is wasted. "Mañana thinking," procrastination, and rumination curtail the power of the mind and are responsible for the strain of depressive moods. The brain hungers for activity.[7] Mind search, mind plunges, and mind refreshment are not just nice exercises for school, but are a human necessity. The active and thoughtful reshaping of passively received impressions is as indispensable to emotional vitality and self-affirmation as fresh air is to the body.

Ideas do not often come to us on their own. They are not given to us, but have to be chased like butterflies. They wait to be invited, they have a startling effect, and they bring on alert moods. Rumination and "busy thinking," by contrast, fall passively upon the individual like shadows produced by someone else's movement

Avoiding Stereotypes

Thought searches cannot rely exclusively on ideas, concepts, and verities that have passed if not from hand to hand then from mind to mind. If thought is to be orderly, constructive, and imaginative, it cannot run in ruts since its very purpose is to avoid old unsatisfactory patterns, to channel and organize new discoveries, and to prepare the way for reaching further into the world.

Concepts resemble bureau drawers. We throw into them things that belong together. But from time to time, when new things are acquired, they must be reordered. New finds, offering new uses and also changing the usefulness of our old belongings, open our eyes to fresh criteria by which to sort the contents of our drawers. Furthermore, some old articles have to be thrown out when new ones arrive.

> Kirby's concept of women worth his attention was based on looks and some stamp of power. If a girl had long legs and a pretty face, was well groomed, witty, rich, or college-educated, then he marked her as a choice article. He would note her name in a little yellow address book under the heading "desirable females."
>
> Soon after Kirby married the most persistent and seemingly most generous among the ladies who had made that list, he became convinced that his sorting system was no good. His wife was endowed with a fresh complexion and a willowy body and was considered to have an important writing talent, but she irritated and bored him and was, in fact, unable to understand her complex, brilliant, and actually warm-hearted husband. Although as a good scientist Kirby had a gift for conceptualization in his field, he realized only now that so far as women were concerned he needed new criteria to evaluate desirability. He had to form the concept of a "woman right for me." While he continued to be attracted by his old type, he fought hard and in the end successfully against the appeal of pretty and rather powerful girls. Eventually he made a very suitable choice: a girl, handsome but not fashionable and, what mattered most, dedicated to him — a loyal follower rather than the captain of the ship. In this second marriage, an old, inadequate sorting system was discarded in favor of a better one.

Among the essential ideas on which we rely to navigate through life is the image of our self. It constitutes a multifaceted abstraction.

It accommodates the feelings we consider most central, personal ethics and other convictions, memories of failures and successes, and much else. When people's notions are packaged and frozen, their image of the self remains much too static, resembling a statue rather than a mobile.

As rigidities gradually wane, thanks to increasing insight, as old theories and notions are discarded and new experimentations are undertaken, the self-image should change to include new evaluations of one's personality, fresh correlations between success and failure, and convictions recently gained. Yet not infrequently, the image of the self remains fixed and static, thus being increasingly at variance with reality. Such stubborn clinging to an obsolete self-image may be caused, for example, by masochistic wishes to continue feigning helplessness, or by continued paranoid ideations that enable the person to be always on the offensive, or by inflexible ego boundaries that resist anxiety-inducing modifications. An important role is also played by a passive, withholding turn of mind that is responsible for a continued "rubber-band" condition in which perceptions snap back to their old shape even after they have been temporarily stretched.

No person can in an ultimate sense be truthful if his own self-image is untrue. Furthermore, a self-image that is distorted — because it overemphasizes the person's destructive and negative qualities or because it is chronologically obsolete or because it does not take account of specific changes — prevents increased mobility and self-enrichment. To become more flexible, more imaginative, and more alive, we must make the mind a nutcracker with which to burst open such confining shells as a distorted self-image.

Kevin, a forty-five-year-old businessman, ripped about like a precocious youngster. Although often told by the ladies that he resembled a Persian prince, he clung to the old self-image of a kid who was much derided because his nose was too large and his lips too full to suit a boy. When new business successes came fast, as a result of his newly organized and highly imaginative management, he experienced each advance as if it were a miracle. He had to be gradually convinced that these accomplishments were of his own doing and that his self-image belonged in the attic — or better, the wastebasket.

Thereupon he began to move out also in other directions. He became able to recognize his truly outstanding potential and to give himself credit for his facility for hard work, and he looked on his own face and figure with new-found pride.

Psychoanalysis has been preoccupied with the significance of dreams and the primary processes that are, by definition, not yet subject to the restrictions of reasoning. It has thus, understandably enough, erred through omission. Extolling the fertile qualities of primary-process thought, it has unintentionally underplayed the inventiveness and excitement of rational thinking.

But an exclusive and divisive distinction between search thinking and creative, imaginative thinking, including thought games, is unwarranted and harmful. For a person to be both efficient and fully alive his mind needs both inclinations. Problem-focused thoughts succeed only if they are inventive. In order to establish new and pertinent connections between causes and results, to burst open obsolete concepts, we need imagination. On the other hand, if creative thoughts are to be not only discovered, but also recalled, recorded, and shaped into form, they must be accompanied by search thinking.

The human mind does not wish to stand still. Even autistic children, with their noted rigidity, fall prey to frenetic activity, fretting and nervous, searching aimlessly, should their defenses be stripped away.[8] Far from seeking adjustments (a much overrated concept), people in general, unless they are seriously damaged, long for fresh shapes and new complexities and will devise novel expressions for nuances of feeling and thought.[9]

Everybody, not only the young, wants to turn on — and by no means necessarily through drugs. Will, flexibility, and competence are fine bases for letting go of old, overpracticed modes of manner and thought. Though older people owe the terminology of "turning on" to the young, the privilege belongs to everyone, as artists, philosophers, and other wise men have always known.

To turn on does not mean to become passive. In the best sense it is a pathbreaking, innovative, and rejuvenating inner experience, leading to productiveness, to perceptual and conceptual enrichment and expansion, and to greater acuity of all senses. It makes possible the free roaming of the surface of the mind as well as the exploration of its rich underland.[10] Psychotherapy at its best should help patients let go of meanderings of old thought and to be open to new impressions and contemplations.

Clues From Discrepancies and Inconsistencies

Many valuable discoveries have been based on the observation of contradictions, inconsistencies, and puzzling facts. Only by studying a person from different angles can we gain full knowledge of his physical appearance. Only if we allow ourselves to combine the different vistas gained from different perspectives can we learn all about his face, figure, and expressions. Similarly, when someone's behavior clashes with the ideas and convictions he has expressed, it behooves the observer not to disregard such inconsistencies but to piece the bits together. The resulting personality profile will be much truer and much more interesting than a single-dimensional one. If exceptions are found to rules set up by oneself or others, they should not be dismissed as bothersome contradictions, for they are likely to lead to more valid explanations and theses. Inconsistencies and exceptions are important signals that the nets we have woven do not catch all the fish they are supposed to haul in.

What makes many people oblivious of even blatant contradictions in their own lives? The explanation is at least threefold. First, there is the well-known desire to avoid dissonance with one's peers. Almost everybody wants to sing in harmony with the choir even if the tunes are unappealing. Second, there is the wish, noticeable particularly in those who feel weak, to agree with others' firmly expressed assumptions. Self-doubt, passivity, and dependence, these states all induce a person to give in to a majority so as to avoid conflict and clash. Third and finally — and all three reasons mentioned are interwoven — there is the wish to stave off tension by settling a question rather than leaving it open for further inspection. Even if it does not account for all observed phenomena, an old theory is often retained because it allows for the fast settlement of issues and the release of tensions created by unfinished business.

The need for the "closure" of a task or a project, although

described as universal, is more pronounced in people who suffer from pressure.[11] Lest further tensions be added to their burdens, those who are disturbed prefer to write finis to chapters they know to be unfinished. Any ending will do, as long as the effort does not have to continue.

Only the unpressured mind tolerates dissonance, disagreement, and incompletion and is willing to inspect and indeed to treasure the incongruities it discovers. Only the mind that is free looks upon puzzling facts and inconsistencies as valuable clues.[12]

Mr. Feer, a passive, vague, and often obtuse man, appeared warm and pleasant to most people because he rarely agreed to disagree. One summer, he and his wife, a rather impetuous person, invited Mr. Count and his family for a weekend at their country home. Mr. Feer advised the Counts to follow the map to the center of the quiet village near which the Feers vacationed, to park there in *front* of the branch of the Botany supermarket chain, and to give him a ring so that he could come and show the way to the house in the woods.

Earlier than expected, Mr. Count, a sharp-minded but volatile man known for his quick decisions, telephoned to say he was parked *behind* the Botany store and that, although the huge parking area was filled with cars, Mr. Feer would easily recognize their green, foreign-make convertible. Mr. Feer said he would be there in just a few minutes, since the house was only a mile away from the store. Off drove Mr. Feer, taking no note that the car was parked behind, not in front of, the store or that there was neither space nor need for a huge parking area in the little village.

A half-hour later, Mr. Count telephoned again to ask where Mr. Feer was. He was interrupted in his talk by the operator, who requested a twenty-cent toll. For a moment Mrs. Feer, who had answered the phone, was amazed about the toll charge, but she immediately dismissed this additional incongruity because she had her mind set on her lunch preparations.

When, after two long hours, everybody finally arrived at the Feers, it became apparent that all the unnoticed incongruities actually contained clear indications of what had happened. Mr. Count, impatient as he was, had indeed parked at the Botany supermarket, but in a factory town thirty miles away. This explained (a) the size and location of the parking lot, (b) the density of the parked cars, and (c) the toll charge. Because the adult participants in this little comedy of errors were impatient — the guests to speed their arrival, the host to meet them, and the hostess to ready the lunch — the incongruities had been hurriedly dismissed although, or rather *because,* they gave such clear clues.

Lateral thinking, which consists of looking for new tacks, of making shifts in emphasis, and inspecting old problems from unorthodox angles, always pays off.[13] The person who thinks laterally, instead of going along with the majority who inspect a problem only from the front or the back, seeks side perspectives and thus obtains insights that can be gleaned only in such manner. He therefore often takes others by surprise and wins his points, because as he emphasizes the side angles he makes a situation more complex and also more interesting.

Beverly was a perfect agreer, since she feared challenge and opposition. But when she began to question ever more energetically "authoritative" statements with which she disagreed, her thinking started to sparkle, and she discovered that she enjoyed displaying the wit she had previously hidden. Not through docile agreement and not through insistent attack but through emphasis on some takeoff point of her own, this girl, who had been an obedient follower, turned out to be an excellent observer and, indeed, a leader, as the whole world now became to her aglow with discoveries.

A previous question is revisited. In order to apply the therapeutic lever under the heavy weight of passivity, dependence, and insipid agreement, do we first have to solve major emotional problems? Must we make the administrative ego, the seat of mental guiding, scouting, and structuring operations, wait until the field is cleared of conflict? Or do we proceed in the opposite direction, encouraging and helping an inert and acquiescent mind to approach its daily assignments with higher skill and ingenuity, even while tensions and problems are unsolved?[14]

Both types of leverage should be applied together. While psychotherapy traces the origins and nature of essential problems, the mind can learn to use its previously unused strength and ingenuity. As the ego becomes stronger — for instance, through clue hunts and lateral thinking — it proves to be a better ally in the dissolution of character problems.

Self-Search Instead of Recrimination

Instead of looking for the actual and complex reasons for failure, many disturbed personalities who have run into troubles of one kind or another raise fruitless accusations and queries. Their aim is not to discover what went wrong but to blame someone or something for the difficulties incurred. Questions like "Who is to blame?" or "Who did it all?" are expected to solve the bothersome problems that face them. Such accusations, often sharply worded or even shriekingly articulated, suggest that the person's thinking, the prime aid in getting extricated from adversity, is indirect, abortive, and off-target.

The true offenders in the case of repeated failure are usually personal shortcomings that can be neither recognized nor remedied by blaming others or by blaming oneself. Those who are bent on blame usually remain unaware of important truths: that inadequacies of the self account for problems in series; that whereas it is essential to diagnose personal shortcomings, they disappear through improvement and change and not through self-reproach; that in this life frustrations are bound to occur every hour and day, and therefore the indignant complaint "Look what is happening to me" is usually out of place. The assumption that someone or something else — fate, for example — is supposed to watch out for the individual is always misleading. External protection and other people are not responsible for personal destiny; rather, one's own strengths and skills carry the burden. Childlike rather than mature notions lead to the supposition that an individual has a birthright to uninterrupted safety and protection and that, in the case of unfavorable events, some supposed protectors who were unduly neglectful are to be blamed. Such recriminations and fixing of blame undermine solid thinking.

Roger, a despotic businessman who despite an arrogant

demeanor was unsure of himself, depended for support and guidance on his kindly and realistic wife. While he clung to her like a puppy, he also blamed her for any wrong turn in his affairs. During a trip to Canada he characteristically telephoned her in the middle of one night to make her the target of his reproaches. "Why did you recommend this Canadian trip?" was his opening question. "No motel or hotel is open at this hour, and I'll have a heart attack if I sleep in my car." The wife, listening to these complaints, suggested that he try a small hotel that she knew. He was infuriated, called this a female, harebrained suggestion, and hung up on her, only to call back in a short while. Without admitting directly that he had found sleeping quarters, he complained vigorously that the hotel his wife had recommended had assigned him a stuffy room. Next morning a third call came through. The husband reported cheerfully that after a fine French breakfast he was about to explore the town's reputed golf course. In this case, which is by no means extreme, petulant reproach rather than objective thought search was the first recourse.

Like this businessman, many people who are talented and even brilliant do not investigate the genuine roots of their difficulties but take to recrimination. In the pursuit of an object of reproach they may become seemingly paranoid, raging at alleged offenders. Irrational, resentful, and self-destructive blamers who censure others or themselves instead of objectively casting about for the causes of defeat can improve through psychotherapy if their thinking is examined in addition to their emotions.

Kevin, a very lonesome and self-derogatory man, ran a successful booking office for performing artists. Whenever he placed a new client — which he did with great perception, launching many beginners on a fine career — he hoped to make a friend. Thus Kevin hoped to make his own loneliness more tolerable.

Invariably, after his first enthusiasm was over (usually after about five months), Kevin was once more confronted with his problems. He rediscovered that he was as isolated, self-critical, and self-effacing as before. But in the course of treatment he also realized and admitted to himself how great was his resentment of those artists he dealt with. As he was thrown back on his personal difficulties he would always think: "Which one is to blame now?" Yet even as he built a case against one of them, he felt guilty over the injustice he was about to perpetrate.

"Blame thinking" is a hangover from a deprived childhood.[15] Initially, all infants and young children, unable to provide even the smallest service for themselves, rely on the mother and regard her as the center of the universe. If something goes wrong, then it must be the fault of that same all-powerful person.

Youngsters who are appropriately protected and guided develop an expanding self on which they gradually learn to rely. But those who are either showered with or deprived of the parental help and understanding that befits each phase of development remain fixed, passive, and helpless. Unable to fend for themselves because the ego stays weak, they continue to hang on to the mother by maintaining a false causality. The vague notion settles in that if a frustration hits, then lamentations and reproaches are the way to get over the hump. The feeling persists that "someone" or "something" (even the self) is to be mobilized by accusation. A primitive causal thinking lingers. Reproach fails to give way to emerging imaginative connections between cause and effect, and hence adult thinking remains gravely defective. Clumsy recriminations are too frequently substituted for subtle reasoning.

When the world of things and people offers to a child proper emotional support, consolation, and explanation, or if psychotherapy makes up belatedly for what was lacking, then peace is made with real life. The fantasy is abandoned that perpetual gratification is possible, and the notion is given up that frustration is the result of an arbitrary letdown by a neglectful or hostile person. Reproaches against others and against the self subside as the idea takes hold that not everything can turn out well and that self-acquired strength and skill are the best protection when difficulties strike.

Magnitude Counts Less Than Meaning

Thinking becomes static and loses its usefulness when attention is focused entirely on externals — on whether something is small or large, dull or bright. Ready-made opinions should be given less consideration than the modifying words that establish connections and suggest implications. "I adore him although his sloppiness drives me crazy." In this statement the key word might well be *although* rather than *adore*. The observer does not get far if he remains preoccupied with the external appearance of people, objects, and events and fails to inquire how things function, how they have become what they are, and what their significance is. Sizes, colors, visible movement, and surface textures are the prime preoccupations of a simplistic and childlike mind. Small children notice first and foremost whether a ball is big or tiny and what its color is, and they are but little interested in to whom it belongs, what it means to the owner, and what can be done with it.

The use of language is another indicator of the level of ongoing thinking. Language aids recall and contributes to the creation of order by supplying labels — that is to say, names for sensory data and terms describing connections between them. If linguistic exaggerations prevail and allusions to the size of events outweigh the concern with connections and relationships, then once more chances are that merely surface phenomena are being observed. Causes, consequences, opportunities, and personal interests are likely to be neglected if the observer refers primarily to appearances.

> Nora called the therapist late one night demanding that she be seen the next day; otherwise, she said, she would commit suicide. After only a few meetings the patient's emotional pangs subsided, but she determined to remain in treatment because of a vague conviction that she had wasted her life.
>
> Nora's speech abounded with expressions such as "Ah," "Oh," "Absolutely terrific," "Fantastic," "It's simply nothing, forget it," which told little about her feelings. Because this quite psychotic patient was undefensive, the therapist was able to establish quickly some of the crucial problems: Nora disliked being a woman and identified with her violent and megalomanic father, although she was better controlled than he; she hated her "dreary" teaching job and wanted to gamble and make big money fast; still, money flowed through her fingers and she was always without reserves; she loved speed in any form and dreamed of riding wild horses across prairies;

she had lesbian desires. She was perfectly ready to discuss these and other problems, but remained unfeeling in their presence.

One of various approaches used to break through Nora's impassive and narcissistic shell was to insist that she stay away from big words and say instead precisely how she felt about a happening rather than dwelling on its catastrophic or negligible proportions. Surprised, often irritated, but sensing that something worthwhile came out of the therapist's suggestions, Nora complied. As she started to admit bit by bit what people and events meant to her, she softened, and her craving for melodrama and the fast-paced life subsided.

Primitive people, as their tales of giants and dragons show, and psychopaths are fascinated by hugeness and power, and are overwhelmed by anxiety if their own supplies and strengths dwindle. Homosexual men and women have a liking for that which shines and is big or else is cute and minute.[16] Obsessive-compulsive personalities are occupied with minutiae because of their fear of the essential facts, namely, the intensity of rage and other impulses. Whatever the many motivations for the concern with size and appearance, the form of this kind of thinking matters. People improve emotionally when thinking is recast into more dynamic and complex molds.

Headline reading, so popular in American civilization, is another manifestation of impetuosity, of primitive thought habits, and of antagonism to inquiry. Because headlines are big and easily legible, they save readers from expenditure of energy and allow impetuous and primitive personalities to keep up with the world the easy way. Because headlines compress (but also oversimplify) complex and intricately related facts into sequential form that is readily comprehensible, they cater to primitive and simplistic thinking.

Passivity, anxiety, and the hyperactivity that is the frequent cover up for both make for extremist, undifferentiated, and static thought. Conversely, if labor is spent on the observation of details and significant connections between them, and if the mind engages in genuine thought search, frustration tolerance is heightened and passivity and anxiety are modified.

8. The Passive Stalemate

Passivity resembles the guest who came to dinner, never to leave the host's home to which he was invited for a brief stay. In the beginning, usually early childhood, passivity evolves into a familiar way of life because it is one form of self-protection. Many a young organism renders itself instinctually inert and insensitive so as to lower the threshold of inflicted pains and pressures. The basic idea is that if you play dead the deprivations and rejections of an unaccepting environment won't hurt as much. But passivity, first adopted as an emergency measure, becomes a way of life that sticks. Unless a changed element of the environment intervenes and offsets early deprivations, inaction and insensitivity become a permanent holdover that paralyzes purpose, initiative, and mental alertness. Protracted passivity then becomes the soil in which such self-destructive and hostile character traits as exploitativeness, sullenness, laziness, and withdrawal take root.

As any psychoanalytically oriented psychotherapy shows, adults adopt a passive way of life against their own deep wishes and will. The inertia and apathy that were originally self-invoked but that eventually become autonomous always go against the grain. People who nurture, usually without conscious intent, their own passive condition do not lose a more basic longing for competence, playfulness, and self-activation.[1] Lingering discontent and depression, which invariably accompany an inert life, are evidence of the yearning for an outgoing and eventful life.

The passivity of the adult is not only often unwelcome and uninvited, but also amazingly tenacious. Its persistence derives from a variety of reasons:

1. Many adults forgo the pleasures of initiative because, though they do not welcome their inertia, they are only vaguely aware of its pernicious existence. There are no clear-cut or resounding signals that passivity is the offender responsible for listlessness and depression. Hence it is fought not at all, or too late, or with inadequate weapons.

2. Apathy permits exploitation. Passive people, through their seeming inability to watch out for themselves, usually force others to offer excessive indulgence and protection. Even though those who are withdrawn and unresponsive irritate nearly everyone, it does not become readily apparent just what it is they do to annoy those who attempt to pull them into activity. Hence efforts to help them to participate in life rarely cease, and the passive person continues to exploit other, more vigorous, people.

3. Passivity equals punishment, primarily of the self but also of others. Remaining inactive and languorous, the passive resister enjoys sweet victories of getting even, for withdrawal of any kind is experienced by other people as a deprivation and discomfort. In every person who insists on apathy there lurks an expert at the passive and vindictive behavior that often instills guilt in others.

4. Slackness, slowness, and the timidity that often accompanies both offer a hiding place. They make it possible for the reluctant one to stay out of any contest that might expose weakness and emotional clumsiness. Indeed, by remaining conspicuously quiet some people even manage to suggest that they have more capabilities than meet the eye.

The Processes of Passivity

The rest and sleep required to relax a healthy mind and body are one thing, but the passivity of which we speak here is a very different matter, as many specific features that accompany inertness show. Healthy rest periods can be compared to intermissions between acts of a play. Despite the break, actors and audience remain alert and become even more curious about what the next scenes will bring. But pathological and protracted passivity * goes hand in hand with some of the feelings that come up when a show is permanently interrupted. Everyone feels deprived and at sea. Since self-awareness is low and ill-defined feelings prevail in states of passivity, both patients and therapists find it hard at times to make the right diagnosis. It can become difficult to decide whether languor is the result of fatigue or of passivity. Hence it is helpful to highlight some of the crucial differences between the two:

1. When a personality who is healthy and put together soundly seeks rest, the desired phases of relaxation are relatively short. A few weeks or even a few days of taking it easy usually reestablish the customary vigor.

2. In rest, as distinguished from apathy, the ego retains enough alertness to enable it to go into action should needs and dangers arise. Many sleepers, for instance, are sufficiently aware of noises and lights to snap into a ready-set-go condition if a burglar intrudes or a fire alarm sounds or lights suddenly go on. The mind does not become completely empty, but stays accessible to remnants of stimuli. These remnants indeed create the interesting and significant structures that we call reveries or dreams.

3. When resting is sound it changes but does not eliminate the processes of memory. In fact, while the acuity and the working of memory are temporarily altered, the mind returns from rest with increased spark, sharpness, and even improved ability to organize facts. Observations of human learning tell us that people who take intermissions during their studies subsequently recall facts better and indeed are often able to rearrange their data more ingeniously so that information acquired makes more sense after interruptions than before. During leisure time and vacation periods, when mind and judgment are encouraged and permitted to wander, the individual often feels enriched and finds that insights pop up with higher frequency. In sum, productivity continues or is even enhanced when (or because) intentional effort and logical thought are periodically suspended.

4. After a good sleep or rest most people are brighter than before. They find it easy to hit on just the right words and expressions. And, more ably than before, they can make discriminations between

---

* Subsequently the term passivity will always denote a disturbed condition.

facts of varying importance and set up in their minds priority lists that make sense and are helpful. In other words, sound rest helps the brain to distinguish which facts are important and which ones are secondary. It helps the brain decide which ideas and tasks should be tackled first and which ones can be postponed.

5. The same thing is true of personal reactions and the self-protective measures that are our chief defenses in case of stress. Following healthy sleep and rest the individual has better judgment as to which kinds of reactions and defenses are suitable in dealing with particular social and work situations.

Pathological passivity (as a rule, a protracted condition all the more insidious because the individual is usually not conscious that he renders himself paralyzed) reveals very different characteristics. Following the unconscious use of widespread repressions, withdrawals, and constrictions of affect, which are forerunners and also nuclei of passivity, the personality forfeits its vigor and snap. Animation and alertness are suspended. An apathetic person, unlike the healthy sleeper, cannot slip swiftly into a ready-set-go condition. In fact, the paralyzing passivity is hard to shake and feels subjectively like an all-enveloping numbness.

The memory span becomes even shorter, and what recollections can be conjured up tend to be indistinct and inaccurate. For example, passive patients often do not remember even fragments of their recent psychotherapy sessions. If any recollections come to mind, the proceedings in both treatment and outside life are recalled in simplistic fashion. Crucial events are leveled off, and few distinctions made between peak events and in-between happenings. Instead of rich and structured memories there are only skeletal recollections. When the passive state ebbs and initiative returns, memory proves to be one of the first faculties to reflect the change. It now extends further back, and its ready recollections reflect the natural complexity of life and are accompanied by feelings of pride and zest.

People who have become submerged in their self-created passivity settle for stereotypes and seem satisfied with facile explanations that require little thought search. They are habitual askers of questions, resembling little children who expect (quite appropriately, up to a certain age) to be fed answers. Trite phrases are used repetitively to describe or explain even the most important happenings, and the bland feelings, the reiteration of words, and identical sentence structures would be striking if they were not so boring.

Many a person who has sunk into the muddy waters of inertness makes spurious and inexact connections between events and their causes. He lacks even basic information that is splashed all over the news media. Both the intellectual and the emotional curiosity is awry. People who have permitted their minds to become slack and inert fail to register even those reactions of others that most directly affect the passive person. Also, instead of responding differently to widely divergent events and to different personalities whose needs and interests are far apart, passive people tend to crank out responses that are fairly equivalent. They also seem incapable of choosing — or are unwilling to choose — the most suitable defenses from a wide range of existing possibilities. Nor is a defense dismissed once it has served its function. Instead, a unitary, pervasive, and persistent defensive front is exhibited. Productivity, creativeness, and the delightful surprises of wit diminish.

Evan, a disturbed, reticent, and rather isolated man, thrived on the satisfactions of his brilliant scientific career. Employed by an electronics laboratory, he had developed two important inventions and had published a much-read paper about his findings. Though the patient's social contacts were sparse, he enjoyed a moderate popularity, making it a habit to observe people carefully and to inquire into their interests. A calm listener, he was pleased to be invited to some of his colleagues' parties.

Shortly after Evan married his second wife, whose easy sociability and initiative he admired, he changed radically. He became angered by what he saw as his wife's frequent psychosomatic complaints and her insistence on small attentions. Fearful of closeness, Evan protected himself by turning into a sullen, uninterested, and eventually inert hermit. His arrivals home were timed ever later. He felt smothered in a dense and impenetrable fog of confusion, and he spent increasing amounts of time in bed.

To his shock, Evan discovered that in the course of his general retreat from activity and participation, many functions of which he was proud and on which he relied at work disintegrated. Formerly a man with excellent recall of both minute and substantial data, Evan found that his memory "evaporated," a fact he attributed not to his passivity but to the irritations he had to endure. At first he could not remember marital spats; then it became a mystery to him what he and his wife had done during weekends. Finally the young scientist was shocked to discover that he could no longer remember his findings at work. Determined to help himself, Evan started to keep voluminous logs of everything that took place in his life. If he began to forget what had happened during a treatment session, he headed for the nearest drug store where he could set down on paper recalled fragments of exchanges between himself and the therapist before they vanished completely.

The worst blow, and one that convinced this brilliant young man that he might have sunk too deeply into the treacle of inertia, came when he recognized that the shadows of unproductivity lengthened. He made diverse and undirected attempts at new experiments, but his attention stayed riveted on mechanical details. He could no longer think of interesting questions to study and pursue. For hours he sat at his desk scribbling on a pad of paper figures that meant nothing to him. Always plagued by tiredness, Evan now felt so fatigued that large parts of each afternoon were spent on the couch in his office.

Whatever happened, Evan had one primary response — a cynical silence. Whether his wife was good-humored and considerate or not, the patient's invariable thought was that she was sloppy and unattractive. He avoided former friends, going over a particular fault of each in his mind many times, especially at night. Everybody appeared to him to be offensive and ridiculous, and his response to each human being was an invariable "Stay away" or "Get off my back."

When people become passive they focus primarily on autocentric sensations within the body.[2] The organs are no longer taken for granted, but their presence and condition, usually a condition of pain, are observed and described. In short, whatever sensations emanate from the self, pleasurable or unpleasurable (and they are much more often unpleasurable), outrank messages from the outside world. Auditory and visual signals, ideas and communications transmitted by other people, all these are of lesser importance. Herein lies another reason for failure of memory and the subjective experience of dullness. It is much easier to remember sounds heard, sights seen, risks encountered, and exchanges experienced than to remember vague notions as to whether an organ or the entire body felt "good" or "bad."

> Evan, always fairly passive and increasingly inert after his marriage, reported in treatment that he was constantly preoccupied with pains. While formerly he had vaguely noticed a tension in the chest and a pressure behind the forehead, he was now also uncomfortably aware of his breathing and his nasal drip. Nearly every part of the head bothered him most of the time. Turning passively inward and almost completely away from the outside world, his attention to physical functions and feelings — his body-consciousness — was so great that he was almost perpetually restless and anxious.

Passivity yields blunt and blurred affects because distinctions between separate feelings get lost. It becomes difficult to tell what is experienced: is it annoyance, curiosity, lack of interest, or suspicion? Moreover, feelings are beamed vaguely either at everybody who happens to come along or at accidentally selected people, so that Peter is blamed or suspected for what Paul did. It is a case of hit-or-miss reactivity.

When and Why Did It Start?

The adult's familiarity with inactivity and inertness harks back either to the "good old days" of infancy or to harsh and injurious beginnings. The continuation or reemergence in mature life of sluggishness and immobility belongs in one or the other of two categories, which occasionally overlap.

Infants, born helpless as they are, depend on the mother for sustenance and comfort. In a setting that starts out "good," the child's life is so closely linked to that of the mother that this early existence is described accurately as symbiosis. But should a mother, for multiple reasons of her own, enjoy this closeness too much and encourage continued leaning on her interventions, rather than growing separateness and independence, as her offspring's body and mind mature, then the child gets stuck. Most likely, too high a level of dependency will persist and leave its mark on adult life, furnishing all the markings of a "give me" or "do it for me" personality. To establish clarity, let us call this kind of inertness *plea passivity*.

The children of deprivation and rejection grow up quite differently and have but little acquaintance with "good old days." These children are the offspring of reluctant and rejecting mothers on whom the role of parent was forced, though this is not always consciously admitted. Only a minimum of care was supplied, and deprivations were rampant. Later, veiled or direct criticisms were added. Such bereft children at first send out SOS signals of screaming and fretting, but eventually switch to those of apathy and depression.[3,4] If their appeals fail to be heeded, they barricade their needs behind an all-encompassing immobility, self-induced insensitiveness, torpidity, and quiescence. Gradually, if deprivations continue, the protective shield of "playing dead" becomes ever more impenetrable. A character fortress, a kind of physical and mental Maginot Line, is erected to seal off needs and feelings. Such impassiveness again continues into adult life, either as a perpetual state of impassivity or a retreat to slip into at the slightest suggestion of new deprivations and rejections in the offing. Let us call this torpid condition *barrier passivity*.

Though both of these two varieties of passivity, single or (more likely) in combination, block self-fulfillment and self-activation, barrier passivity seems the more pernicious. Perhaps it does not produce more difficulties, but it certainly is responsible for problems that are more tenacious. Patients displaying barrier passivity render themselves insensitive and impenetrable so as to avoid pain and rejection and thus are likely to make slow progress in therapy.[5] The reaction potential of all their senses has to be reawakened.

It is true that inertia and passivity are more often caused by deprivation — for instance, too little relief of tension and too few opportunities for gratification and for the exercise of such functions as perception.[6] Yet to say only this is an oversimplification of a complex problem.

Since, as we have seen, both self-awareness and discrimination among external facts are poorly developed in passive people, it is as though heavy shades are pulled down over the eyes and the mind much of the time. Whether a person is pleadingly petulant or hides behind the barrier of impenetrability — and from here on the distinctions between the two kinds of passivity will be made only when they are significant — life is staved off. Dangers and joys together are buried by the weight of apathy, lowered awareness, and reduced sensitivity. Confined and almost strangled by torpidity, many adults only occasionally reveal in flickers of thought, associations, or dreams their nascent longings for stimulation and contact.

> The patient Lee, who spent four or five hours each day in a small closet-like room with the shades pulled down to shut out both light and noise, rarely addressed more than a few sentences to her husband when he returned from work at night. However, on her most silent days she insisted on being taken out for dinner to a restaurant where the atmosphere was friendly. On such occasions the impersonal courtesies of a doorman or waiter substituted for the contacts of which she deprived herself. Night dreams following such visits to eating places often centered on a large woman, a mother figure. This woman offered fruit, but after placing it before a blond little girl, representing the patient, quickly whisked it away. The brief restaurant contacts pursued by Lee never permitted anyone to become too intimate. Consequently, both glimmers of lasting interest and the beginnings of irritation were carefully avoided.

Passivity is an offense of omission rather than commission. This is one reason why it has been given relatively little attention and has been looked upon as pathological only when it leads to specific symptoms or failures in work and love. Whatever the origins and underpinnings of passivity, resentment, which is an ever-present component, is not displayed openly. Though passive people invariably harbor anger and are skillful in irritating others, their misdemeanors are so veiled and their infractions appear so slight, especially upon initial acquaintance, that many appear innocent even to very astute observers. Yet, in the long run, few people are so bound to ruin friendships and intimate contacts, few arrest their own lives as seriously, and few create in others as deep a sense of entrapment as do passive individuals.

Does Passivity Have a Purpose ?

The mind, as has been described and proved,[7] avoids and indeed abhors a vacuum, seeks out stimulation, and reacts with joyous emotions to initiative. Why then, and to what end, are so many adults caught in the web of inaction, emotional inertness, and mental immobility? To unearth some to-the-point answers to these important questions, with the hope that as a result passivity can be uprooted, dispersed, and replaced by action, we must be ready to look in several directions. In fact, a triple understanding is required. To achieve a dynamic explanation that promises change, we have to set our sights on the passive person's past, his present, and his future. To undertake such a multifaceted examination of passivity, therapeutic help is usually necessary.

When patient and therapist together look backward at infancy and childhood, they discover roughly *when* stagnation began to set in. They find out *who* was responsible for the onset of the depleting human quiescence. And what is probably most essential, such reviews establish just *how* the problem was initiated. Was is through encouragement of *plea passivity* or through traumatic deprivations that led to the protective bulwark of *barrier passivity?* Such reviews of the past build perspective, relieve some guilt (though not all), and add considerably to self-knowledge.

Yet to accomplish liberation of the passive sufferer, to set him free to act and to enjoy strong and unfettered feelings, the psychotherapeutic review has to be extended into additional and crucial perspectives. The *present and future* must also be scrutinized. Explorations primarily of the past are too limited. People don't stick with their doldrums and torpor merely because in this manner long-repressed feelings can remain unconscious. And the notion that such behavior is "inherent" in a person's makeup, thus holding him back from new life patterns, avoids essential questions.

Dynamic answers that dig up the roots of unnatural, inert behavior so that new seedlings can be planted in the human soil are forthcoming if we ask questions pertinent to the present: Are there any essential rewards to be reaped through continuing passivity? And if some secondary gains are made by those who remain on the sidelines of action, then just how great are these winnings? What is the on-going psychological price paid for the safety of inertness? And what, finally, are some superior alternatives to which the patient has access, should he be willing to escape the morass of apathy and sluggishness and acquire new, alert skills?

Such questions probe the *present-day* reasons for perpetuating dreary habits, outmoded solutions to pressing problems, and what must surely be considered primitive and outwardly unappealing modes of self-protection. Such questions uncover the scant profits the sluggish life provides and hold up finer, more exciting, and much more durable gains. When patients look at the other side of their supposed gains from passivity, they discover that the price they are paying is much too high since it amounts to at least a partial extinction of life itself.

A dynamic approach combines the historical method with a curiosity about present function. Like a classic historian, we look at the ruins and rituals of bygone times, adding to the store of knowledge by keeping a log of the findings. We make sure, however, to discover the function of customs and methods that continue in use. The usual explanation of these continuing traditions is that they are maintained because they serve the purpose of groups that staunchly defend their perpetuation.

Similarly, patients stick with old mental and emotional habits because these habits do a lot for them. Patients dress up in the mental costumes of yesteryear because old trappings can still be put to use. But above all, unless psychotherapy intervenes, many such patients simply do not know how to develop faculties that will give them access to modern and less self-destructive satisfactions.

Evan, who was discussed earlier, was the only surviving son of a mother who, having given birth when she was only sixteen, never weaned her son psychologically. She demanded that he stay close to the kitchen where she spent most of the day in useless and restless activities. She insisted that the boy keep her company after dinner and listen to the weepy accounts of her loneliness and physical discomfort. In return, Evan received many maternal assurances that he was especially bright and destined for greatness.

Even by the time he was nine or ten he waited for the evening, not because he enjoyed the mother's complaints but because he desired her praise. Much later in life, as a not very masculine man in his twenties, Evan behaved meekly and quietly with the women he courted, not only because he transferred such behavior from the mother to the women friends, but also because he knew that certain compliments would be forthcoming to reward him for his seemingly undemanding manner.

Both this patient's self-pitying mother and his silent, embittered father were incapable of offering their only child physical affection. In infancy body contact was minimal. During feedings the child was held stiffly and in uncomfortable positions. Discipline was stern. Evan protected himself against his own sensitive expectations by developing an antagonism to body contact and closeness, and even as he kept the mother company during the after-meal sessions he moved his chair to a corner.

When as an adult Evan married twice, he still used this same kind of avoidance (which went hand-in-hand with an unadmitted craving for body contact) to punish both wives to the point at which they raged and sobbed in despair. In the second marriage, for example, Evan, who was vaguely aware of his combined wish to be close and yet far away from the physical presence of his wife, always created unmerciful confusion. Should his wife kiss him, he withdrew into another room to remain sullen and remote. Should he put his arm around her and get a warm response, he invariably turned impassive and silent, complaining that he was disappointed and had become uninterested. Though Evan, of course, perpetuated old forms of body isolation through his erratic ways and avoided feared closeness, his ideas and dreams showed that one prime purpose was punishment.

Evan's stern father had always demanded that the boy keep the large grounds raked and the cellar clean, even when the son was far too young to possess the tenacity and strength to obey these orders with any ease. Resentful over these pressures, Evan became apathetic and morose. As an adult employee with an expanding professional career, he deliberately clung to his sulky and uncooperative ways. Knowing that he wanted to get back at the world for pressure that he allowed to be put on him, he struck about him wherever it did not hurt his career. Evan refused to make personal phone calls; he ate at the houses of others but never issued an invitation to have a meal; he refused to give even token gifts or to send Christmas cards; but he hoarded wires, electric plugs, and parts of machinery that he had removed from the office.

Even well-trained and otherwise perceptive therapists, as well as the patient's friends and acquaintances, are often trapped by the quiet implied demands, the punishing withdrawal, and the veiled exploitations that emanate from the apathetic and passive individual. Hardly any patients are so likely to evoke irritation and anger in a hospital staff as those who remain stubbornly and punitively inert. It is not unusual that the passive patient is prematurely discharged, largely because of the dormant resentments he creates in others.

In such patients, the slow but important forward movement toward activeness usually comes about when the reasons for continued learning, inertia, impassivity, and depression are made explicit. After such a start, the patient becomes interested in acquiring personal ways that promise, and indeed produce, more enjoyable, more lasting, and more affirmative rewards, rewards that invariably lead to reciprocal love.

9. The Subjective Advantages of Passivity

The majority of people who render themselves temporarily or permanently passive extract distinct psychological benefits from their quiescence, inaction, and the extended standstill of emotions and capabilities.

The exception is that unfortunate group of autistic human beings whose apathy signifies total resignation and an almost complete abdication from life. So thick is the wall of inertness and insensitivity that surrounds the autistic person that neither the pain against which the fortress is built [1] nor any gratification can penetrate.*

Excepting this singularly isolated autistic group, other nondoers are not merely victims but also users of their own passivity. They make sure, though often unconsciously, that their inertness works for them and relieves some of their problems.

The World Owes Me Indemnity

The show of helplessness, sadness, and resentment which passive people display exerts pressures on others, whether the show is subtle or dramatic. If such pressures are not distinctly felt on first contact with passive personalities, the continuous claims for sympathy, solicitousness, and assistance that are sent out eventually

---

* The subgroup of passive people that displays what has been called barrier passivity resembles the autistic group in kind but not in degree.

leave the imprint of irritation. Mates, children, friends, and colleagues, initially puzzled and guilty because of their negative feelings toward the seemingly innocuous passive person, eventually comprehend that the flow of oblique requests that the passive ones channel toward them accounts for the felt vexation.

Passivity is made out of frequent silences, a seeming inability or unwillingness to shift for oneself, depressions of various degrees, and, above all, ever-present intimations of experienced maltreatment. Essentially, these various manifestations amount to perpetual complaints, the purpose of which is a form of psychological blackmail. The passive individual's basic intent, usually unconscious unless psychotherapy intervenes with explanations, is to prevail on the cast of characters who constitute the here-and-now world to make up for the passive person's deep deprivations. Mates, offspring, friends, teachers, and employers, all are exposed to the mentioned pressures of sadness, helplessness and quiescent resentment. The hope of the passive person is that the exhibited suffering will evoke in them lasting concern. Deprived in the past in various ways, and still occupied with damage suffered long ago, the passive person tries to extract unlimited indemnity for the mistakes made by parents, caretakers, and later substitutes.

If parents, in the sensitive period of infancy and childhood, are too self-centered and insensitive to the child's varying needs to provide the proper kind of caretaking, the child frequently displays apathy and inertness. Although he is not necessarily as isolated as the autistic child who lives on an inaccessible island, a barrier is nevertheless gradually erected. Its original purpose is to make the nonfulfillment of needs less painful by fending off arousals precipitated by the exciting world, both external and internal. Where such barrier passivity is formed and later perpetuated by the adult, contradictory desires vie one with the other. Deep, though unadmitted, nascent desires for nurture clash with urges to slap any extended hand offering compassion and help.

If, on the other hand, the parental offense that is responsible for ensuing passivity in the offspring is overindulgence and a reluctance to unloose the symbiotic tie, then the inert mind seeks different achievements. The residual passivity in the adult expresses a reluctance to let go of the effortless life. Wishes to lean, to get, and to be protected — not through self-effort but through "foreign aid" —

continue. In this case, the condition is one of plea passivity.* The childlike and protection-seeking adult looks on the disappearance of passive childhood and on the call for effort as an affront. Compensation is demanded through implicit pleas and appeals to make up for the paradise lost.

Not infrequently, barrier passivity and plea passivity are both found in one person. The emerging character profile reveals alternations between insatiable demands for indulgence and stubborn refusals of friendly gestures that are offered. Indemnification is either not enough or not worth having at all.

Noah was the eldest son of an adoring mother who expected her boy to become a celebrity. She deprived her five younger children of the impoverished family's limited food supplies, and of her attention, to channel all treats to her firstborn. Spoiled, self-indulgent, and expecting the world to go his way, the adult Noah could never get enough comfort. He amassed considerable wealth and equipped his home with luxuries, especially precious imported carpets and lush fabrics that he loved to touch. Reluctant to spend energy, especially on physical movement, Noah was driven to and from work in a limousine. He watched his weight and looks carefully to maintain a beguiling appearance and thus to solicit adoration and acclaim from the advertising world in which he worked. Though this patient had much success and comfort, his mouth watered for more. Frequently in dreams he stroked an Aladdin's lamp to provide him with treasure. As psychotherapy showed, he was still submerged in demands that fate itself make up for the paradise of his youth from which he felt prematurely expelled.

Yet there was another side to this patient. As a young boy he suffered sharp ridicule from his rough father who was jealous of the love the mother squandered on the puny boy. The father called his son a sissy and refused to take him along when he made his (unsuccessful) sales rounds.

In his adult life, Noah underwent several metamorphoses. Responding to the appetite for a comfortable life his mother

---

* See chapter 8, "The Passive Stalemate."

had whetted, he demanded extra solicitude from his wife, sons, and employees. But Noah also was frequently immobile and impenetrable. If his carefully groomed appearance was praised or his creative work acknowledged, he pooh-poohed the much-desired compliments. None of the praise that he carefully secured sufficed to make up for his father's erstwhile derision. Despite his business successes, this passive man almost dragged himself to work. The ultimate feeling in the late evening when Noah sat in his big living-room chair was exhaustion, fatigue, and vague despair. No praise gained made up for the good old times when his mother had spoiled him; none was strong enough to penetrate the thick wall of indifference that Noah built around himself as a shield against his father's contempt.

Passive people are accusers, no matter how sluggish their words. They are among the most demanding of personalities, insisting that the present-day environment compensate them not only for old pangs, but for the lacks of the moment as well. Passive people, having withdrawn too early and too often into inertness, are strangers to reality. The seemingly innocuous, undemanding, inactive nondoer is unreasonable and greedy. Absent from his nature is awareness that frustrations, both past and present, are inherent in the exposure to the flux of life and have to be borne with intestinal fortitude and imagination. To avoid having to take a good look at realities and the inevitability of disappointments, passivity is used as the means by which a pleasing fantasy picture is maintained and indeed clutched close. Holding on to passivity, the nondoer, indulging his apathy, rebels, accuses, and points the finger at present-day figures, no matter how close, who have the audacity to deny him things.

The search for new love objects, which looks at times deceptively active, has roots in passivity. The hope and intention is again to obtain indemnification. If a beloved one has had the audacity to commit a negligence or an offense, a substitute person is sought, often in fantasy and at times in reality.

Jerry was the indulged only son of a childlike mother who divorced her first husband and feared her second mate. He felt that the world owed him atonement if he could not have everything his way. He was not willing to face up to the idea that his cozy childhood bed could ever be rumpled. Defeat and disappointment in work or love led to an immediate but ill-conceived search for restitution. If this Don Juan was disappointed by one girl in the afternoon he would make a date with another young lady at night. And if the second one expressed too little admiration or gave Jerry too much trouble, he left for a weekend with a third girl to dispel any lingering disappointment. Yet in psychotherapy it became clear that the sequence of girls resembled a string of paper dolls, for all were faceless and seemed alike. As a result of such passive acceptance of any female who came along, provided she promised to heal a wound, Jerry became engaged to a young woman utterly unsuitable as a marital partner.

Those who eventually become pronouncedly passive have had in childhood either too much uninterrupted human company or else too little. In either case an essential human faculty or process remains underdeveloped. *Overprotected* children who are not separated periodically from the parents know little about the need for building up an internal image or a set of representations that reflects the beloved person in his or her absence. Rarely alone, because of parental overindulgence, they do not come to realize that in solitude comfort is found by reviving living memories and internal representations of the beloved object.[2]

For different reasons but with similar results, the *rejected* young organism also fails to form inner images of beloved persons and to learn to revive them when alone. If there are no internal representatives of a beloved person, separation is borne through the aid of apathy. The absence of a clearly formed image of a treasured person makes possible the shift, in either fantasy or reality, from one person to another, each of whom is expected to hold out promise of gratification. Attachments fluctuate.

The key psychoanalytic concept of fixation suggests that when childhood needs remained unfulfilled and basic childhood rights were snatched away, the individual continues demands for indemnification. The deprived who are fixated will not relinquish claims that were frustrated or only partially fulfilled. Rather than move beyond the mental and emotional territory from which they were expelled as children, they hover near the lost land, reiterating their rights to access, regardless of the passage of time. Innocent as passivity looks, it is a form of blackmail. It reinforces both pleas and barriers.

Silent Punishment Through
Passive Resistance and Sulking

Passive people make angry but soft-spoken antagonists. The resentment they carry inside is pervasive and tenacious and calls for the punishment of others through the dogged use of silent weapons. Common clinical labels suggest the existence of intricate connections between passivity and hostility. Leaning, dependent, inert, and apathetic patients are described as "passive hostile," "passive aggressive," and "hostile dependent." The inherent anger, rarely revealed in full force except during occasional unplanned ruptures, is aimed indiscriminately in many external directions, nor is the self spared. The punishments dealt out by the seemingly unthreatening passive plaintiffs are frequently disguised so subtly that one's chief clue to their existence is the observation of one's own counterreactions. It is only by catching glimpses of the irritations and anxieties that such personalities arouse that vague proof is provided of the injury or offense being perpetrated.

Anyone who stays confined within the straitjacket of the inactive life resents the early sources of the passive problem, the present company, and the whole world. Despite constant self-punishment, the passive person's reservoir of hidden rage is so vast that constant though silent punishment and reproof are meted out to everyone around. Like most disturbed persons, the sufferers from inertia blame others, especially the people who are closest. They take their environment to task for the shackles of stagnation that encumber them — shackles that they do not want, but do not try (or do not know how to try) to shed: work blocks, social paralysis, sexual inadequacy, and fruitless thought expeditions. All these failures, which are suffered because of self-restriction, are laid with sullen anger at the door of the external world.

The punitive weapons inherent in self-restricting behavior are passive resistance and the silent strike. Behind the facade of bland, though often ominously charged, quiescence, veritable vendettas are carried out through "say nothing, do nothing, feel nothing" behavior that refuses participation and communication. Passivity in itself is a punitive method that has a pernicious effect and outlasts the patience of well-intentioned people. Perhaps in Gandhi's India it occasionally had a liberating and constructive effect but in relations with family and friends and in small group settings the tactics of passive resistance are most deleterious.

The distress that passive resistance and the silent strike evoke are best summed up as a wholesale arrestation in the victims: the emotional atmosphere is rendered heavy, dense, and unpleasant; the flow of banter and humor is halted; proposals, plans, and initiative are brought to a standstill, partly because the emphatic non-participation of the passive resister defeats teamwork and partly because the other members, through identification, fall in with the halting footsteps of the resister and lose their level of energy and involvement. The brick-wall quality of passive resistance gives those who approach with warmth and friendly propositions a bump on the head. Getting nowhere with their invitations, they eventually feel ineffective and useless.

On a ward in a community mental health center that opened its doors to patients punctually at 9:00 A.M., the patient, Arthur, arrived regularly at 10:45, boycotting the institute's schedule with his well-timed tardiness. Dragging his feet as he entered, bent on resistance, he sat himself in a corner and refused all invitations from staff and patients to participate in the ongoing activities. Yet should any ward project planned to last a certain time be terminated even a minute early, Arthur held up his watch, staring accusingly at the responsible member of the staff. Silent, reproachful, and contemptuous, he suggested — nay, emphasized — that the patient population, including himself, was being neglected.

Arthur's regular refusal of invitations to participate in activities, his sullen standoffishness, and his accusatory clock-watching had a perturbing effect upon the staff. They felt angry, guilty that their ire was aroused, ineffective on their

job, and increasingly paralyzed. Arthur's passive resistance
achieved its purpose of punishing.

Gradually the staff, aided by consultations, comprehended
how their continued invitations to participate in the ward
program merely increased Arthur's passive torpor and its
punitive intent. Indeed, the staff realized that they had allowed
themselves to become stooges who, by their repeated encouragements, merely furnished the patient with ever new opportunities for inflicting punishment through passive resistance.
When such understanding was acted upon and staff invitations
ceased to be forthcoming (though the atmosphere remained
polite), the first round was won. The next step of progress
came when Arthur was told laughingly that he had better
take out his anger on a game of darts or on a punching bag.
When it was clearly spelled out that everyone was on to the
angry and punitive engagement Arthur aimed for and that
no one minded any longer, the recalcitrant patient changed
within the short span of two weeks. His "conversion" came
just in the nick of time, for plans had been made to transfer
him to a stricter, more confining institution should the mental
health center setting continue to prove ineffective.

The retaliatory intentions of those whose passivity aims at
inflicting pain on others through resistance and the silent strike
can be diagnosed if a few rather faint clues are heeded. People
who use passive behavior as a way to get even follow up the
rejections, silences, and displays of indifference that they practice
with *emphatic* withdrawals to niches, sidelines, and corners which,
though somewhat remote, remain well within view. The furtive and
sidelong glances directed toward those who are meant to be chas-
tised are a subtle but reliable clue. The visual inquirer wants to
establish whether the type of punishment he inflicts "takes" and
whether the supposed victims are hurt, discouraged, and deflated.

Another clue that helps to detect retaliatory though silent rejection is feelings — or rather, gut sensations. The innocent victims
of passive resistance and the silent strike become irritated, fretful,
restive, even queasy. These reactions should serve as an indication
that trouble is afoot. The signs point to the underground workings
of an interloper who smuggles in hostility and blocks emotional

(and even physical) movement so as to bring the optimism and initiative of others grinding to a halt.

Another form of punishment through passivity is sulking, which in effect castigates both the self and the environment. Sluggish individuals slide into sulks to get even because they were interrupted, given too little attention and admiration, or underrated altogether. Sulkers are quite frequently unaware of their tightly closed lips, moody facial expressions, and sullen behavior. In fact, some heavy sulkers who undergo psychotherapeutic treatment are rather relieved to discover the existence and purpose of the taciturnity that shuts them off from reciprocal communication with others.

The silent, punitive, and often unconscious sulk has several conflicting aims. One is to withhold thoughts and actions of supposedly high caliber so as to deprive the ungrateful environment of unique contributions. Yet almost invariably the passive sulker has yet another contrasting feeling. It is the fearful expectation that were he to take a chance and open up in front of the crowd, his pronouncements would prove to be but meager fare. Hence the sullen passivity has a double function: to deprive the unappreciative world of important enlightenments and, at the same time, to hide ineffectiveness in an aura of promising mystery.

> Emery, the silent member of a therapy group, overrated his brilliance and indulged various unwarranted ambitions. He told the therapist that he could narrate every detail of medieval history and could remember all important historical dates. Whenever this obsessive-compulsive patient began one of his frequent, extensive, yet halting recitations of some past event, the rest of the group tended to become restive and to interrupt. Noting that Emery remained silent for the remnant of each session at which he had been stopped, the therapist inquired whether the silence was a form of sulking. Emery, a patient with much insight, agreed thoughtfully and remarked humorously: "I really want to deprive the others of singular facts I know through my unusual news sources and my uncanny memory. I am a medieval knight who holds up the shield of powerful knowledge. And I want no questions asked."

To give up the practice of passive resistance and sulking makes the passive person feel fragile, enfeebled, and embarrassed. Although the disadvantages are many, autonomous silence, impenetrable passive resistance, and the stubborn "say nothing, do nothing" strike supply a rocklike feeling. They shore up the loose and fluctuating ego boundaries of the people who are habitual leaners and clingers (addicts of plea passivity). And they add strength to the seemingly inflexible yet actually brittle self-containment of those passive people who wrap inertness around themselves like a protective cocoon (the addicts of barrier passivity).

When the silent plaintiff abstains from his punitive battles and warms up to human contact, he at first feels anxious and denuded of a helpful defense. The transition from punitive silence to frank communication is as difficult as that from hate to love. In both instances, the widening ego boundaries and ensuing softening sensations create some regret that the impervious arsenal of autonomy is lost.

> The accomplished musician Lee was often sent by her agent on interviews for prospective engagements that she clearly did not desire and had no intention of accepting should concrete offers materialize. Nevertheless, she almost invariably went to what she called "fool auditions." Equally invariably she turned taciturn, and the few words she uttered were purposely lacking the information requested of her. When the therapist asked whether her conduct had the purpose of making the interviews, the agent who worked for her, and the concert managers who interviewed her ridiculous, she smiled impishly. She was pleased both at her powers of non-communication and at the discovery that she did indeed possess her own secret weapons.
>
> When she finally broke her silence in the therapy session she covered her blushing face with both hands, and eventually a few tears ran down her cheeks. She then stamped her foot and said, "Damn you for weakening my barricades."

Resistant, silent, passive, and sulking patients who learn that their nonparticipation is understood as a form of punishment and strike often feel pleased. It gratifies them that their powers of retaliation and opposition are acknowledged. At least, so they feel, the force and purpose of their negative existence, once understood by others, bolsters their feeble identities. It is therefore always important to help silent and sulking patients whose isolating cocoons are being broken to discover and develop latent talents of a constructive kind to be substituted for lost power.

Passivity as a Psychological Alibi

Quiescence, inertness, and a withdrawn existence provide a hideaway for people who wish to lay low, to remain inconspicuous so as to conceal their psychological inadequacies. In this sense, one of the uses of passivity is to provide a shelter toward which to retreat whenever demands are made for ego skills that the psyche does not possess and whose absence the individual wishes to hide. The very people who seek the shelter of a passive life are exactly those whose character, and particularly whose ego, was paralyzed, restricted, truncated, and warped because of early childhood passivity. The lacks and frailties of the ego that were caused by childhood passivity are later covered up through a passive style of adult life. Many people with weak, vacuous, and warped egos hide out like wallflowers. They stay on the sidelines of action and avoid competition and participation lest they be found clumsy and ineligible should they enter the action. The idea is to stay out of the running by choice, lest exposure reveal psychological ineptness and backwardness. At times, the shortcomings that retreat and passivity are meant to hide are merely imagined. Yet in many instances they do exist, and since most underdeveloped or warped ego functions can be corrected (for instance, through the learning experiences of psychotherapy), it is self-destructive to hide behind the shielding walls of passivity.

The poorly developed or faulty faculties that people try to hide by doing and saying nothing that might give them away are usually basic: thinking, life's psychological steering device, remains unclear, aimless, or rigid if passivity has its source in childhood.* Perceptiveness, similarly, often remains unprecise and lacks daring. And such an important ego skill as being able to carry on lively, observant, and understanding human relations is disturbed by excessive

* See chapter 7, "Active Thinking."

self-absorption * if in infancy and childhood passivity had an upper hand. If the child's free-roaming exploration of the world was curtailed, then his command of mobility is poor.

> Frederick was a strikingly handsome and well-built man, endowed with such physical advantages as long limbs and a slender body. This patient was the son of an early-widowed mother who adored her boy and babied him. When he was old enough to run about, climb trees, explore streets and fields, suffering the usual childhood knocks and little injuries, he was restricted to the home and watched carefully. He became a physically, and also mentally, timid young man whose whole body was clumsy and poorly coordinated. He moved about as slowly as an old man, was a flop at sports, and was a poor dancer. When Frederick's friends invited him to play tennis or join them on the ski slopes, he excused himself by pleading fatigue or asked to be exempted on account of an old leg injury (which he might have incurred unconsciously so as to have a reason to stay inactive at home). His various alibis prevented exposure of his body awkwardness, but also deprived him of improvement through practice and new learning.

Alibi passivity perpetuates itself and spreads like a weed. At first employed to hide ego deficits, the hiding habits prevent correction of whatever skills are feeble or warped. And eventually other skills, too, are no longer properly practiced. People who stay away from four or five social or business occasions out of fear that their lacks might be showing end by avoiding many other situations and tests. And some of these people in fact become recluses.

Remaining incommunicado to hide their ineptness, people do spare their self-esteem. But the narcissistic injuries are avoided only for a short while. Since it is only through exposure, through admission of defeat and learning, that skills are enhanced, the sheltering isolation and passivity that preclude new learning inevitably lower self-esteem in the long run. Self-esteem is the inner measure of personal competence, and this competence grows through admission of defeat, provided such admission is followed up by practice and learning.

* See chapter 5, "Active Loving," and chapter 6, "Creative Human Contacts: The Case of Marriage."

One of the most reliable means of strengthening the ego and enriching its faculties — for instance, thinking, planning, observing, and relating — is psychotherapy. Often patients who have just begun treatment are reluctant to take a good look at their ego flaws. Not able to foresee as yet how they can acquire better tools for living rather than the ones they have and are used to, they hold on stubbornly to their old methods. It is, therefore, important to make possible, within the therapeutic setting, small ego gains whose presence and force can be experienced immediately. For example, a moderately advanced patient with meager abilities in argument can find out convincingly, if he is encouraged to test and question what the therapist says, how to set up more fruitful and incisive discussions. With every ego gain accomplished, the flight into hideaway passivity is slowed down.

Other Advantages of Passivity

Like masochism, which employs the technique of self-defeat to minimize personal competence lest it antagonize needed protectors[3,4] or grow into ominous proportions,[5] passivity serves the purpose of minimizing certain personal forces. Behind every apparent milksop and every seemingly impassive starer into space there lives a person with grandiose ideas. The passive person, filled with low self-esteem, compensates by harboring wishes and intentions to dominate his protectors or oppressors and indeed to destroy them. Often the omnipotent wishes are so great that the fantasy aim is to blow up the whole universe.

Other secret attitudes hidden behind the apparently innocuous passive front (though intuitive people can sense ominous undertones) are aggression, hostility, and even murderous intent. Proof of the aggressive undercurrents that run below the surface of meekness are actual murders. Many an incarcerated man who lives out his life behind bars because he has killed used to be known in his neighborhood as a quiet and harmless person.[6] And to a lesser degree we not unfrequently witness the explosive anger that bursts like an atom blast from a person who usually conducts himself with circumspect and silent composure.

Passivity, then, often has the purpose of covering up impulses of grandiosity and tendencies toward violence, as well as less pronounced aggression. Suppressing feelings of omnipotence and rage, urges that instill anxiety since they bode ill for others and in the final event for the self, passivity is a hideaway not only for failure, but also for explosive mental weapons.

By remaining passive a person who feels excessively deprived and whose facilities for relating to others are too limited to express or elicit love can stock the inner storehouse with solicitude, attention, and love reserved for the self. To supply itself with love and consideration that the individual cannot manage to obtain from external sources, the passive self indulges the self. Masturbation, especially when every semblance of a relationship to another is omitted and no fantasies accompany the autoerotic activity, is an example of extreme passive self-giving.

Treatment Implications

Clinical results show that modern treatment approaches to masochism, which is a widespread and near-universal symptom complex, are effective. Among the factors that account for the positive results that have been observed and confirmed, a big role is played by the use of a double-pronged approach: (1) The causes of masochism in the individual past of the patient are clearly explored but not exclusively emphasized; and (2) the immediate, up-to-date gains the patient gets from the suffering, self-pity, and dwelling on catastrophe are studied in detail.

As for the causes in the individual's past, we find invariably that the bent toward masochism was first started by rage when dependency needs were not fulfilled, by grandiose omnipotent expectations that were not put into perspective, by submission for the sake of placation, and by self-paralysis lest childhood figures who were close be attacked and injured. As to the present bittersweet gains that the adult masochistic patient reaps, we find a whole variety. Masochistic behavior allows the sufferer to punish others with his complaints and recriminations; it allows him to ventilate rage; [7] it permits the perpetuation of delicious self-pity; it protects the individual against attack; and it protects him against sudden trauma through perpetual preparedness for it.[8]

Such a bifocal approach, which considers, at one pole, the genesis of the specific emotional disturbance and, at the other pole, continuing secondary gains that the perpetuation of the symptom complex guarantees, has decisive advantages. The disturbance is understood globally, and its dynamic effect, partly profitable but primarily pernicious, is comprehended vividly. Cures are frequently both fairly quick and lasting when the bifocal approach is applied systematically.

For the treatment of passivity, such a bifocal concentration is strongly recommended. The genesis and persistence of passivity have been delineated variously in preceding chapters. Major benefits of passive conduct have been described in this chapter. The hope is that by tracing and stressing the specific rewards of passivity — all of them pathological in the long run — bifocal treatment will be useful and practicable. The patient always needs to discover how heavy the price is which he pays for what he considers the advantages of passivity. Of course, he needs equally to find out precisely what steps he can take to escape the paralyzing confinement of passivity and to assure that its enveloping threat will recede.

10. Escape From
Semantic Jungles

Some measure of self-deception is a human necessity. We need to blind ourselves to some stark truths of the primitive lusts within the psyche, as well as to some external dangers, lest we be overwhelmed, paralyzed, and discouraged. These necessary falsifications assume different forms. One category of camouflage, the defenses, has been much discussed and is of prime concern to the psychotherapist. We know only too well, for instance, that even healthy and forceful personalities must wipe from their consciousness some of the disturbing aspects of life by the use of the customarily unconscious defenses such as denial, repression, and projection, to mention but a few. To these therapists are highly attuned. But another category is frequently shrugged off too lightly.

Simplifications of thought and expression, in one form or another, belong to this category of protective devices. We resort to a variety of simplifying measures to ensure the safe feeling that the complexity of the world can be comprehended. It is through certain tricks of thought and language that the multiple currents of the mind, often at cross purposes, and the infinity of outside happenings are brought within the practicable scope of mental vision. In this chapter it is these rather neglected linguistic-semantic simplification devices that will be scrutinized.

Such simplifications as generalizations, stereotypes, and common maxims serve as an umbrella under which one can bunch varieties of events that have certain resemblances. If the similarities are genuine and basic, then the simplifications serve a legitimate purpose.

"Bad" and "good", for example, are concepts that permit extraordinary simplifications. So vast indeed is the range of phenomena that can be covered by these words that the effect can be either the creation of order or the injection of prejudice and confusion. To take one pole of the dichotomy, if a wife calls her husband good, and the implication is that he is responsible, kind, and considerate of friends and colleagues, the conceptual adjective does save time and effort, at least on occasions. But if the term good is meant to suggest that the mate gives in to every whim, is subservient to others, and depletes the family's financial resources through lavish gifts that cannot reasonably be afforded, then the conceptual abbreviation is likely to be confusing.

What distinguishes the healthier people from the more disturbed is the difference in the quantity and quality of semantic devices. If the world is simplified too much and too idiosyncratically by the use of generalizations, clichés, maxims, and proverbs, we are being penny-wise and pound-foolish. A too large price is paid, in such instances, for the supposed mental economy and the functions it is supposed to serve. Thinking becomes static, and misunderstanding is aided by semantic imprecision.

Language, that unique human invention and tool,[1] becomes a ruin serving only mental blindness and confusion. The individualistic explorations that are among the highest achievements of the mind are either nipped in the bud or gradually crippled. With this destruction there also wanes the subjectively exhilarating experience that accompanies the search for facts and connections.

When generalizations are undertaken with careless abandon and for the purpose of denying essential distinctions so that phenomena as divergent as birds of different species are thrown into one pigeonhole, a clouded view of the world results. Clichés, too, if they are used with inattention, become the linguistic vehicles for passive indiscriminateness. They perpetuate the effortless thinking that was earlier described as one of the pitfalls of searching thought. As to commonplace sayings, popular maxims, or proverbs, their effect is harmful in a nonrigidified society, such as the Western one, that draws on a conflux of individualistic, imaginative, and courageous ideas and convictions to keep affairs running and to gratify its citizenry through self-expression and productivity. The situation is quite different in primitive societies that rely on ritual passed on from person to person through commonly shared proverbs and popular sayings.

Thus, while a certain amount of automaticity is necessary and, indeed, protects real creativity — after all, we cannot every morning set up entirely new expressions for that day — flexible, active, and individualized thinking must balance or, preferably, outweigh routine. Brain-damaged persons who lose their mental flexibility survive through automaticity. Organically healthy personalities fail to develop or else lose the precious qualities of pliancy, observation, and expression through disturbances in development. Especially, those disturbed people in whom narcissism, dependency, and passivity were fostered through circumstances not of their own making tend to give up the human talent of discriminatory linguistic expression. To avoid pain and to save energy, they avoid the effort of investigation by hiding behind easy generalizations, clichés, and maxims. In the treatment of the passive patient the therapist does well to be on his toes to spot these protective strategies, through which many patients avoid familiarity with the very ground upon which they tread.

> Bruce, whose self-indulgent and ambitious parents overprotected their son, not by excessive personal attention but by buying him off with worldly goods and the services of a team of obedient servants, was always late. He was never on time for business meetings, therapeutic sessions, or even his own fifth wedding anniversary, to be celebrated in the midst of the family.
>
> When Bruce was asked to talk about his lateness, he replied indolently, "Why can't I be late like everybody else?" This instant generalization was meant to get him off the hook of self-inquiry and to leave him to pursue his self-indulgent tardiness without any kind of intrusion. Yet when this and other semantic devices that Bruce used to the point of absurdity were countered with a smile or a question, a first step was taken toward rendering his passivity questionable, and eventually moving it out of the way to make room for activeness.

The Study of Language Belongs in Psychotherapy

Once mannerisms of speech — which signify habits of thought — are considered an integral part of the patient's production in treatment,[2] then false generalizations, the excessive use of clichés and adages, and rationalizations help to refine the accuracy of diagnosis. Moreover, psychotherapy itself is aided. Two principles that have been stressed throughout this book in the treatment of inertia must be followed: (1) to understand and dissolve the conflicts that are the fuel of deadlock, and (2) to take the route from the specific to the general and to encourage, explain, teach, and practice in the treatment situation active mental activities, at the same time identifying (but otherwise responding as little as possible to) everything that is false and sluggish.

It has been pointed out in these chapters that the weak, fearful, and inert become strong and independent if they do what is difficult. The confrontation with emotional and mental challenge, the plunge into the turbulent waters of inner life, the pursuit of lively and discriminating language are great fortifiers, provided they are tried under the guidance of a therapist who can gauge just when the patient can afford to hop from the diving board into the water — and how deep the water should be. If a patient who has been too anxious to be able to look at his unconventional impulses and thoughts or at surrounding dangers is encouraged to clear away the verbiage and clichés that helped him hide, his strength and creativity are increased. Every time he is dissuaded from covering up a specific and unique truth with the cloak of an unspecific and meaningless generalization, he gains independence. All avoidance of a verbal cloak develops the capacity to find pathways into the mind, to make contact with the emotions, and to look straighter at life.

Despite Freud's clear warnings, it is probably too often assumed that the disturbances most deeply removed from consciousness are the most harmful and hence most worthy of the patient's and therapist's prime attention. But semantic falsehoods, inaccuracies, and strategies, while more accessible to consciousness than, say, the mechanism of projection and the wishes it disguises, are important therapeutic stuff. It pays to take heed of them, to understand their purposes, and to bring them to the patient's attention. Deeply disturbed people strew self-destructive semantic strategies around willy-nilly like a wind that scatters the dry leaves of fall.

Patients, usually resisting therapeutic attempts to discourage defenses that throw a haze over reality, are particularly nimble when it comes to preserving semantic and logical strategies. So fast is their verbal footwork — which is often unknown to the patient though it is not necessarily lodged deeply in the unconscious — that it takes much watchfulness on the part of everyone to stay a step ahead. It takes some study of language and meaning to detect where verbal confusions are brought to bear on sectors of life that patients wish to shield from examination. The fact that, apart from some recent isolated attempts,[3,4] relatively little attention has been paid to communication in therapy is a handicap. The therapist who alerts the patient to his "lazy phrases" and the parallel logical confusions faces another pitfall. In an understandable desire to hang on to the long-effective and protective tactics of phrase-pathology, the patient jumps quickly to the next tack, and, of course, it is important that the therapist not go along with the race. When a person is made aware that he has just used a particular semantic strategy — say, a false generalization — he is as quick as a merchant in an oriental bazaar to haul new semantic merchandise from under the counter. Incidents are quoted, often from poorly known areas of experience, to prove that the pronouncement made is indeed correct. It helps to repeat the original refutation of the generalization and to promise that future semantic confusions will be pointed out so as to sharpen the good mind that is indulging itself in expeditions that are both fruitless and blinding. The therapist thus focuses on the emotion that prompted the protective generalization, and emphasizes that the real truth is far more interesting than the vaporous and spreading haze.

Evan explained at length how he had stopped working on a paper during the weekend because "all writers take breaks when they run dry." The generalization was a notification that the patient was in trouble. He was about to make denser the fog that already surrounded him. Not only was this man, whose scientific papers were excellent only when he faced every fact, unmercifully strewing obstacles into his already narrow path, but he was also covering up through the stratagem of generalization important feelings that he felt too weak to face. In this instance the therapist did not go into the truth, often discussed between Evan and himself, that successful scientists and writers set to work regularly no matter how they feel. Instead he asked the patient to help him understand some of the objectives of the paper in question. Evan mentioned immediately that he doubted the originality of his ideas and then went on to examine his gigantic ambition to make only such contributions as would startle the conference at which he was scheduled to speak.

Classical ego defenses such as denial and projection, if they are maintained for long, initiate far-reaching self-alterations. Semantic distortions and simplifications, on the other hand, do not so much change the self as they change the world around, so as to permit the continuation of self-indulgence and passivity. To choke out the weedlike growth of counterfeit communication — worn-out concepts, words, and rationalizations — the efforts of scientists and artists can be given an ever-expanding hearing and viewing. The vocation of scientists and artists is to break through futile and frozen thought. They are the minters of new semantic currency. They do for society what the therapist so far does primarily for the single person. Their work might create anxiety, as does everything that is truly new, but the final outcome is strength and truthful communication.

False Generalizations Obscure Reality

Generalizations not based on accurate observations represent serious infractions of reality. They stem from pathology and in turn reinforce psychological disturbance. What makes them fairly palatable and often immune to criticism is that they resemble inductive reasoning, which we respect as valid and useful. Yet inductive reasoning calls for the patience and skill of scientifically inclined observers, while false generalizations come out of the do-it-yourself kit of lackadaisical amateurs.

Careful observers study specific details and connections under controlled circumstances until they have collected a bagful of observations. If they find, for instance, that most people who eat clams dug in specific waters contract hepatitis, they conclude that seafood from these quarters, delightful though it tastes, may be infected. But the amateur observer, going for indulgence and conservation of effort, bases a thesis he advances on two or three instances, and often nonidentical ones at that. His samples are too small to permit valid inductions. Moreover, as we invariably find, certain emotions and needs prompt premature generalizations. Quite possibly, had we less respect for inductive reasoning, we would object faster to such neurotic and unwarranted findings.

Thought and language develop gradually in the human being, with the early phase characterized by a kind of clinging to the "old-fashioned way." Everything novel that is discovered and named is fitted into a preexisting mold. This kind of equalizing has been termed *accommodation.*[5] The newcomer to thought and language — namely, the child — gets the hang of something new by finding a similarity to something familiar. Only later does his mind allow itself to be startled, so to speak, and welcome the new discoveries he has stumbled on, new ideas, and new explanations.

People who guard their inertness proceed like the young. As they come across new and unprecedented objects, people, events, and ideas, they hesitate to recognize that a discovery has been made. What prevails is the primitive and passive mode of thought in which nothing comes as a surprise. No novelty or discovery calls for revision of old notions, attitudes, language, and thought. Stasis prevails. One event is likened to another. This mode of expression is a tributary, feeding into the swamp of false generalization. Events, partially or totally different, are unobservantly equated.

> Beverly was helped by both therapy and a stirring love relationship to exchange her passive and melodramatic ways for alacrity. After a fight with her accusatory lover she was, as often before, apologetic, depressed, and blank. The first dejected words she uttered were, "Listen, dear, we've had these troubles before, and we'll have more." Suddenly Beverly stopped herself in the middle of this untruthful, glib, and, to herself, dull sentence. She found herself yelling at her lover: "I'm not circumscribed. I am not self-trapped and don't want to look on each day as a repetition of the previous one. So why do you keep asking me to monitor your moods?" Later the patient explained the significance of this breakthrough. She had become tired of regarding each quarrel as her offense. Uncertainty had been the wellspring of her old equations and generalizations, but now she was clear and excited about the new and

strange. Her lover's negligence, not her carelessness, was the issue this time, and what was more, she could invent settlements through means other than quarrels.

Generalizations abound so conspicuously in the speech of disturbed people that their presence is a fairly reliable indicator of pathology. They can be spotted by key words that are common introductions, little verbal beginnings that spearhead the coming generality. "All people have . . . ," "Nobody needs to . . . ," "It always happens that . . . ," these are some examples.

Key words and generalizations are partly meant to evoke and support the notion that certain events occur normally and inevitably in everyone's life, following natural laws about which nothing can be done and, therefore, not calling for responsible action. Distinctions are not needed, individual choices become unnecessary, and initiative, a skill that is almost unknown to the passive person (though it can be acquired through therapy), can be dispensed with. A fatalistic, passive, inert, dependent orientation appears justified.

Quentin, a forty-year-old narcissistic and passive patient, was charming, strikingly handsome, and very talented, though his gifts lay dormant because of lack of initiative. Quentin's narcissism and passivity had many roots. His mother, a beautiful, childish, and wealthy woman who had married very young, had borne five children. She did not possess sufficient selflessness and independence to rear her offspring as autonomous individuals and especially overprotected Quentin, her oldest child. She did not send him to school or camp, but provided private instruction at home. She habitually caressed her son, even when he was well over seven. Above all, she remained unaware of her children's individual characteristics, needs, and distinct talents, and, indeed, usually confused their names. Naturally, Quentin had oral, symbiotic, and narcissistic tendencies as well as being oedipally attached. Owing to previous therapy he was well aware of his pathology, but was not able to institute significant changes.

One of the many difficulties the patient had to face was avoiding procrastination about his work. Anxious and self-critical, he took refuge in easy generalizations: "No one ever gets anything done on time" or "Every job that is any good takes long." These pet phrases had for him a near-magical effect.

Quentin seemed to be tolerant, placid, and eager to avoid friction. If he encountered injustices or if much-needed repairs on his decaying country home were left undone, he relied on a familiar backlog of generalities to spare him the anxiety of protest: "People want their peace." "I'm not going to push anybody." "Everyone hates an argument." Such easy-to-come-by generalities as these took this man quickly off the hook of action.

Quentin eventually married Claire, a firm, well-meaning woman. Recognizing her husband's dormant talents, she tried carefully to crank up his lagging initiative. In the home setting, unlike other places, Quentin's reactions were acrimonious, but even so, he still took refuge in generality: "You always pester me." "Women always nag." "Like all women you want trouble." "You never give me a chance." Such was the generalized invective with which Quentin, even in anger, preserved the passive status quo. But the assemblage of these phrases also clouded his view of his devoted wife.

Quentin's love of generality had a counterpart in his social and political philosophy. He was of a utopian persuasion and demanded that all people be given economic and social equality. The desire for this utopian state was clearly the outgrowth of narcissism, passivity, and dependency and not of a thoughtful sociological and economic analysis, which the patient did not attempt.

In Quentin's treatment, consistent investigation of his passive language proved effective. As his vague generalizations were examined, and as it was pointed out that they let him perceive life as a reassuring, uniform process without painful distinctions between individuals and without specific responsibilities, dents were made in the patient's passivity. Gradually Quentin recognized that he rendered all people equal not out of kindness, but out of the desire to obscure his own serious problem, which was by no means a universally shared affliction. Instead of continuing to humor his passivity and to regard it as a form of original sin which everyone shared, he discerned that he was responsible for his dependence and inertia. Deprived of reassuring phrases, the passivity and symbiotic condition became ego-alien and unacceptable, and resistance diminished greatly.

Impressions, expressions, and conclusions are valid and growth-promoting to the extent that they are individualized and unique. Active inquiry, images conjured up from the depth of individuality, and verbal connections that are not inherited but newly made are the soil in which living and life-giving language grows. Even physical activity that accompanies self-expression — for instance, the back-and-forth pacing that many people practice when they are intent on getting to the truth — tones up semantic practice through which, in turn, individuality and truth are reinforced.

The mind that produces and uses false generalities is frequently unequipped to make discriminations even in mental areas in which fear and conflict play almost no role. A general blunting and lack of discrimination creep in so that even food flavors, arrangements of living quarters, and widely divergent levels of theater and art works are not distinguished with adult discernment and sophisticated taste. Anything goes, as it were. The passive mind, having spared itself the chores of fact-finding, of making valid comparisons, of establishing meaningful personal categories and concepts into which events are carefully fitted, colors everything the same dull gray.

This result of passivity suggests interesting questions for research. Has a person with this kind of outlook and language not *learned* to distinguish different events sufficiently? Or, having learned to discriminate, does he *abstain* from using existing capacities out of fear — fear, for example, that discrimination will eventually throw too much light on dangers and call for underdeveloped personal skills?

In Western society, one of the primary aims of psychotherapy is to assist the process of individuation. We make the explicit assumption that in becoming aware of individual needs, assets, and liabilities, and in balancing and developing them, and in creating harmony with others, something that we call happiness is achieved. Psychotherapy is a method by which the patient discovers and evolves belatedly very personal — though, it is hoped, not selfish — thoughts, feelings, and modes of behavior.

Exemplifying this, the patient Quentin, for many reasons, lacked

individuation and protected the vacuum in himself. In psychotherapy Quentin became discriminating. He discarded *a priori* assumptions and descriptions of women and learned to use special and
exact words for occasions when his wife was, in fact, reflecting the
generosity and maturity he so admired when he married her. Modes
of evaluation and designation that had become highly generalized,
automatic, and sloppy became refined, specific, and discriminating.

Clichés and Proverbs:
A Sanctuary of Passivity

Clichés, proverbs, and popular sayings, persuasive and occasionally colorful as they seem, are produced partially by mental indo-
lence. They are well-suited to perpetuate lassitude of the mind and
language. They contain many obsolete facts and connections, vague
promises, and a bloated body of half-truth. The sluggish mass of
prefabricated sayings fills a paramount need of the passive consumer
in supplying him with supposedly philosophical underpinnings to
justify his unadmitted needs and to spare his torpid mind the effort
of accurate perception and articulation. As a passive patient, inclin-
ing toward anxiety, withdrawnness, and depression remarked, "I
don't like to do my own thinking and talking, especially when I get
home. I resent my wife when she pulls me into a 'think argument.'
Talking is waste. That's why I'm getting a color TV."

For almost every cliché, and especially for every proverb, there is
an equally trite opposing expression. Take, for example, two attempts
to explain what makes for attraction between lovers: "Birds of a
feather flock together" and "Opposites attract." The reason for the
sharp clash is the absence of truth in either saying. Like other simple
maxims, both sayings fail to reflect essential psychological complexity. Some people are attracted by similarity because chances are
good that frictions will be minimal when needs, tastes, and habits
are alike. Probably narcissistically inclined, such partners go for
someone "just like me." But those who get together on account of dis-
similarity hope that their mate's mental-emotional assets, differing
from their own, will make up for their own lacks and shortcomings. The undisclosed valid truth underlying both proverbs is
that disturbed people tend to base their selection of a mate on their

own neurotic needs. The very common clashes between proverbs within one culture underscore the fact that astuteness, deep understanding, and real wisdom are absent from these popular sayings.

A fascinating large-scale program recently undertaken to collect the proverbs of many cultural groups was launched in the hope of unearthing common denominators of human thought.[6] Undoubtedly this project will shed much light on the vast variety of human attempts, especially in earlier times, to discover and describe the essence of things, but it is not likely that this collection of the verbal molds of magical and primitive thought will shed light on the highest possible level of discovery and articulation.

Interestingly, people who are eager and frequent users of the prefabricated phrase often are wary of simplifications and distortions when expressed by others. Injected with the serum of the half-truth, they often have the capacity to resist the brainwashing techniques of others. But healthier persons, bent on the struggle to come to their own understandings and verbal expressions, often have less immunity. Only occasional users of semantic devices, they are readily taken in by them, at least for a while. Independent, healthy personalities and schizophrenics, contrary to various psychoanalytic assumptions,[7] are active speakers in the sense that they make up their very own and often carefully selected terminology. Remaining individualistic and shunning the commonplace, they seek truth in their fashion and search for the appropriate words. But as listeners, such people, and especially the healthy and independent individuals, are often too easy and fail to probe the verity of clichés and sayings with which they are inundated. Attentive listening is not the same as critical listening to verbal deceptions.

> Quentin's wife, Claire, though firm and independent in many ways, tended to accept too often the veritable barrage of generalities, clichés, and popular sayings with which her husband bombarded her. Entering couple therapy with her husband when the marriage became very rocky, Claire discovered that one of the chief reasons for her all too speedy acceptance of her mate's statements was her fear of the violent outbursts and abandonment threats of which this inwardly passive man was capable.
>
> Holding on to such insight and making concrete attempts to

liberate herself from the damaging brainwashings, Claire discovered and used several specific methods to hold her head above water when fear seized her. Quite often when she had an inkling — usually of a physiological kind — that Quentin was up to a verbal trick, Claire pulled herself up into a questioning attitude. She behaved somewhat like a rider who, glimpsing some hurdles, pulls his body up on the horse better to survey the obstruction from an elevated vantage point. This was an effort, but well worth the try since Claire began to prevent her mental collapse when showered with verbal confusion.

Another policy found and practiced successfully by this wife, who was too readily snowed under, was to look in directions other than those suggested by her husband when he became verbose and pulled out the clichés. In quality and nature the tactics used by Claire resembled the negativism of a three-year-old who says no to nearly everything because the strength to discover, express, and assert his own preferences is so weak.

One day, Quentin, planning to present a gift to a superior who had done him a favor, said, "Whoever gives fast gives double," Claire, about to agree and, indeed, to admire her husband's pretty little speech, turned it the other way. "Gifts that ripen slowly can be as good or better," she said firmly, convinced that the little summary she had just invented and phrased was valid.

The clichés and slogans that permit half-truth to prosper have permitted vaguely grandiose politicians and dictators to pursue dishonest goals. The half-truths, spread widely and irresponsibly, are initially accepted because of the relatively healthy trust of those who become believers. Putting their own motives second and possessing an ability for relatedness and for making sacrifices, the believers lack the immediate suspiciousness that would expose dissimulation. Good and loyal students, employees, mates, and groups have to study and practice watchful rationality in order to defend against the debased, overgeneral, and untrue language used by the exploiters, who are always cowards at heart.

Other clinical facts, many under study by the social psychologist, are responsible for the ready acceptance of the cliché and catchword, always deceptive in some measure. As a rule, the prefabricated statement either is widely known or, if it is new, gets immediate broad distribution. The impression is created that there exists a consensus. To go against consensual validation, as we know, creates anxiety. To withstand common opinion requires an extraordinary and nearly unique conviction as to the verity of the disputed truths one holds, a conviction which, quite often, geniuses or certain schizophrenics possess. Again, if there are to exist a greater readiness and ability to dispense with consensual validation, questioning and testing rationality will have to be taught to individuals and groups. It should be added that group psychotherapy is an excellent setting for this purpose.

Many proverbs and sayings are the heritage bequeathed by older generations. Personalities who have not completed the emancipation from parental authority — and this includes the majority of human beings — are not only reluctant to raise questions pertaining to the truth of tradition, but feel guilty when they do so. The massive opposition of the young generation of this time undoubtedly has, among many other purposes, the aim of lending strength and support to the anxious dissenter. The method, like that employed by the three-year-old, is to say no much of the time in the hope that widespread negativism will lend support to discriminate objections.

Life demands economy of time. If we want to move on to new developments and projects we must rely on certain automatisms in relationships, thinking, and language. Communication would be unbearably burdened by perpetual semantic investigations. Sometimes, therefore, it is with the intent of sparing energy and time that we let clichés and phrases slip by, allowing a person to use the word "freedom," for example when the term "license" would have been far more accurate. The way out of this trap is to beware particularly of those words and phrases that are most widely sanctioned and hence most likely to be passed off as authentic verbal currency. Also, since the body frequently responds more swiftly and reliably than does the mind, the tiny twinges that are felt when verbal twists conceal truth deserve careful attention. They are reliable clues that can be felt distinctly even though fleetingly when verbal boondoggling goes on.

Our own passivity is a quiet enemy within us, nurtured unwittingly, as a rule, in the hope that it will yield an easy life and permit us to express our grudges. But we have traced throughout these pages how passivity stifles truth, growth, expansion, and passion. It resembles a quiet plague infecting more and more life all the time. It damages communication and thinking. It weakens the human struggle against anxiety. It corrodes human contacts and makes a mere shadow out of love.

To live passionately, creatively, and in the spirit of a youthfulness that is not tied to chronological age, we have to learn to spot passivity and to go against it in the direction of activeness. Many emotional, mental, and body skills described here can be acquired to help us find the way toward new perceptions, live on higher energy levels, and reap the joys of a mind that is alive.

References

1. The Basic Need for Activeness

1. Erik H. Erikson, *Insight and Responsibility*. New York: Norton, 1964.
2. R. W. White "Competence and the Psychosexual Stages of Development," *Nebraska Symposium of Motivation*, ed. M. R. Jones. Lincoln: University of Nebraska Press, 1960.
3. Sandor Ferenczi, *The Development of Psychoanalysis*. New York: Dover, 1956.
4. Michael Balint, *Primary Love and Psychoanalytic Technique*. London: Hogarth Press, 1953.
5. W. H. Miller, F. Ratcliffe, and H. A. Hartline, "How Cells Receive Stimuli in Psychobiology," in *The Biological Basis of Behavior*. San Francisco: Freeman, 1967.
6. Harold Kelman, "Psychoanalysis: Some Philosophical and International Concerns," in *Modern Psychoanalysis*, ed. Judd Marmor. New York: Basic Books, 1968.
7. George R. Bach and Peter Wyden, *The Intimate Enemy: How to Fight Fair in Love and Marriage*. New York: Morrow, 1969.
8. Margaret S. Mahler, *On Human Symbiosis and the Vicissitudes of Individuation*. New York: International Universities Press, 1968.
9. A. H. Maslow, *Toward a Psychology of Being*. Princeton, Van Nostrand, 1962.
10. Charlotte Bühler, "The Social Behavior of the Child," in *Handbook of Child Psychology*. Worcester: Clark University Press, 1931.
11. Ernst Kris, *Psychoanalytic Explorations in Art*. New York: International Universities Press, 1952.
12. Edrita Fried, "Ego Functions and Techniques of Ego Strengthening," *American Journal of Psychotherapy* 9 (1955).
13. Sandor Rado, "The Psychic Effects of Intoxicants," *International Journal of Psychoanalysis* 7 (1926).
14. Otto Fenichel, "Early Stages of Ego Development," in *The Collected Papers of Otto Fenichel*, vol. 2. New York: Norton, 1954.
15. Willie Hoffer, "Psychoanalytic Comments on the Psychology and Psycho-

therapy of Depression," in *Depression,* ed. E. B. Davies. Cambridge: Cambridge University Press, 1964.

16. B. Berliner, "On Some Psychodynamics of Masochism," *Psychoanalytic Quarterly* 16 (1947).

17. Esther Menaker, "Masochism: A Defense Reaction of the Ego," *Psychoanalytic Quarterly* 22 (1953).

18. Frieda Fromm Reichmann, *Psychoanalysis and Psychotherapy.* Chicago: University of Chicago Press, 1959.

19. Hyman Spotnitz, "Techniques for the Resolution of the Narcissistic Defense," in *Psychoanalytic Techniques,* ed. Benjamin B. Wolman. New York: Basic Books, 1967.

20. H. Hartmann, E. Kris, and R. Loewenstein, "Comments on the Formation of Psychic Structure," in *The Psychoanalytic Study of the Child,* vol. 2. New York: International Press, 1946.

21. Mahler, *On Human Symbiosis.*

22. J.-P. Sartre, *Being and Nothingness.* New York: Citadel Press, 1965.

23. Martin Heidegger, *Introduction to Metaphysics.* New York: Doubleday, 1961.

24. Edrita Fried, "Combined Group and Individual Psychotherapy With Passive-Narcissistic Patients," *International Journal of Group Psychotherapy* 15 (1955).

2. Female Passivity: A Half-Truth

1. Sigmund Freud, "The Psychogenesis of a Case of Homosexuality in a Woman," *Standard Edition of the Complete Psychological Works of Sigmund Freud,* vol. 18. London: Hogarth Press, 1955.

2. Leo Salzman, "Psychology of the Female," *Archives of General Psychiatry* 17 (1967).

3. Edrita Fried, "The Fear of Loving," in *Modern Woman,* ed. G. D. Goldman and D. S. Millman. Springfield, Ill.: Charles C Thomas, 1969.

4. V. M. Masters and V. E. Johnson, *Human Sexual Response.* Boston: Little, Brown, 1966.

5. M. Bass, *Meaning and Content of Sexual Perversions.* New York: Grune & Stratton, 1949.

6. Marie Robinson, *The Power of Sexual Surrender.* New York: Doubleday, 1959.

7. Edrita Fried, "Reactions to the Sexual Anatomy," *Quarterly Journal of Child Behavior* 4 (1952).

8. Sigmund Freud, "The Ego and the Id," *Standard Edition of the Complete Psychological Works of Sigmund Freud,* vol. 19. London: Hogarth Press, 1961.

9. Salzman, "Psychology of the Female."

10. Matthew Besdine, discussion in *Modern Woman,* ed. G. D. Goldman and D. S. Millman. Springfield, Ill.: Charles C Thomas, 1969.

11. Edmund Bergler, *The Basic Neurosis.* New York: Grune & Stratton, 1949.

12. Henriette Glatzer, "Neurotic Factors of Voyeurism and Exhibitionism in Groups," *International Journal of Group Psychotherapy* 17 (1967).
13. Esther Menaker, "Masochism: A Defense Reaction of the Ego," *Psychoanalytic Quarterly* 22 (1953).
14. Margaret S. Mahler, *On Human Symbiosis and the Vicissitudes of Individuation.* New York: International Universities Press, 1968.
15. Jule Nydes, "The Paranoid Masochistic Character," *Psychoanalytic Review* 50 (1963).
16. Edrita Fried, *The Ego in Love and Sexuality.* New York: Grune & Stratton, 1960.

3. Passive Men and Their Partners

1. Edmund Bergler, *The Basic Neurosis.* New York: Grune & Stratton, 1949.
2. Norman Mailer, *An American Dream.* New York: Dial, 1964.
3. David Rappaport, *Organization and Pathology of Thought.* New York: Columbia University Press, 1951.
4. Lauretta Bender, Paul Schilder, and Sylvan Keyser, "Studies in Aggression," *Genetic Psychology Monographs* (Worcester, Mass.) 18 (1936).
5. Sandor Ferenczi, *The Development of Psychoanalysis.* New York: Dover, 1956.
6. I. Bieber et al., *Homosexuality: A Psychoanalytic Study.* New York: Basic Books. 1962.
7. Ibid.

4. Mastering Danger and Anxiety

1. Konrad Lorenz, *Evolutions and Modifications of Behavior.* Chicago: University of Chicago Press, 1965.
2. Anthony Storr, *Human Aggression.* New York: Atheneum, 1968.
3. Earl G. Witenberg and Leopold Caligor, "The Interpersonal Approach to Treatment," in *Psychoanalytic Techniques,* ed. B. Wolman. New York: Basic Books, 1967.
4. Sigmund Freud, *The Problem of Anxiety.* New York: Norton, 1963.
5. Max Schur, "The Ego in Anxiety," in *Drives, Affects, Behavior,* ed. R. M. Loewenstein. New York: International Universities Press, 1953.
6. Otto Fenichel, "Early Stages of Ego Development," in *The Collected Papers of Otto Fenichel,* vol. 2. New York: Norton, 1954.
7. Lewis R. Wolberg, *Techniques of Psychotherapy.* New York: Grune & Stratton, 1967.
8. Frieda Fromm Reichmann, *Principles of Intensive Psychotherapy.* Chicago: University of Chicago Press, 1950.
9. Sören Kierkegaard, *The Sickness Unto Death.* New York: Doubleday, 1954.
10. Rollo May, *The Meaning of Anxiety.* New York: Roland Press, 1950.
11. Edrita Fried, "Self-Induced Failure: A Mechanism of Defense," *Psychoanalytic Review* 9 (1954).

12. Arnold H. Modell, *Object Love and Reality*. New York: International Universities Press, 1968.
13. Lawrence Kubie, "The Central Effective Potential and Its Trigger Mechanisms," in *Point Counterpoint*, ed. H. S. Gaskill. New York: International Universities Press, 1963.
14. Ernest G. Schachtel, *Metamorphosis*. New York: Basic Books, 1959.
15. W. R. Bion, *Learning From Experience*. New York: Basic Books, 1962.
16. Melanie Klein, *New Directions in Psychoanalysis*. London: Hogarth Press, 1956.
17. Bion, *Learning From Experience*.
18. Edrita Fried, *The Ego in Love and Sexuality*. New York: Grune & Stratton, 1960.

5. Active Loving

1. Edith Jacobson, *The Self and the Object*. New York: International Universities Press, 1964.
2. Sandor Ferenczi, *The Development of Psychoanalysis*. New York: Dover, 1956.
3. Sandor Rado, "The Psychic Effects of Intoxicants," *International Journal of Psychoanalysis* 7 (1926)
4. Otto Fenichel, "Early Stages of Ego Development," *The Collected Papers of Otto Fenichel*. New York: Norton, 1954.
5. Frederich Perls, Ralph F. Hefferline, and Paul Goodman, *Gestalt Therapy*. New York: Delta, 1951.
6. D. W. Winnicott, *The Maturational Process and the Facilitating Environment*. London: Hogarth Press, 1965.
7. W. Ronald D. Fairbairn, *An Object Relation Theory of the Personality*. New York: Basic Books, 1954.
8. Sandor Ferenczi, *The Further Development of an Active Therapy in Psychoanalysis: Further Contributions to the Theory and Technique of Psychoanalysis*. London: Hogarth Press, 1950.
9. Sigmund Freud, "Lines of Advance in Psychoanalytic Therapy," *Standard Edition of the Complete Psychological Works of Sigmund Freud*, vol. 17. London: Hogarth Press, 1955.
10. Erik H. Erikson, *Insight and Responsibility*. New York: Norton, 1964.
11. Phyllis Greenacre, "The Role of Transference: Practical Considerations in Relation to Psychoanalytic Therapy," *Journal of the American Psychoanalytic Association* 2 (1954).
12. Ernest G. Schachtel, *Metamorphosis*. New York: Basic Books, 1959.
13. Jule Nydes, "The Paranoid Masochistic Character," *Psychoanalytic Review* 50 (1963).
14. Sidney Tarachow, *An Introduction to Psychotherapy*. New York: International Universities Press, 1963.
15. Matthew Besdine, "Jocasta and Oedipus: Another Look," *Pathways in Child Guidance* 10 (1967).
16. Perls, Hefferline, and Goodman, *Gestalt Therapy*.

17. Jean Piaget, *The Origins of Intelligence in Children.* New York: International Universities Press, 1952.
18. Leon Festinger, "An Analysis of Compliant Behavior," in *Group Relations at the Cross Roads,* ed. M. Sherif and M. D. Wilson. New York: Harper, 1953.
19. Nathan W. Ackerman, "Psychoanalysis and Group Psychotherapy," in *Group Psychotherapy and Group Function,* ed. M. Rosenbaum and M. Berger. New York: Basic Books, 1963.

6. Creative Human Contacts: The Case of Marriage

1. Heinz Hartmann, "Psychoanalysis and Developmental Psychology," in *The Psychoanalytic Study of the Child,* vol. 5. New York: International Universities Press, 1950.
2. Nathan W. Ackerman, *The Psychodynamics of Family Life.* New York: Basic Books, 1958.
3. Edith Jacobson, *The Self and the Object World.* New York: International Universities Press, 1964.
4. Rubin and Gertrude Blanck, *Marriage and Personal Development.* New York: Columbia University Press, 1968.
5. Theodore Lidz, *The Person.* New York: Basic Books, 1968.
6. Margaret S. Mahler, *On Human Symbiosis and the Vicissitudes of Individuation.* New York: International Universities Press, 1968.
7. Walter B. Cannon, *The Wisdom of the Body.* New York: Norton, 1932.
8. Mahler, *On Human Symbiosis.*
9. Sigmund Freud, "Formulations on the Two Principles of Mental Functioning," *Standard Edition of the Complete Psychological Works of Sigmund Freud,* vol. 12. London: Hogarth Press, 1958.
10. W. P. Bion, *Learning From Experience.* New York: Basic Books, 1962.

7. Active Thinking

1. Eric Berne, *Games People Play.* New York: Grove Press, 1964.
2. Sigmund Freud, "Formulations on the Two Principles of Mental Functioning," *Standard Edition of the Complete Psychological Works of Sigmund Freud,* vol. 12. London: Hogarth Press, 1958.
3. Joost Meerloo, "Writing: That Lonely Dialogue," read before the American Medical Writers Association, October 1967, unpublished.
4. David Rapaport, "Toward a Theory of Thinking," in *Organization and Pathology of Thought,* ed. David Rapaport. New York: Columbia University Press, 1951.
5. Jean Piaget, *The Origins of Intelligence in Children.* New York: International Universities Press, 1952.
6. D. C. Levin, "The Self: A Contribution to Its Place in Theory and Technique," *International Journal of Psychoanalysis* 50 (1969).
7. Erich Fromm, *The Heart of Man.* New York: Harper & Row, 1964.

8. Esther Menaker, "Will and the Problem of Masochism," *Journal of Contemporary Psychotherapy* 1 (1969).
9. Paul Schilder, "On the Development of Thought," in *Organization and Pathology of Thought*, ed. David Rapaport. New York: Columbia University Press, 1951.
10. William Wilson. "Prince of Boredom: The Repetitions and Passivities of Andy Warhol," *Films and Filming* (March 1968).
11. Bluma Zeigarnik, "Ueber das Behalten von Erledigten und Unerledigten Handlungen," *Psychologische Forschung* 8 (1927).
12. Jerome S. Bruner, Jaqueline J. Goodnor, and George A. Austin, *A Study of Thinking*. New York: Wiley, 1956.
13. Edward de Bono, *Studies in Lateral Thinking*. Cambridge: Cambridge University Press, 1968. "Dr. E. de Bono discusses his theory of two kinds of thinking, lateral and vertical," *New York Times* interview, November 10, 1968, 32:1.
14. Edrita Fried, "Ego Functions and Techniques of Ego Strengthening," *American Journal of Psychotherapy* 9 (1955).
15. Esther and William Menaker, *Ego in Evolution*. New York: Grove Press, 1965.
16. Edrita Fried, *The Ego in Love and Sexuality*. New York: Grune & Stratton, 1960.

8. The Passive Stalemate

1. Erik H. Erikson, *Insight and Responsibility*. New York: Norton, 1964.
2. Ernest G. Schachtel, *Metamorphosis*. New York: Basic Books, 1959.
3. René Spitz, "Hospitalism: An Inquiry Into the Genesis of Psychiatric Conditions in Early Childhood," in *The Psychoanalytic Study of the Child*, vol. 1. New York: International Universities Press, 1945.
4. D. W. Winnicott, *Ego Integration in Child Development*. New York: International Universities Press, 1965.
5. Edrita Fried, *The Ego in Love and Sexuality*. New York: Grune & Stratton, 1960.
6. Sylvia Brody, *Passivity*. New York, International Universities Press, 1964.
7. Louis Breger, "Motivation, Energy and Cognitive Structure," in *Modern Psychoanalysis*, ed. Judd Marmor. New York: Basic Books, 1968.

9. The Subjective Advantages of Passivity]

1. Bruno Bettelheim, *The Empty Fortress*. New York: Free Press, 1967.
2. Edith Jacobson, *The Self and the Object World*. New York: International Universities Press, 1964.
3. Esther Menaker, "Masochism: A Defense Reaction of the Ego," *Psychoanalytic Quarterly* 22 (1953).
4. B. Berliner, "Role of Object Relations in Moral Masochism," *Psychoanalytic Quarterly* 27 (1958).
5. Edrita Fried, "Self-Induced Failure: A Mechanism of Defense," *Psychoanalytic Review* 41 (1954).

6. Lauretta Bender, Paul Schilder, and Sylvan Keyser, "Studies of Aggressiveness," *Genetic Psychology Monographs* (Worcester, Mass.) 18 (1936).
7. Edmund Bergler, *The Basic Neurosis*. New York: Grune & Stratton, 1949.
8. Jule Nydes, "The Paranoid Masochistic Character," *Psychoanalytic Review* 50 (1963).

10. Escape From Semantic Jungles

1. Lili E. Peller, "Freud's Contribution to Language Theory," in *The Psychoanalytic Study of the Child*, vol. 21. New York: International Universities Press, 1967.
2. Ernest G. Schachtel, *Metamorphosis*. New York: Basic Books, 1959.
3. Thomas S. Szasz, *The Myth of Mental Illness: Foundations of a Theory of Personal Conduct*. New York: Hoeber, 1961.
4. Jean Piaget, *The Origins of Intelligence in Children*. New York: International Universities Press, 1952.
5. L. P. Bradford, J. R. Gibb, and K. D. Berne, *T-Group Theory and Laboratory Method*. New York: Wiley, 1964.
6. George B. Milner, Report on a study of the School of Oriental and African Studies, University of London, 1969.
7. Arnold H. Modell, *Object Love and Reality*. New York: International Universities Press, 1968.

Index